Dreams for a World in Harmony

DREAMS FOR A WORLD IN HARMONY

NANCY HAWKINS

With contributions from confirmed atheist Barbara Coddington
Illustrator of front cover is 12 year old student Anna Dalton
with cartoon of 'the world' by Dennis Garlick.

To order additional copies of this book, contact:
Xlibris Corporation
1-800-618-969
www.xlibris.com.au
Orders@Xlibris.com.au
500785

CONTENTS

SECTION ONE

SECTION TWO

A Glimpse of Twelve Major Religions and Beliefs

SECTION THREE

Two year discussion program

Dedicated to...

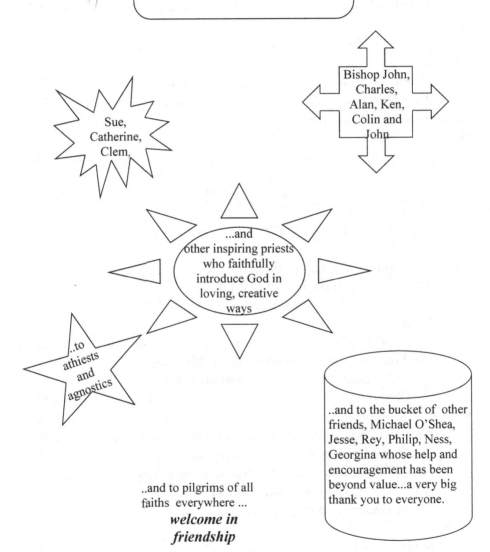

Sue, Catherine, Clem.

Bishop John, Charles, Alan, Ken, Colin and John

...and other inspiring priests who faithfully introduce God in loving, creative ways

..to athiests and agnostics

..and to the bucket of other friends, Michael O'Shea, Jesse, Rey, Philip, Ness, Georgina whose help and encouragement has been beyond value...a very big thank you to everyone.

..and to pilgrims of all faiths everywhere ...
welcome in friendship

From The Right Rev John Parkes,
Bishop of Wangaratta,
The Anglican Church of Australia.

"Dear Nancy,

I have opened it (Dreams for a World in Harmony) more than a few times, spent time reading and found that it too me to a place of recollection and prayer. Each page geve me a lot to think about! And that can be difficult for a busy Bishop. You have brought a wealth of resources together in Dreams for a World in Harmony, which feels like a retreat or a visit with a trusted spiritual friend—a series of encounters, reflections, and questions and answers, which both enlighten and dazzle with their depth.

The book seems to me to be more than a book; instead, it is, in my experience, more like a recollection of conversations with beloved companions. It makes me wonder of the original settings, meetings with family and friends, Frank and others, as you try to speak the truth in love in telling the stories of the mighty acts of God in our language, our cultural configuration, our place and time.

You have moved into deep water here, with an ambitious undertaking that demands as much from the reader as it did from the writer, where each of your questions calls for a deeper answer, and for further questions as well. I find that my several diving episodes into this font of resources left me, to quote you, in an 'interior haven of peace, like mist on the water in the morning.' And I thank you for that. I do honor your accomplishment. I wish you well in this and further publications. I thank you for your kindness in sharing this fruit of your ministry with me."

In Christ,

The Right Revd. John Parkes
Bishop of Wangaratta, Victoria, Australia

Also by Nancy Hawkins, *O My God! Where Are You?*
www.theworldinharmony.com

Acknowledgments

I am grateful to Bishop John Parkes, the Rev. Colin Goodwin, the Rev. Alan Hoskin, the Rev. Ken Parker, the Rev. Catherine Easton, John Waller, Meryl Batson, Carlin Bruce, Manar Chelebi, and Professor John Lambooy for their energy, wisdom, and comments in helping to develop one or the other of *Dreams for a World in Harmony* and *O my God! Where Are You?*

To Michael O'Shea of Soon Fixed, our friend and computer wizard, without whom I could not survive, to Philip Sarthou and Rey Barnes, my two wonderfully helpful Xlibris personal support representatives for their unfailing patience, to Linda Lambooy for her enthusiasm and bubble, to Anne Findlay from Editing Works, Melbourne for her generous and thoughtful remarks on both books.

My sincere gratitude also goes to two especially wonderful atheists, Mrs Barbara Coddington, and Mrs Mim Sargood, who steeled themselves to go beyond the bounds of friendship, to read and comment on the manuscript, overcoming any feeling of "crispness" at being asked to do such a strange task.

Barbara Coddington, a retired lawyer, who is a **R**eally **I**ntelligent **A**theist, Ria for short, is a companion through the book.

The biblical text included in this book is acknowledged gratefully. It is printed with compliments from Wikipedia from their version of the bible, the World English Bible.

The delightful cartoons by Dennis Garlick have been copied from over 200 illustrations in the earlier book, *O my God! Where are You?*

I am proud of the artist, Anna Dalton, who painted the front cover. She is our granddaughter, aged 12, and along with our other three grandchildren, our three children and Sally, are the most cherished people in our lives.

Finally, many unsaid thanks to my husband for being my best friend, and author companion through the years of writing.

FOREWORD

Dreams for a World in Harmony, along with the author's earlier *O My God! Where Are You?* was originally written for an atheist son-in-law, Frank. He asked quite sincerely one day, after dutifully attending a church service, 'Do you really believe in all this?' Later he picked up a Bible only to groan in despair, 'Where do you begin with all this stuff?'

Frank is no longer a part of our family life, but it was he who inspired the writing.

He came back to be baptized in the sea on a very cold wintry day on 22nd September 1996. He said he didn't feel the cold, as we pulled up trousers and robes to douse him in the freezing waves. It was an emotional, moving moment.

Something happened to Frank, because with a firm faith in God, he went on to write and sing gospel songs on his guitar, in pubs or to anyone who will listen. But that is another story, and this book has moved—to dream on.

O My God! Where Are You? reflects on St. Luke's gospel, while *Dreams for a World in Harmony* focuses on the Book of Acts. The dreams aim to cross two bridges—to fill two serious gaps which are apparent in the Christian church.

Both books are available from the web site *www.theworldinharmony. com*

INTRODUCTION

As I sit by my window, looking at our small, beautiful garden, I wonder why I ever started to write a book about God in this secular age. Was it madness? *Dreams for a World in Harmony* is a call—a plea—to Christian leaders to embrace two groups of people—to fill two yawning gaps—the generation gap, and to cross inter-faith bridges to make realistic connections and friendships with those who believe in a different way.

It is apparent by the lack of numbers in most churches that the needs of the last two generations of young Christians have been largely ignored by the traditional church, although there is an exciting groundswell of young believers, who, like tiny pockets of seedlings, are growing and facing the challenge to bring the love of God home again in a way to which they can relate.

Dreams for a World in Harmony is a journey to find the richness waiting to be explored through the dreams for hordes of young and disillusioned ones, and a pathway to connect with inter-faith fellow travellers through St Luke's wisdom.

The dreams are designed as tools for building bridges through music, listening, and talking together, while sailing through a two year learning program.

The two year learning program

Details of the programs with notes for the group leaders are found in section three.

The first year's program takes readers through the author's first book, *O my God! Where are You?* which journeys through St. Luke's complete gospel. The second year's study taken from *Dreams for a World in Harmony,* not only travels through the Book of Acts, but also introduces fresh approaches to celebrate Advent and Lent.

The Dreams

No. 1 Dreams of celebrating a school choir's competition.

"Let all the world in every corner sing . . . ."
George Herbert 1593-1633

Within a chosen district, an enthusiastic coordinator invites schools in the area to participate in a choir competition. They choose three songs for the competition—one from each section of a carefully pre-selected list of songs from three cultures—Jewish, Muslim and Christian—songs which express world peace, harmony, and 'oneness'.

To add to the student's experience, each year the judicators will be encouraged to judge the competitions in different places—a church, a mosque, a temple, a barn, a park, a hall. A sponsor or two would help to get the competition going. Television stations are invited to follow the competition, and may even offer sponsorship.

The students could be encouraged to write their own school's song—the '(school)'s Harmony Song' about their own values, and those of their school.

This competition may start in a small region, gather momentum to statewide, nationwide, and even spread worldwide one day. Further details: *www.theworldinharmony.com*

oo0oo

No. 2 Dreams of teenager leadership in church and chapel . . . .

. . . for lead they will, when given the opportunity—because the present and the future belongs to them.

Three or four young people, probably fourteen or upwards, are invited to help a coordinator lead a section of a church service—perhaps on the first and third Sundays for a few months. The goal is to encourage them to be creative, and feel the excitement of searching for their souls, by contributing and belonging to a great faith.

Planning:
1. Choose a relevant theme for the season.
2. Choose a relevant section from either *O my God! Where are You?* (Luke) or *Dreams for a World in Harmony* (Book of Acts) to fit the theme.
3. The Readings.
   a. The first person reads the bible text portion.
   b. The second reads the commentary section.
4. The Answers.
   a. The third, who is the main spokesperson this time, reads the question, and invites about three (is probably enough) people in the congregation to reply. Initially these people could be warned to think about their answers beforehand.
   b. One or more of the youngsters follow by giving their thoughts to the question.
   c. The leader thanks everyone for listening, encouraging them to come again on the next allocated Sunday, when other young people will share their thoughts and opinions.
5. Singing.
   The young people, having chosen the singing into a song or hymn of their choice (they need not be hymns, but songs with appropriate words to their theme). They lead the singing—at the end of a microphone if they feel comfortable to do this. Karaoke here we come!
   Songs such as 'Climb every mountain' . . . or 'Bring him home' from Les Miserable—or am I being a bit old fashioned? The young people will have some wonderful songs to contribute.

6. Action.

As the congregation sing along from the words on the overhead projector if available, while some or all of the three leaders go around the church greeting members of the congregation during the hymn/song, making both eye and action contact for a significant moment, before coming back to their places for the last verse.

The action may take a bit of getting used to, but will become valuable after the initial 'newness' has worn off.

7. Prayer. One or more of the leaders lead the prayer(s) they have written.

8. Making a song book. This is a useful exercise, providing a resource of songs, loved by the young, encouraging them to come back again.

The two books *O my God! Where are You?* and *Dreams for a World in Harmony* may be used of course, but the young people may prefer to explore other books which have inspired them, and enjoy the excitement of creating and thinking through their own comments, and questions.

Very soon friends will be invited along to help, support, contribute, and watch a while, as numbers grow as now the church sometimes resounds with the sound of their music.

ooOoo

No.3 Dreams of the freedom to express spirituality.

The Park Dream.

This dream provides an opportunity to high school or university students to express their spirituality, devoid of denominations and church walls in a celebrating event of their own choosing.

The event is held in the Park, football oval, Cathedral precinct, town square, or other suitable open space, on a Sunday. In colder weather, the town hall, theater, school hall or—even better—a large barn would be suitable. Families sit on the grass, on BYO chairs, rugs, or on bales of hay—while toddlers potter about happily.

The organizing Committee—enthusiastic people who understand teenagers—are represented by church denominations, students, schools, university, and community.

The event will hopefully be held several times a year.

Initially the Committee decides:

1. How many schools, university and colleges are there in the district?
2. Which dates in the educational diary and church calendar would be suitable to offer each establishment at least one 'Sunday in the

Park' event to coordinate during the year? (Be sure some of the ministers and school representatives are present for this meeting.)

3. A committee member approaches the schools, colleges and university, and notes those who are willing to be adventurous. If it is useful please feel free to copy the format below for a simple hand out.

The Plan.

Having had the idea explained, each host school, college, or university willing to be involved, discusses the following topics:

a) A theme for their celebration on their allotted date.
b) Someone to choose and organize the music with the students which will be a prominent part of the celebration.
c) A 'cool' guest speaker of their choice for the celebration may be an author, actor, priest, Muslim, plumber, Buddhist, builder, teacher, pop star, carpenter, or other, who is invited to share his or her spiritual or inspired story—in words of hope and encouragement. As a courtesy the arrangements should obviously be discussed with the Committee.
d) For a project or homework, the students are invited, in advance, to express their feelings by writing about the theme in song, music, poetry, or prose.
e) The students may have a piece of prose or poetry that inspires them to contribute to the program relevant to the theme, on which they are prepared to stand up and explain why it is important to them.
f) The event is rehearsed at some stage, and the student's program and contributions compiled into a small book each year.

In the park or large space, the musicians and singers can make as great a noise as they like—filling the air with their own created praise to the Creator. No religious affiliation is necessary, but again the songs and writings are chosen to fit the theme.

Everyone is encouraged to bring a picnic, to stay on afterwards, making new friends in a relaxed, non-threatening atmosphere—airing their thoughts, and hopes for the future.

One day, perhaps at the end of the second year when everyone feels familiar with the program, the schools and universities may wish to come back to be a church or chapel, and could now be excited to gather together in a church.

ooOoo

No. 4. dreams of crossing interfaith bridges through a Q&A panel—celebrating cultural diversity by learning from each other, and learning about each other.

In this dream the organizers, who may be Christian ministers, chaplains, pastors or lay people from schools, university, prison, mothers club, youth club or anyone else, invite 'guests' to take part in a panel for a Questions and Answers discussion—a Q&A panel.

The program can be flexible, perhaps for an hour a week during recess, a lunch break, over a cuppa, or any suitable time, and take place anywhere except in a church or chapel, to work through the first year series program for Advent, Lent or the Ordinary Sundays or simply to work through the book from the beginning. There are further details in section three at the end of this book.

O my God! Where are you? or *Dreams for a World in Harmony* become the catalyst for the debates. The Q&A panel work through the chapters, airing thoughts and hopes, ignited by the comments and questions at the end of every few verses.

Lapsed Christians, atheists, agnostics, and members of other religions, particularly those people from historically the same faith-based families, the Jews and Muslims, make perfect guests. The greater the mix, the better the debate will be.

Barbara Coddington, a retired lawyer and confirmed atheist, has generously given her time to provide another point of view at the end of many small segments of scripture and comments. She can be quite 'feisty', and stands up for the atheists in the group. I hope you enjoy her company.

The questions address many of the challenges that face Christianity, the world, and each of us today, so expect to find interesting discussion, laughter, maybe healing tears and disturbances along the way.

Dreams for a World in Harmony is designed to be read with a journal at hand, to record thoughts, answer questions, and note possible action. Different versions of the Bible would highlight the miracle that the content is still largely the same after so many translations have dipped into the original 'pie'. Where there are Jewish and Islamic members in the group, it would be wonderful if they brought their Holy books along, to enable thoughts from the bible text to be extended to hear what the Torah or Koran have to offer on a given question—enabling all members of the group to learn from each other.

It is a good idea to put a small advertisement into the local paper, church, school, prison, wherever, news sheets, something like:

St. Somebody or The Rev . . . . or Chaplain or Jo Bloggs
Invite(s) interested people/students of
any faith or no faith at all,
to join in a
Q&A (question and answer) session
to share their thoughts and, beliefs, at an initial (? public) meeting in ?the
Scout Hall/? in the gym . . . wherever
At 6.30pm/10.00am/during recess/lunch break/
on Tuesday, ?? June . . .

Meet the Eclectic Panel

Sip—Seriously Important Person, the group leader
                (sounds good if pronounced with a 'zing').
Ria—Really Intelligent Atheist.
Winc—Wonderful Intelligent Non-Christian members of the group.

A&A Atheists and Agnostics who are included with Wincs unless stated otherwise.

Sees—an easy and short way to refer to 'C' for Christians.

Tinc—a Truly *Imaginary* Non-Christian.

+ other invited guests, who will hopefully include members from both the Jewish and Muslim faiths.

ooOoo

No 5. Dreams that 'a little child shall lead them' . . .

. . . and takes place in the church that I love, to encourage younger children to begin taking a leadership role.

Children, perhaps ten years and more, are invited to create their own form of Sunday school, using their own ideas and choice of music. The game of 'being teacher' is exciting and generates serious thought as they teach the younger ones (under the guidance of one of the congregation, preferably a school teacher or retired teacher) to care for and teach the smaller ones.

This idea came about in our church because our grandchildren said that church was boring. They were told that if something is boring in life, they need to take some responsibility to change it, so "do something about it if you can". They asked if they could take Sunday school. And they did!

The children come into the church for the first ten minutes or so, and then retire to another room with a whiteboard and an adult. Later they return to the church with a 'show and tell' to the congregation.

The young leaders take it in turns to organize the program with help from a parent, friend or teacher, and bring support from their friends on the day—a sort of BYO growing Sunday school.

A variation of this dream may be to invite young families to get together with the children, and work through a chosen theme away from the church, in a warm room with a carpet and rug for little people. The families may like to take it in turns to lead, with a reading from the bible, this book or any other, with symbols, songs, and games from *www.teachsundayschool. com* or join up with Mary Kate Warner *marykate@teachsundayschool.com* and enjoy her creative programs, while the families explore their spirituality informally together.

Keep an eye open on *www.theworldinharmony.com* for developing card, board and other games for young people related to the scriptures.

ooOoo

No. 6 just dreams . . .

       . . . of the people spent reading this book,
with a hope, a wish and a prayer
that their time turns into leaps
and bounds . . .

ooOoo

These first six dreams may flirt with parks, choirs, and Q&A panels, but the ultimate goal is three-fold.

That new and lapsed Christians come to embrace their church, feeling comfortable, excited, familiar, refreshed, enthusiastic, and committed.

Secondly, that strong and lasting friendships have been made with pilgrims of other faiths.

And thirdly, many people will continue to dream on through further dreams in section three.

ooOoo

SECTION ONE

Planet earth began with a bang....

5000 my's later—another bang, a sun exploded in the universe, and one part flew off to illuminate the foggy ice ball—earth.

God made two great lights –the greater light to govern the day and the lesser light to govern the night Gen 1:5

BANG
About 13700 mya a star in the universe exploded and hot gases, dust and atoms formed a large ball of mist.
Genesis 1: In the beginning, when God created the universe, the earth was formless and desolate. Gen.1:1

4600 mya
...a meteorite crashed into the earth. A bit of the earth flew off and formed the moon.

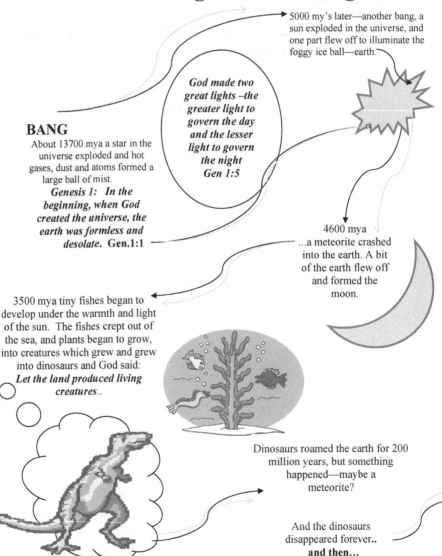

3500 mya tiny fishes began to develop under the warmth and light of the sun. The fishes crept out of the sea, and plants began to grow, into creatures which grew and grew into dinosaurs and God said:
Let the land produced living creatures..

Dinosaurs roamed the earth for 200 million years, but something happened—maybe a meteorite?

And the dinosaurs disappeared forever..
and then...

Diagram of the Beginning of Time

...and now there is an amazing journey waiting to be explored....

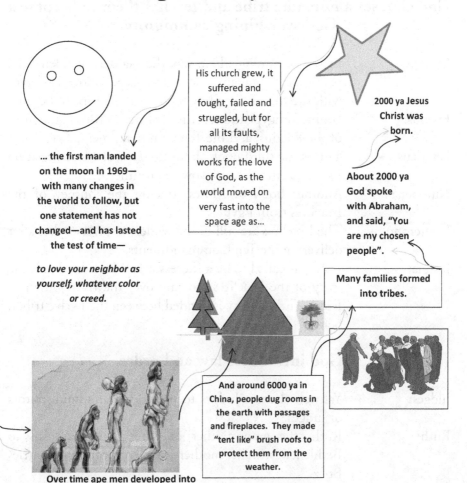

His church grew, it suffered and fought, failed and struggled, but for all its faults, managed mighty works for the love of God, as the world moved on very fast into the space age as...

... the first man landed on the moon in 1969—with many changes in the world to follow, but one statement has not changed—and has lasted the test of time—

to love your neighbor as yourself, whatever color or creed.

2000 ya Jesus Christ was born.

About 2000 ya God spoke with Abraham, and said, "You are my chosen people".

Many families formed into tribes.

And around 6000 ya in China, people dug rooms in the earth with passages and fireplaces. They made "tent like" brush roofs to protect them from the weather.

Over time ape men developed into humans about 3 mya.

Note: mya =million years ago   ya=years ago

The Bible in Miniature

Old Testament

God chooses a nomadic tribe and teaches them to become a God-worshiping community.

Genesis:	In the beginning, there was the Garden of Eden. The patriarchs, Abraham, Isaac, and Jacob, move to Egypt with their families to buy food during a time of famine.
Exodus:	Begins in Egypt and records the birth of Moses, the story of the Exodus, and the Ten Commandments.
Leviticus:	This is the third book about the Law of Moses, relating to the sacrificial Laws, vows, and tithes.
Numbers:	Another book of Moses, tracing the journey of the Israelites from Egypt.
Deuteronomy:	The Israelites are still in the wilderness; Moses dies after delivering the Ten Commandments.
Joshua:	Joshua is called to be a successor to Moses, and tells the story of the Israelites crossing over the river Jordan to Israel. The territory is divided between the twelve tribes, before Joshua dies.

God introduces law and order.

Judges:	Yahweh chooses Judges to provide local administrators or judges.
Ruth:	Ruth, the grandmother of King David, returns to Bethlehem with her mother-in-law Naomi. Ruth marries Boaz.

1 Samuel:	Records the life and death of Samuel. Saul, chosen to be king, while David is secretly anointed to be the next king.
2 Samuel:	Saul dies; David reigns victoriously.
1 Kings:	Records the death of David, the life and death of Solomon, and the separation of the kingdom. Elijah the prophet enters the story
2 Kings:	Elijah is succeeded by Elisha. War with Syria. The Israelites are exiled to Babylonia.
1 Chronicles:	From Adam to Abraham, many people are begat. David dies.
2 Chronicles:	Solomon reigns, builds a temple, and dies; Cyrus of Persia permits the exiles to return home from Babylonia.
Ezra:	Ezra the scribe and Nehemiah the governor begin to restore the nation. The Temple in Jerusalem is to be re-built.
Nehemiah:	Originally, Ezra and Nehemiah was one book. They tell the continuing story to rebuild the Temple.
Esther:	A young Jewish girl, Esther was chosen to be queen. She miraculously reverses the near extinction of the Jews.
Job:	Job asks, 'Why do the righteous suffer?' Job's trials and his fortunes are eventually restored.
Psalms:	A well-loved and well-known collection of poems of praise.
Proverbs:	The wisdom of Solomon gives valuable instruction for practical living.
Ecclesiastes:	This strange book is about the vanities of the human species.
Song of Solomon:	a love poem.

He promises to send a Savior to the tribe.

Isaiah:	Isaiah receives a message—God is going to restore the nation.
Jeremiah:	A day of redemption. is prophesied after terrible judgment on the people for their sins.
Lamentations:	Records an outpouring of grief over a fallen city.
Ezekiel:	The judgment of God has arrived. Only a faithful few will be restored to their land.

Daniel: Daniel appeals for faithfulness in the midst of adversity.

Hosea: Hosea's message of wisdom leads the people to repentance.

Joel: A call for repentance—for God will surely judge the nations.

Amos: 'The lion roars.' This book records five of Amos's visions of judgment.

Obadiah: The old animosity between the tribes of Esau and Jacob continues through the centuries. Warnings are given to Judah and the Edomites.

Jonah: A struggle to accept God's forgiveness.

Micah: Judgment will come—but mercy will be shown if the people repent.

However, God expects obedience in the meantime.

Nahum: Tells the story of the impending doom of Nineveh—a message of consolation.

Habakkuk: The prophet Habakkuk cries against violence—God's answer to a prophet's prayer.

Zephaniah: The terrible day of the Lord is announced.

Haggai: The priorities of the people are challenged.

Zechariah: The people are inspired to trust God and rebuild their lives in response to that trust.

Malachi: A prophet's call to stop cheating God—with an announcement of the coming judgment.

New Testament

The Savior arrives, but the chosen race does not listen to him; the Savior is a nuisance.

Matthew: The life of Jesus Christ is written according to St. Matthew—Jesus fulfills the Old Testament prophecy of the long-expected Messiah

Mark: The story of Jesus of Nazareth written for the Greek Community—Christians speak in tongues—then scatter to the four winds throughout the Mediterranean region.

Luke: Luke 1:3-4: 'since I myself have carefully investigated everything from the beginning, it seemed good also to me to write an orderly account of the things of which you have been taught.'

So they kill him.

John: John 20: 31: 'these things are written that you may believe that Jesus is the Christ, the Son of God, and that by believing you may have life in his name.'

Acts: Christianity is born, along with the beginning of the early church.

But the news and his teaching travel like wild fire . . .

Romans: Paul writes to the church in Rome preparing them for his visit. He explains God's overall plan of forgiveness for both Jews and Gentiles.

1 Corinthians: Another letter from Paul to the Corinthian church, he answers questions on immature and unspiritual practices.

2 Corinthians: In a letter, Paul tries to heal the wounds of a divided and troubled church.

Galatians: Paul establishes a new policy that allows Gentiles to become Christians without being bound to the Jewish law.

Ephesians: Paul addresses a letter to every church, in every age, on the timelessness of God's plan for life in the Spirit.

Philippians: This 'thank you' letter from Paul and Timothy acknowledges generous support while he was in prison; Paul encourages a resolution to their problems, by living lives close to Christ.

Colossians: While still in prison, Paul and Timothy write to assure their readers that Christ alone is completely sufficient for every human need.

. . . throughout the world . . .

1 Thessalonians: A letter from Paul, Silas, and Timothy with a gentle theme of the last days stresses the need for thanksgiving, honesty, and prayer.

2 Thessalonians: A stern follow-up letter from Paul, Silas, and Timothy deals with problems of steadfastness and the need for discipline.

1 Timothy: Paul's first pastoral letter to Timothy provides guidance on how to handle the difficult situation in the Ephesian church.

2 Timothy: A second pastoral letter—written in prison not long before Paul's death—advises Timothy on his evangelical and teaching work and asks him to come to Rome.

Titus: A third pastoral letter from Paul—offers an instruction manual for officers and members of the church.

Philemon: This letter is a masterpiece from Paul to the slave owner Philemon—expressing the nature of love, which must be the base of all Christian relationships

Hebrews: An uncertain author proclaims Jesus Christ as the final, perfect, and eternal sacrifice.

James: The author is probably the brother of Jesus—who explains that trials test faith and the power of prayer.

1 Peter: A letter calling upon Christians to bear suffering with patience and unwavering faith in Christ.

2 Peter:	This letter, probably written by Peter although only ascribed to him later in Origen's time (AD 185), reminds his reader the basics of faith and warns of false preachers.
1 John:	A letter from the apostle John, first cousin of Jesus, calls the church to obedience in love.
2 John:	Another letter from John, it encourages traveling evangelists and teachers to stand fast in the faith.
3 John:	John commends his friend Gaius for his work supporting the teachers.
Jude:	A warning against false teachers and doxology. 'To him who is able to keep you from falling . . .' (Jude 1: 24). Probably written by Jude, brother of Jesus, but there is no indication to whom it is written.
Revelation:	The author, identifying himself as John the apostle, describes a series of visions, symbolically revealing the future triumph of God over the forces of evil.

. . . and now in the twenty first century, is anyone listening to the young ones today?

WALKABOUT WITH LUKE, PETER, AND PAUL

Welcome to the book of Acts, hopefully with a notebook at hand to reflect on the questions at the end of many segments in this section.

Christianity has weathered many storms since the time of Luke, Peter, and Paul. Some say that it faces its greatest challenge today, competing with the wonders of science, cyber technology, and the 'simply too busy' syndrome. Atheists, critics, and authors such as Richard Dawkins and Christopher Hitchens are strongly challenging believers, perhaps unwittingly doing Christianity a favor, and like a large pair of bellows, fanning the embers to reignite the spirit of Christianity.

Journalist Madeleine Bunting, reporting on the World Atheist Conference in Melbourne in March 2010, headed her article in the *Melbourne Anglican* newspaper, 'Religion has been invigorated by those who came to bury God.'[1] Certainly, God has seldom had such splendid media coverage to rekindle the flame.

Dawkins's energetic and enthusiastic search for the truth is not far removed in many respects from the unbiased, open-minded religious believer, as both look together at the Great Spirit of Creation with wonder and awe.

As we begin this journey, Luke, the gentle, 'beloved' physician and friend of Paul, is excited to be writing a letter to his friend Theophilus, who was probably Roman and a person of high rank and wealth. Luke was a

---

[1] Journalist Madeleine Bunting writing in *The Melbourne Anglican* newspaper, Tuesday 6 April 2010 page 11. Her article "Atheists win a battle but may lose the war" reported on the World Atheists Conference held in Melbourne, March 2010.

pioneer in the defense of the Jesus story, recorded some thirty to forty years after the death of Christ.

Significantly, Luke is the only non-Jewish author to write a Gospel, although he may well have embraced the Jewish faith during his lifetime.

The archaeologist Sir William Ramsay, after intensive research in the nineteenth century, wrote, 'Luke's history is unsurpassed in respect of its trustworthiness . . . In short this author should be placed along with the very greatest of historians.' [2]

The dominating theme in the Book of Acts is the presence and work of the Holy Spirit, the Great Spirit who guided his messengers, giving clear instructions as to where and when to go to spread the Christian gospel through the Middle East and Europe.

The Book of Acts records the story of Peter and Paul, their failures and successes, with vivid descriptions of people and places at that time. Luke picks up the story in his letter to Theophilus at the same moment he finished his Gospel of Luke, the day of the ascension of Jesus into heaven. Jesus had appeared to the apostles several times during the month after his death and had given them a clear message about the work ahead.

---

[2]   The New Bible Commentary Revised, published by Inter-Varsity Press, page 970. Contributor to the Acts of the Apostles F.F.Bruce, DD, formerly Rylands Professor of Biblical Criticism and Exegesis, University of Manchester wrote the quote about the nineteenth century archaeologist, Sir William Ramsay summing up Luke's qualities as a historian.

CHAPTER 1

Election Time—the Foundation of the Christian Church

Acts 1: 1-2

The first book I wrote, Theophilus, concerned all that Jesus began both to do and to teach, until the day in which he was received up, after he had given commandment through the Holy Spirit to the apostles whom he had chosen.

Luke felt impelled to write this story about the first Christian evangelists. Theophilus and Luke had a strong bond, but it probably never occurred to either of them that we may be reading his letter two thousand years later.

We seldom know what effect our actions may have for good or bad, or even what chain of events a seemingly insignificant remark or act may spark. Many thoughts were shared with Frank, for whom this text was originally written, while wandering over the paddocks or sitting on a log, trying to fathom the great mystery of the Spirit of God. God knows where those talks will take us. They were good times—gone now, but my life would have been poorer without them.

Now Frank and I are each on a different course. Having walked through the pain, this is the place to say thank you and farewell to Frank, for there are new horizons and adventures ahead with this amazing God, who mercifully never gives up on us.

Q. As Luke was impelled to write his story of Peter and Paul's journey, so a new journey begins for the group. Will you write in your journal a few paragraphs about your life so far—in three sections—your childhood, young teenage years, and for those who have left school, recount your story since leaving school.

Acts 1: 3

To these apostles, he [Jesus] also showed himself alive after he suffered, by many proofs, appearing to them over a period of forty days and spoke about the kingdom of God.

Who was Jesus? People have battled over this for years. The Bible says he was the Son of God. Was he divine, a sort of living 'spiritual being' on earth, or totally human like the rest of us? With his great insight, he was able to learn, heal, and communicate with God and people on a highly developed spiritual plane. Has God sent other sons and messengers to this earth?

The Dalai Lama is a fine example of a spiritually healthy man. He is calm, in harmony with himself, gentle, strong, and free of sharp edges. He has a lovely chuckle and radiates compassion and peace. Thousands flocked to hear him. Can anyone truly believe he is not a 'son of God' because he is a Buddhist?

Q. Who was Jesus? Historically, he was a man. Will you write in your journal and describe to Tinc (your Truly Imaginary Non-Christian) who Jesus is to you?

Acts 1: 3b

(from Peter) . . . and speaking about God's Kingdom.

Peter speaks to his friends about God's kingdom being here on earth. The kingdom of God means a *present reality and a future hope.*[3] This expression is central to the teaching of Jesus, mentioned many times through the gospels. A present reality presumably means 'here and now.' Today, this moment, Peter is saying, we either are or are not living in the kingdom of God. But where is this kingdom?

Are the times of unexpected thoughts that come to mind that simply will not go away something to do with it? Or when an unexpected incident triggers a reaction? Do these moments indicate that we are walking with God?

However it happens, Peter confident enough to trust his visions, dreams, and angels and follow the advice he was given. He apparently had both feet firmly in the kingdom of God.

Perhaps, it takes practice to walk in God's kingdom, like tennis or playing an instrument or any other skill. It takes a commitment to stick to it, to be still with God regularly, and to find the space to listen and understand. Lucky Peter had been with Jesus; no wonder he found it easier.

This excerpt was lying in my "squirrel box" from where it came, I know not:

"The Kingdom of God is *a space*. It exists in every home where parents and children love each other . . . .

The Kingdom of God is *a time*. It happens whenever someone feeds a hungry person, or shelters a homeless person, . . . or whenever we overturn an unjust law, or avert a war . . . .

The Kingdom of God is *a condition*. Its symptoms are love, justice, and peace.

Q. Sees (Christians), can you describe to the Wincs (Wonderful Interacting Non-Christians) what you think Peter meant when he talks about 'the Kingdom of God'? Have there been moments when you feel you were 'walking in the kingdom of God?

Wincs, can you share a particular moment when, like Peter, you had the conviction you were unexpectedly, absolutely on the right path?

---

3   Ralph Earle, contributor to St Matthew's Gospel commentary in the NIV Study Bible chapter 2:3: page 1444 Published by the Zondervan Corporation in 1985.

Acts 1: 4-5

Being assembled together with them, he (Jesus) commanded them, 'Don't depart from Jerusalem but wait for the promise of the Father, which you heard from me. For John indeed baptised in water, but you will be baptised in the Holy Spirit not many days from now.'

The apostles were asked not to leave Jerusalem until they had received a spiritual gift. They thought this would mean the arrival of the Messiah to deliver them from the political oppression of Roman rule.

Jesus promised his friends the gift of the Holy Spirit, but his friends did not know what to expect. We don't know either what to expect from our unpredictable God. We don't ever know where he might lead us. But life with God is often exciting and always filled with loving concern. It is difficult to understand, but there lies the mystery.

Q. 'John indeed baptized in water, you will be baptized (by Jesus) in the Holy Spirit . . . '

Everyone can try this one.

The symbols of baptism are water, light, and life. What is the significance of these symbols? Describe how the baptism from John differs from the baptism with Jesus?

Acts 1: 6

Therefore, when they had come together, they asked him, 'Lord, are you now restoring the kingdom to Israel?'

It would be interesting to know how the apostles were coping with the risen Jesus, not knowing from one day to another whether Jesus would turn up or when he would go again.

Q. List at least five emotions that these disciples may have been feeling just now.

Acts 1: 7-8

He [Jesus] said to them, 'It isn't for you to know the times or seasons which the Father has set within his own authority. But you will receive power when the Holy Spirit has come upon you. You will be witnesses to me in Jerusalem, in all Judea and Samaria, and to the uttermost parts of the earth.'

'You will receive power . . .' From what source do you receive your power, energy, integrity, leadership qualities, etc. Is 'hope' powerful?

Pope Benedict XVI said in his address at the World Youth Conference in Sydney, 2009, 'But what is this "power" of the Holy Spirit? . . . in this great assembly of young Christians from all over the world, we have had a vivid experience of the Spirit's presence . . . a living community of love, embracing people of every race, nation, and tongue, . . . an underground river which nourishes our spirit and draws us ever nearer to the source of our true life. We have to let it break through our hard crust of indifference, our spiritual weariness, our blind conformity to the spirit of the age . . .'[4]

And the disciples were the first to experience this 'living power.'

Q. 'You will receive power.' In which areas of your life do you feel intellectually and emotionally powerful—professionally, at home, at school, in your relationships?

Acts 1: 9-11

When he had said these things, as they were looking, he was taken up, and a cloud received him out of their sight. While they were looking steadfastly into the sky as he went, behold, two men stood by them in white clothing, who also said, 'You men of Galilee, why do you stand looking into the sky? This Jesus, who was received up from you into the sky, will come back in the same way as you saw him going into the sky.'

---

[4]   Pope Benedict XVI's address at the World Youth Conference in Sydney, 20 July 2008 printed in the Australian newspaper on Monday, 21, 2008.

If we say that Jesus was wholly human, this scene is difficult to understand, as eleven men stood on the side of the hill overlooking Jerusalem, watching Jesus disappear 'into the sky' like a helium balloon. Whatever occurred during that encounter made such a huge impression that we still talk about it annually two thousand years later on Ascension Day.

The Ascension occurred on the eastern slope of the Mount of Olives, between Jerusalem and Bethany. Standing on a bend of the road on the side of that fairly steep hill, Jesus may have stopped to catch his breath here as he climbed up the hill on the way to see his friends, Mary, Martha, and Lazarus. He looked down across the Hedron valley to the walled city of Jerusalem and wept for the city he loved. To stand on that hill today gives one a sense of timelessness—of standing on holy ground.

Q. Have any of you had a special spiritual transcending moment lately? Can you share it?

Acts 1: 12-14

Then they returned to Jerusalem from the mountain called Olivet, which is near Jerusalem, a Sabbath day's journey away. When they had come in, they went up into the upper room, where they were staying; that is Peter, John, James, Andrew, Philip, Thomas, Bartholomew, Matthew, James the son of Alphaeus, Simon the Zealot, and Judas the son of James. All these with one accord continued steadfastly in prayer and supplication, along with the women, and Mary the mother of Jesus, and with his brothers.

Set by Jewish law, a 'Sabbath day's journey' was a permissible distance the Jews were allowed to walk on the Sabbath.

This was a sad moment for the disciples as they walked back to Jerusalem, realizing they had finally said goodbye to Jesus as they knew him. They went upstairs, possibly to the same room they had used for the last supper. What poignant memories this room would bring back.

In these few verses, we say goodbye to Mary in the Bible; she is not mentioned again.

It is interesting to imagine the bond that must have built up between Mary and her boys and their friends. The bonds that build up between people going through dreadful times in life seem much stronger than any other. We see it among servicemen and women, marching on War

Memorial Days—a bond we may be forgiven for almost envying—a love that nothing can destroy, a comradeship above value. They too had to say 'goodbye' to so many in the theatre of war.

God is sometimes hard to find in bleak, depressing moments. The apostles must now learn to find Jesus in spirit, having lost the privilege of being with him physically.

This poem seems to have the answer. It was found in the pocket of a soldier who died as a prisoner of war while working on the Burma Railway during World War II:

> I sought my soul, my soul I could not see,
> I sought my God, but he eluded me,
> I sought my brother, and I found all three.

Ria's comment: My reaction to all this (assuming it is correct in the first place) is how sad that she (Mary) was written out of biblical history and what a pity her gospel is still hidden from sight as it were.

Q. Who knows what happened to Mary after this time? Perhaps a member of the group will fill in the story. Mary, with her sons and other disciples, found solace in 'continued steadfast prayer and supplication'.

Where or in whom do you find solace?

Acts 1: 15-17:

In these days, Peter stood up in the midst of the disciples (and the number of names was about one hundred and twenty), and said, 'Brothers, it was necessary that this Scripture should be fulfilled, which the Holy Spirit spoke before by the mouth of David concerning Judas, who was guide to those who took Jesus. For he was numbered with us, and received his portion in this ministry.'

As Jesus predicted, Peter emerged as the first church leader of the establishing church and is now held as the first Pope by the Roman Catholic Church.

Strong Peter, devastated by the death of Jesus, filled with guilt at his own denial at the trial, and appalled by Judas's betrayal yet, after only a few weeks he was able to bravely put it all behind him to get on with the job.

It had been an emotional month for them all. Mary and the others may have winced at the name of Judas. Before that black Friday, Mary may have been very fond of Judas. Could she manage to forgive him?

Q. Is there a story of betrayal you can share?

Acts 1: 18-19

Now this man obtained a field with the reward for his wickedness, and falling headlong, his body burst open, and all his intestines gushed out. It became known to everyone who lived in Jerusalem that in their language that field was called 'Akeldama', that is, 'the field of blood'.

This is a gruesome story. It is believed that after Judas hanged himself, the gory corpse was left to decompose.

It was an ugly end to a seemingly devious character. Poor Judas; how interesting that Jesus, who had such insight, chose him for a friend. Judas saw the worst side of himself too late.

Many people believe Judas never imagined for a moment the situation would get so out of control—or that Jesus, his friend, would actually be killed; he was simply giving Jesus a push to call down legions of angels to rid the Jews of Roman occupation. Poor man. Perhaps Amy-Jill Levine could write a sequel to *The Misunderstood Jew* debating the misunderstood Judas.

From Ria: If there is such doubt about Judas, is it appropriate to 'assume' that he was guilty as charged.

Would it be possible to have a two sided question—the second being on the basis of Judas not being guilty?

Q. By committing suicide, Judas apparently condemned himself as 'guilty'. In your journal, describe the character of Judas as you see him. If he were brought to trial today, what charge would you bring against him? Would your verdict be 'guilty' or 'not guilty'?

Acts 1: 20-26

For it is written in the book of Psalms, 'Let his habitation be made desolate. Let no one dwell therein and let another take his office. Of the men therefore who have accompanied us all the time that the Lord Jesus went in and out among us, beginning from the baptism of John, to the day that he was received up from us, of these one must become a witness with us of his resurrection.'

They put forward two, Joseph called Barabbas, who was surnamed Justus, and Matthias. They prayed, and said, 'You, Lord, who know the hearts of all men, show which one of these two you have chosen to take part in this ministry and apostleship from which Judas fell away, that he might go to his own place.' They drew lots for them, and the lot fell on Matthias, and he was numbered with the eleven apostles.

Peter, the chairman, began to look for a new committee member to replace Judas. 'Of the men therefore that have accompanied us . . . one must become a witness with us of his resurrection,' he said. It seemed a pity that Joseph and Matthias couldn't both take over ministry, but twelve members of the ministry team were needed to identify each person with one of the twelve tribes of Israel.

The Jews made their decisions by casting lots (commonly pebbles or sticks were used). We may be forgiven for feeling skeptical that these decisions were made by coincidence.

Have you ever thought what a lot of coincidences we have in life? Think for a moment of the interesting things that have happened after some tiny event turned out, on reflection, to have brought about an amazing change in your life.

A while ago I was asked to write a paper on 'coincidences.' Here are just a few.

1. A chance meeting in a vegetable shop changed my career path.

2. We bought our present home because I met a stranger in this street and asked if she knew if any houses were for sale. She said, "Yes mine will go on the market tomorrow."

3. Yesterday I went to an Arts Festival and met a stranger from among a fairly large crowd, who works in a government department to help immigrants assimilate. She was excited about promoting religious intolerance. We had lunch together, and will work together to start establishing one of the dreams.

Ria's comment: remember coincidences can be good and bad—I assume you are talking about good ones.

Q. Have any of you had any extraordinary coincidences that have changed the direction of your life? Do the Sees feel they could be spiritual directions—they happen so often?

What about the Wincs? What do you feel about coincidence?

Considering Ria's point, reflecting on your life, is there some unpleasant coincidence that has affected your life? What is this conundrum telling us?

Summary of Chapter 1

The apostles begin to organize themselves after Jesus' ascension; Peter emerges as the first church leader; Judas is painfully replaced by Matthias as one of the twelve apostles; and Mary, the mother of Jesus, fades out of the Bible story. According to tradition, the apostle John took Mary to live in Ephesus, in Turkey. Certainly, there was a church of the Holy Virgin Mary there, which played a key role in the beginning of Christianity.

CHAPTER 2

Explosive Beginnings

Acts 2: 1-3

Now when the day of Pentecost had come, they were all with one accord in one place. Suddenly there came from the sky a sound like the rushing of a mighty wind, and it filled the entire house where they were sitting. Tongues like fire appeared and were distributed to them, and one sat on each of them.

Imagine that you are sitting with your friends when a 'sound like the rushing of a mighty wind,' not a whispering wind this time, but a gale, filled the room. Then tongues like fire seemed to rain down—did they look like leaves that separated into match-sized flames?

The whole thing sounds crazy, really. It is as difficult to understand and yet, they received an incredible feeling that 'passes understanding,' of peace and joy, wonder and excitement. It seems to be a hallmark of the Holy Spirit. It is too big to understand, is too big to ignore, and was too wonderful for the disciples to forget. Something changed their lives that day, and it can happen to anyone.

Q. Lewis Foster wrote '"fire" is a symbol of the divine presence' (Exod. 3: 2)[5] Are any of you able to explain a moment of 'divine presence' to the Wincs in the group from your personal experience, or have you done it already? In which case 'pass'.

---

[5] Lewis Foster contributor to the NIV Study Bible, Book of Acts commentary Chapter 2.

Acts 2: 4

They were all filled with the Holy Spirit, and began to speak with other languages, as the Spirit gave them the ability to speak.

Some years ago I worked in a church retirement village. It belonged to a charismatic Christian denomination. Speaking in tongues was new to me, and I thought, quite honestly, it was a whole lot of hooey.

However much 'hooey' it seemed, these Christians had more energy and excitement in their Christian lives than I.

As time went by, out of curiosity and diplomacy, I went to some of their church services. It was an interesting experience that I found rather threatening, isolating, embarrassing, and uncomfortable, as everyone else clapped their hands and worshiped God with all the energy they could muster. They broke into unrecognizable 'speakings.'

These people were able to forget themselves in their love and worship of God; they were free to show their emotions, to shout and laugh and praise the Creator in crazy joyfulness, and although nobody would notice or care what I was doing, I was still unable to get past my own ego and feeling of foolishness to praise God in their way. At last, I almost learned the freedom of the dance but stayed with my own traditional church, albeit changed—freer, more open-minded, and less critical of the way others worship God.

Q. Can you all write and share your thoughts about 'speaking in tongues' with your group?

Ria's comment: After the last few years of fire and flood dramas one could argue that something like that might have happened and been superimposed later when the stories were actually written down.

After all the first Bible wasn't *printed* until about AD 330 as I recall. (scholars date the Acts as possibly being *written, but not printed,* between 63 or after AD 70,). Can you imagine anyone being absolutely sure about what happened some 300 years before, say in 1711 if it was not written down! Even now that would be virtually impossible.

Q 2. Interesting thought Ria, what do you all think about that? Would even forty years ago stretch our memory?

Acts 2: 5-13

Now there were dwelling in Jerusalem Jews, devout men, from every nation under the sky. When this sound was heard, the multitude came together, and were bewildered, because everyone heard them speaking in his own language. They were all amazed and marvelled, saying to one another, 'Behold, aren't all these who speak Galilean? How do we hear, everyone in our own native language? Parthians, Medes, Elamites, and people from Mesopotamia, Judea, Cappadocia, Pontus, Asia, Phrygia, Pamphylia, Egypt, the parts of Libya around Cyrene, visitors from Rome, both Jews and proselytes, Cretans and Arabians: we hear them speaking in our languages the mighty works of God!' They were all amazed, and were perplexed, saying one to another, 'What does this mean?' Others, mocking, said, 'They are filled with new wine.'

What an interesting example of God's incredible sense of occasion, setting the scene at the perfect time to deliver this good news to the world. Not a quiet house or temple in the suburbs but choosing a house in the crowded marketplace early in the morning, among people who came from a vast area of the Middle East.

These people would spread the story to Italy, Turkey, Egypt, Iran, Iraq, and Syria, as well as along the north coast of Africa to Libya, Morocco and Algeria, providing a communication explosion, without any newspapers, in one hit. Brilliant.

Acts 2: 16-17

But this is what has been spoken through the prophet Joel: 'It will be in the last days,' says God, 'that I will pour out my Spirit on all flesh. Your sons and your daughters will prophesy. Your young men will see visions. Your old men will dream dreams.'

Peter explains again that the prophecy of the Old Testament had come true. The theologian Augustine of Hippo (d. 430 AD) put it very neatly when he said, 'In the Old Testament the New (Testament) lies hidden; in the New Testament the meaning of the Old becomes clear.'

In the same way that nothing can stop the sun from rising on some part of the world every minute of the day, so nothing can stop the Spirit of

God from blowing over it, however much humans try to stamp it out in the cruelest forms of torture and evil. We are invited to prophesy, to have visions, to dream dreams in the service of God. It is a challengingly invitation.

Q. What dreams do you have in the service of humanity? Can you share them?

Acts 2: 18-21

'Yes, and on my servants and on my handmaidens in those days,
I will pour out my Spirit, and they will prophesy.
I will show wonders in the sky above, and signs on the earth beneath; blood, and fire, and billows of smoke.
The sun will be turned into darkness, and the moon into blood, before the great and glorious day of the Lord comes.
It will be that whoever will call on the name of the Lord will be saved.'

The thought of blood and fire and billows of smoke before the coming of the Lord sounds rather frightening.

Jesus tells us that God's spirit is built into each of us. It comes with life itself when we are conceived. As we grow, the spirit waits to be recognized much as a seed in the ground waits for the right moment to recognize the rain and the sun to begin to sprout and grow. We are invited to respond and begin our journey through the mystery of faith.

Joel says, 'Everyone who calls on His name,'

will become truly alive–grow to their full potential—with a sense that they are not alone, someone is looking out for them. It sounds easy enough to just call his name, and it is.

Q. It is no secret that we live in a scientific age of rapidly changing technology. Do you recognize any signs in these verses that the 'great and glorious day of the Lord' is coming? Which signs are they?

Acts 2: 22-24

Men of Israel, hear these words! Jesus of Nazareth, a man approved by God to you by mighty works and wonders and signs which God did by him in the midst of you, even as you yourselves know, him, being delivered up by the determined counsel and foreknowledge of God, you have taken by the hand of lawless men, crucified and killed; whom God raised up, having freed him from the agony of death, because it was not possible that he should be held by it.

'You killed this wonderful man,' Peter says, but death can neither destroy Jesus nor can it destroy any of us. If we truly believe the Gospels story, then death is only a gateway to the invisible.

Only the disciples had the privilege of meeting Jesus alive 'after death.' This is surely the ultimate point that sets Jesus apart from any other person who has ever lived.

The apostles had the confidence to talk and preach about a life after death, because they knew beyond a shadow of doubt that Jesus was not separated from them. Death had not obliterated him into darkness. He loved them. In a slightly different way, I believe, everyone who has died is beside and encouraging those they love, never to be apart again, only out of sight.

Q. What are your thoughts of life after death?

Acts 2: 25-28

> For David says concerning him,
> 'I saw the Lord always before my face,
> For he is on my right hand, that I should not be moved.
> Therefore my heart was glad, and my tongue rejoiced.
> Moreover my flesh also will dwell in hope; because you will not leave my soul in Hades, neither will you allow your Holy One to see decay.
> You made known to me the ways of life.

King David wrote this psalm about a thousand years before Jesus' time. His psalm is a perfect summary of how to live in the kingdom of God on earth.

'I saw the Lord always before my face, for He is on my right hand,' as my companion and supporter.

'Therefore my heart was glad and my tongue rejoiced.' I am happy; I no longer nag or bully or criticize, because there is joy in my life, a spring of well-being, feeling that 'all is well.' I'm not alone; I feel secure in him, loved, and cherished.

'My flesh also will dwell in hope.' He gives me self-confidence.

'Because you will not leave my soul in Hades.' He will not leave us in hell. David talks about the joy that is in store for us after this life.

'You will make me full of gladness with your presence.' You show me how I can live and experience moments of the joy of heaven while I am still on earth.

Sometimes there are patches of life that feel so wonderful for no apparent reason, just a feeling of being close to the source of all energy. It may be easier to *feel* these places, which 'You made known to me,' than to understand.

Q 1. Let's look at walking in the kingdom of God again.

Wincs and Sees, are Sees different? Are they generally happy people? Do they gossip? A friend of mine commented the other day that, looking around, she felt most 'successful' people seem to have a faith. Have any of you observed this?

Ria's Comment: Methinks you are talking about a very small proportion of people that this could apply to in this day and age—people who say they are Christians display right left and centre very 'unchristian' behaviour'.

Q2. OK Ria, sadly you are right. Does this need discussing or acknowledging by the group?

Acts 2: 29

Brothers, I may tell you freely of the patriarch David, that he both died and was buried, and his tomb is with us to this day.

Maybe you have visited Jerusalem and have seen the house that is said to contain the tomb of this classic poet and visionary, David. He wrote the lovely verses above (25-28).

There is a huge ancient paving stone in the main street of Jerusalem that was too huge to be moved when the road was remade. It has probably been there for millions of years. To stand on that spot is awe inspiring, knowing that David, and certainly Jesus, stood on that same stone—Jesus would have walked over it many times, even carrying a cross on his shoulders on the way to be crucified.

Today the noise and jostle of the traders would be very similar to the noise David and Jesus heard. Maybe you have, or will one day, walk through those streets and go on to wander through the hills of Galilee. You may swim in the waters of the lake where the disciples fished, wander along the beach where Jesus collected dry sticks to light a fire early in the morning, knowing Peter and the others would be along shortly (John 21) and imagine the smell of the wood smoke and fish cooking on the beach.

To be there is yet another place to feel the sense of timelessness. The hills are the same, the lake looks the same, and many of the trees were there in Jesus' day. Jerusalem's old city is almost the same—suddenly, you belong in a small part to the whole plan.

Q. Wincs and Sees, have you had a similar experience when you felt you were a small piece of the whole of Creation's jigsaw puzzle, the Great Plan? Can you all share the 'piece' you have contributed to it, however big or small?

Acts 2: 30-31

Therefore, being a prophet, and knowing that God had sworn with an oath to him that of the fruit of his body, according to the flesh, he would raise up the Christ to sit on his throne, he foreseeing this spoke about the resurrection of the Christ, that neither was his soul left in Hades, nor did his flesh see decay.

Peter describes David's prayerful relationship with God. The question 'How is prayer answered?' sometimes comes up in sermons. The answer I remember most vividly is often threefold.

The first step is to tell God about the situation, listen quietly for the whispering wind to blow into the mind, and then pray again. For to pray is to set a chain of events in place; something in the cosmos moves—like a breeze through fallen autumn leaves, the leaves never go back to the same place again. Something has changed, however small, forever.

Secondly, talk the situation over with someone whose judgment is to be trusted. The wise person may not advise at all but will help by listening and talking through alternatives.

Finally, if the situation is unresolved, it may be wise to just wait for circumstances to become clearer. The answer will come—in the fullness of time.

Q. Are there other thoughts on answers to prayer to share?

Acts 2: 32

This Jesus God raised up, to which we all are witnesses.

Peter is still talking to the crowd after the extraordinary episode earlier that morning when the Spirit of God descended on the eleven disciples in the market place. They were so filled with happiness, excitement, and effervescence that the people in the crowd thought they might be drunk.

Jesus, the man they had welcomed into Jerusalem only one month ago, and condemned to death a few days later, was in the news again—this same Jesus was alive.

It was common knowledge that the Old Testament prophets promised God would send a Messiah (a rescuer, a savior) one day, not only to be a great prophet but also to overcome death. The Jews did not know how or when this was going to happen. They were waiting expectantly and are still waiting today. While they were waiting, Peter says, the Savior had come and gone under their noses, and they did not notice.

Q. Peter was making an amazing statement about the apostles having seen someone who was no longer alive. Have you experienced such a person, even in a dream? Can you share your event?

Acts 2: 33-35

Being therefore exalted by the right hand of God, and having received from the Father the promise of the Holy Spirit, he has poured out this, which you now see and hear. For David didn't ascend into the heavens, but he says himself,

'The Lord said to my Lord, "Sit by my right hand, until I make your enemies a footstool for your feet."'

The promised Holy Spirit is within me, Peter says, and the Spirit is speaking to you all. The Spirit may speak through any one of us to another. For all our faults, God asks us to be his messenger. He has no other.

Q. Sees, have you delivered any 'God messages' lately? A priest or minister may prefer to miss this one. For Wincs, have you delivered a thought which came from a dream or intuition lately or at all?

Acts 2: 36

Let all the house of Israel therefore know certainly that God has made him both Lord and Christ.

What does it mean to say 'God has made Jesus both Lord and Christ'? It is a question that has baffled theologians for centuries. The German theologian Paul Tillich (1886-1965) wrote: 'Christianity is what it is through the affirmation that Jesus of Nazareth . . . is actually the Christ, namely, he who brings the new state of things, the New Being . . . Christianity was born, not with the birth of the man called 'Jesus,' but in the moment in which one of his followers was driven to say of him 'Thou art the Christ,' and Christianity will live as long as there are people who repeat this assertion.'[6]

God appointed Jesus to be his representative on earth; to save people from being swamped, defeated, and crushed; to save them from fear, anxiety, and hopelessness; and to save them into hope, confidence, and love. We are offered the chance to become a 'New Being' if only we can let go of all the petty rubbish and doubts that crowd in and spoil so much of our time. He offers calm, strength, and peace if only we care to accept it.

Q. Is it easy to except this concept? Is it worth trying? There is nothing much to lose, except worry and problems. Wincs, do you think it is easier to be a Winc than a Christian?

---

[6]   Tillich the German theologian 1886-1965

Acts 2: 37

Now when they heard this, they were cut to the heart, and said to Peter and the rest of the apostles, 'Brothers, what shall we do?'

No wonder they were unsure what to do. It seems remarkable that the people did not react defensively to Peter's accusations, '*this Jesus whom you crucified.*' One could imagine the lawsuits today if an evangelist accused some politicians, for example, of murdering someone. There would be enough material to keep the lawyers going for a lifetime.

So what was it about Peter, this man on whom Jesus founded his church that he was able to get away with such a provocative statement as 'you murdered Jesus'? He made the whole crowd feel guilty! Only a few weeks before, the same crowd had cried for Jesus' death.

A crowd in an angry mood is frightening. A crowd in a happy appreciative mood after a great performance is exhilarating. Peter must have been a master performer, to have kept control of the crowd at this moment.

God chooses so carefully when he wants a job done. No wonder Jesus picked Peter to carry on after he had gone.

Q. What did you do, when you had a serious dilemma? To whom did you go to say 'What shall I do?' What happened?

Acts 2: 38-39

Peter said to them, 'Repent, and be baptised, every one of you, in the name of Jesus Christ for the forgiveness of sins, and you will receive the gift of the Holy Spirit. For the promise is to you, and to your children, and to all who are far off, even as many as the Lord our God will call to himself.'

Peter answers their question—accept the fact that we are all far from perfect—show it by being baptized—ask God for forgiveness, and then freely accept complete forgiveness which is available to everyone.

To 'repent' and apologize, or to accept an apology with warmth, is a gracious thing to do, and shows a generous spirit. So it seems that living in the kingdom of God on earth means giving portions of forgiveness generously.

Q. Do you have any unfinished business in the need to forgive department? Would you care to share it, or do something about it?

Acts 2: 40-41

With many other words he testified, and exhorted them saying, 'Save yourselves from this crooked generation!'

Then those who gladly received his word were baptised. There were added that day about three thousand souls.

Do you feel the present generation is crooked? Or maybe confused, lacking direction, feeling a bit lost if unemployed? Maybe God put us here on earth in the hope that the beauty of this world would change us.

Jesus and Peter both believed God's message of hope for their 'crooked generation' so passionately that they were prepared to die for it.

Q. Pretend you are today's Peter, what would you say to this generation of young people to encourage them? But unlike Peter, you luckily do not have to risk your life doing it, so feel free. Peter advised them to be baptized. What would you say to them that would make them gladly want to accept your advice?

Acts 2: 42-43

They continued steadfastly in the apostles' teaching and fellowship, in the breaking of bread, and prayer. Fear [or Awe] came on every soul, and many wonders and signs were done through the apostles.

Through the ages billions of people have found indefinable wonder and fellowship from belonging to a faith. The Christian church is not perfect we know, because it is made up of imperfect humans, but even so, God still manifests his love through it.

The breaking of bread was a custom regularly used by the Jews at a meal to symbolize two things. The breaking signified the breaking from bondage and slavery in Egypt to lead them to the Promised Land. The eating celebrates the manna from heaven given to feed the Jews during their escape through the desert.

But now, the apostles explain, the breaking of bread had taken on new significance. Jesus taught his friends and followers that a way to be free from spiritual bondage is to be spiritually fed through the mystical act of communion with God—a touch from the holy, a touch from the power of God, which says 'all is forgiven, let's start again, you are clean and whole, and I love you.'

Q. I am not sure how to coin the questions for the Wincs here. I want to ask how do you describe a spiritual episode?'

Ria comments: Have you defined the meaning of the word 'spiritual'?

The dictionary definition of spiritual is 'spirit as opposed to matter; of the soul especially.' And spirit is described as 'intelligent immaterial part of man, soul etc.' While over lunch in the garden, my husband, Richard's definition of spiritual was this, 'a thought that comes into your head from somewhere you cannot put a finger on.' Please all nut out your own definitions of 'spiritual' and then answer the question—how would you describe a spiritual episode, and have you had one? ☺

Acts 2: 44-45

All who believed were together, and had all things in common. They sold their possessions and goods, and distributed them to all, according as anyone had need.

What a great team at work. Can you relate to that team spirit, the warm feeling of joy at having the privilege of doing something useful for other people?

Ria's comment: It seems as though you are inextricably linking goodness with Christianity/Spirit of God etc.

Somehow I think it is not as simple as that. You and I will know many people who are not religious who do good deeds—are you assuming that somehow God is directing them. Sorry Nancy I find that a bit patronizing. Also, sometimes the giving, the assisting, comes back and bites the giver—I have seen that happen and a nasty feeling it is too.

I think those nonbelievers you refer to are decent human beings who just do not need Christianity or some other religion to do good deeds. And some Christians I know I'd not trust at all. Yes, you can say they are not true Christians, but they often believe they are.

Q. What would you all say to that?

But Ria is right, I do link goodness with the Spirit of God whether consciously or not, because to me God is goodness.

Please think about Ria's remarks seriously, and see if you too agree that Christians can sometimes, albeit unwittingly, be very patronizing. It is not an uncommon criticism. And of course, there are bad apples in the Christian bucket too. How do you respond to Ria?

Acts 2: 46-47

Day by day, continuing steadfastly with one accord in the temple, and breaking bread at home, they took their food with gladness and singleness of heart, praising God, and having the Lord added to the assembly day by day those who were being saved.

This is a happy scene filled with companionship, close friendships, and bonds growing out of this newly formed group. It is an interesting description of the social life they were enjoying as they entertained in their homes—not lavishly, I'm sure, because they were very conscious of community needs—but sharing simply and generously what they had.

From Ria: I refer again to my last paragraph . . . one reads of tribes in various parts of the world who take visitors in and feed and care for them . . . Maybe you are not endeavoring to put such a proposal but that is how it looks to me.

Q. How does it look to you? It is interesting that diverse opinions produce conflict, but this maybe a lesson with which the group is coming to term. I am hugely grateful for Ria's opinions, because many of people will feel like her, and conflict is associated with solving diversity. I have lost the question. Perhaps you have one.

Summary of Chapter 2

The chapter began with the promised gift of God's Holy Spirit descending on the believers in tongues of fire at Pentecost. They immediately began to speak in strange languages and feel the joy and excitement that comes from the gift of the Holy Spirit.

The results were dramatic, as thousands of people responded to Peter's teaching, and the Christians infectious joy, generosity, and friendship spread rapidly.

CHAPTER 3

The Age of Miracles

Acts 3: 1-5

Peter and John were going up into the temple at the hour of prayer, the ninth hour. A certain man who was lame from his mother's womb was being carried, whom they laid daily at the door of the temple which is called Beautiful, to ask gifts for the needy of those who entered into the temple. Seeing Peter and John about to go into the temple, he asked to receive gifts for the needy. Peter, fastening his eyes on him, with John, said, 'Look at us.' He listened to them, expecting to receive something from them.

Money occupies such a large part of our thinking. Just enough of it certainly makes life more comfortable. Too little makes it pretty stressful, and too much so often seems to destroy people altogether.

God may not always give us silver and gold on demand, butcourage to carry on when things seem to be against us.

Again in these scripture verses, we find this moment of eye contact, spiritually looking through the window of the soul.

Q. Occasionally 'one of those moments' happen when someone you meet looks straight into your eyes—there is a connection and you are not sure what is coming! Can you share such a moment? There may be laughs or tears here.

Acts 3: 6-10

But Peter said, 'Silver and gold have I none, but what I have, that I give you. In the name of Jesus Christ of Nazareth, get up and walk!' He took him by the right hand, and raised him up. Immediately his feet and his ankle bones received strength. Leaping up, he stood, and began to walk. He entered with them into the temple, walking, leaping, and praising God. All the people saw him walking and praising God. They were filled with wonder and amazement at what had happened to him.

Peter held out his right hand in a simple gesture to help the beggar get to his feet, as the wonderful spiritual hallmark of dancing for joy, excitement, and wonder is clearly visible again.

Sit quietly for a moment with eyes closed, while the Sip reads on to the end of this commentary.

Imagine your legs are crippled, unable to move; you're stuck, needing help to do everything, and, with a heavy sigh, you just watch others busily enjoying life, and suddenly someone touches you—and a life time of crippling emotional pain disappears.

The beggar, unable to believe what was happening, looked at smiling Peter, and just for a second, there may have been a moment of holy recognition as these two men made eye contact—as if they were the only two people in the world—a tiny moment through those heavenly windows again, as the beggar saw God in Peter. Would they have had a wonderful strong hug—a moment the beggar would treasure for the rest of his life?

Many of us experience less obvious healing—of being self-centered, the healing of relationships, or any one of our weaknesses, which are possibly the greatest healing of all. Are you able to identify something that needs self-healings?

Q. Share or not as you will.

Acts 3: 11-12

As the lame man who was healed held on to Peter and John, all the people ran together to them in the porch that is called Solomon's, greatly wondering.

When Peter saw it, he responded to the people, 'You men of Israel, why do you marvel at this man? Why do you fasten your eyes on us, as though by our own power or godliness we had made him walk?'

What a poignant, emotional moment. Then bedlam—the moment passed, and the beggar leapt into the air. Whoop-i-doo. Suddenly, people are running—excitement in the air. What are they missing? Incredible! Peter speaks to the people while the beggar is probably still leaping about. 'Why are you amazed?' asked Peter. But surely they had good reason to be astounded.

Q. Has there been an unbelievably miraculous point in your life? Can you record and share it?

From Ria: Here is a crunch point. There are marvelous things that happen and there are frauds perpetuated which may look as if there is something marvelous happening. We can never know what happened on that occasion and how that was re-written—it only works if you accept what has been said, and again as I said before hundreds of years after it purportedly happened.

Q. Any thoughts on Ria's 'crunch'?

Acts 3: 13-21

Peter goes on to say: The God of Abraham, Isaac, and Jacob, the God of our fathers, has glorified his Servant Jesus, whom you delivered up, and denied in the presence of Pilate, when he had determined to release him. But you denied the Holy and Righteous One, and asked for a murderer to be granted to you, and killed the Prince of life, whom God raised from the dead, to which we are witnesses. By faith in his name, his name has made this man strong, whom you see and know. Yes, the faith which is through him has given him this perfect soundness in the presence of you all.

Now, brothers, I know that you did this in ignorance, as did also your rulers. But the things which God announced by the mouth of all his prophets, that Christ should suffer, he thus fulfilled.

v 19 'Repent therefore, and turn again, that your sins may be blotted out, so that there may come times of refreshing from the presence of the Lord, and that he may send Christ Jesus, who was ordained for you before, whom heaven must receive until the times of restoration of all things,' which God spoke long ago by the mouth of his holy prophets.

These verses give us the threefold message and recurring gospel theme preached by the apostles.

First comes *prophesy* from the Old Testament. Secondly, the Jesus story, and thirdly, in verse 19, comes the need for repentance, baptism and the healing forgiveness. Peter said, 'you did wrong in ignorance.'

'It is finished,' Jesus said, as he died a horrible death on the cross—the price he had to pay for persistently preaching God's unconditional forgiveness, which allows us to leave the past behind and begin again, forgiven and refreshed. And we owe it to him to do just that, Peter says.

Q. Peters remark 'I know that you did this in ignorance' brings me to the huge problem of global warming. Enormous damage has been done to the earth in ignorance, but what will we say to the children when they grow up and ask, 'What did you do about it?' Are we doing everything possible to help—using electricity sparingly, trying not to use the car unnecessarily, taking as many passengers whenever possible, recycling conscientiously, re-using paper and envelopes? Has anyone other suggestions to contribute?

Acts 3: 22-23: For Moses indeed said to the fathers, 'The Lord God will raise up a prophet for you from among your brothers, like me. You shall listen to him in all things whatever he says to you. It will be that every soul, that will not listen to that prophet, will be utterly destroyed from among the people."

People gathered around Peter, after the healing of the crippled beggar, he tells them they need to listen to Moses' stern warning—obey the word of God, follow, listen, then you and your children will be blessed, or ignore God and bear the consequences. God chose a tiny nation to bring his great message to the world. He chose strong, insular, proud people, who are fiercely independent, disciplined, dedicated, and determined survivors. He trained them for two thousand years.

But the trouble was the Jews believed that God belonged to them alone. God had to 'crack the nut' of the Jews exclusive possessiveness to allow this good news of hope to spread out to all nations. The Jews were not happy.

The 'cracking of the nut' began at the crucifixion and resurrection of Jesus. It continued at Pentecost, and carried on through the courage and bravery of hundreds of martyrs who gave their very lives to carry God's message abroad.

Later for centuries the Christians took over from the Jews to believe they owned God alone. Some still do.

Madeleine Albright writes in her book, *The Might and The Almighty* ' . . . peace between nations and peoples cannot be achieved without reconciliation between religions and cultures . . . '

Q. To each person in the group—do you accept people of other faiths, cultures and even different denominations within your own religion, with unconditional acceptance? Or is there a particular group of people you find difficult? Or do you respect their difference, but simply 'know' they are wrong? We probably all have our prejudices. It could be useful to unbury them honestly to share in this nonjudgmental gathering.

Acts 3: 24-26

Yes, and all the prophets from Samuel and those who followed after, as many as have spoken, they also told of these days. You are the children of the prophets, and of the covenant which God made with our fathers, saying to Abraham, 'In your seed will all the families of the earth be blessed.' God, having raised up his servant, Jesus, sent him to you first, to bless you, in turning away every one of you from your wickedness.'

God said to Abraham: 'Through your family, all people on earth shall be blessed.' As parents, one of the greatest joys in life is to see good things coming from our children. Their qualities and care each other, and for others, is a great reward.

There is nothing most of us would not do for our children in gratitude and love, but God's love is unimaginably even greater than loving parents for a precious child. The enormity of that love is staggering.

Q. Our children and children's children are presumably the ones referred to as 'in your seed.' Is your community blessed by them? Maybe there isn't any 'seed,' and that's fine. Is your community blessed by you? How? Don't be humble; jot down your harvest, describe your personal piece of the Great Planner's jigsaw puzzle. Share as you will.

Summary of Chapter 3

The chapter began with the crippled beggar at the Temple Gate called Beautiful asking Peter and John for money. Peter said they will give him something better than money. Peter stretches out his hand and tells the beggar to get up and walk. He is completely healed. They dance through the temple and sing with joy. Peter and John are questioned by the amazed people. Peter explains that it is by the healing power of God, the same God of their fathers, and through the name of Jesus Christ that this beggar was healed and that through the teaching of Jesus, the rest of the world will be blessed.

CHAPTER 4

Peter and John in Trouble

Acts 4: 1-4

As they spoke to the people, the priests and the captain of the temple and the Sadducees came to them, being upset because they taught the people and proclaimed in Jesus the resurrection from the dead. They laid hands on them, and put them in custody until the next day, for it was now evening. But many of those who heard the word believed, and the number of the men came to be about five thousand.

The Sadducees, the keepers of peace in the temple, did not believe in a life after death (Acts 23: 8) tension was rising as the authorities listened to talk of the resurrection of Jesus? They were greatly disturbed by Peter's message and quickly tried to stop the spread of this 'false teaching' by seizing Peter and John and putting them into custody.

They did not understand, because they did not want to hear. They knew they knew best! And yet the uncomfortable fact remained that Peter had healed a man. The Sadducees were trying to defend their fundamental Jewish beliefs without acknowledging the evidence—unprepared to change or even listen. Does this ring a human bell?

From Ria: Reminds me of the peaceful protests in Egypt! Makes you feel very sorry for the peoples in the other Arab countries right now.

Q. The Sadducees were not prepared to listen. Listening skills are important enough to be taught in many professions. Can you think of some important points to remember when listening to someone? Just for fun, a few clues may be found by filling in the spaces below.

1. Give qu _ _ t f _ _ l at _ _ _ tion 2. Don't int _ _ r _ _ t
3. E _ _ c_ nt _ _ _ 4. C _ nc _ _ t _a _ _.
    (Answers at the end of this chapter.)

Acts 4: 5-12

It happened in the morning that their rulers, elders, and scribes were gathered together in Jerusalem. Annas the high priest was there, with Caiaphas, John, Alexander, and as many as were relatives of the high priest. When they had stood them in the middle of them, they inquired, 'By what power, or in what name, have you done this?'

Then Peter, filled with the Holy Spirit, said to them, 'You rulers of the people, and elders of Israel, if we are examined today concerning a good deed done to a crippled man, by what means this man has been healed, be it known to you all, and to all the people of Israel, that in the name of Jesus Christ of Nazareth, whom you crucified, whom God raised from the dead, in him does this man stand here before you whole. He is 'the stone which was regarded as worthless by you, the builders, which has become the head of the corner.' There is salvation in none other, for neither is there any other name under heaven that is given among men, by which we must be saved!'

The Sanhedrin was the supreme court of the Jewish nation, made up of rulers, elders, and teachers of the law. They were alarmed by the effect Peter and John were having in the town, so they immediately called an assembly of important people for an emergency meeting. They were unwilling to accept the overwhelming evidence of the healing power of God.

Peter, filled with great authority and confidence, was fulfilling Jesus' promise in Acts 1: 8, 'you will receive power,' and as bold as brass, he pointed an accusing finger at them, warning the court that the same name by which the cripple had received bodily health was the name through which they, too, could receive spiritual health—salvation.

Salvation is a subjective word. The Oxford dictionary says salvation is 1) 'Saving the soul; deliverance from sin and its consequences, and admission to heaven, brought about by the merits of Christ's death. 2) Preservation from loss, calamity etc.'

Right or wrong, my simple definition of salvation would be that my only hope of coping in this busy, aggressive world is to claim the companionship of the Holy Spirit, which is expressed through the teaching of Jesus of Nazareth, the one on whom I lean, talk, and listen, because from experience, it brings me comfort and creates a greater degree of harmony in my life.

Q. What does 'salvation' mean to you? Write your own definition.

Acts 4: 13

Now when they saw the boldness of Peter and John, and had perceived that they were unlearned and ignorant men, they marvelled. They recognised they had been with Jesus.

The High Priest and his colleagues were amazed at this articulate, bold, and courageous Peter—he was only a fisherman, after all. Here he was standing in the temple preaching, making the authorities feel bewildered. Peter had not been to the right school, and he certainly was not recognized as a religious leader or scholar. Peter and John obviously had no ordinary teacher, and the court took note that they had been with Jesus—there was something different about them.

There seems to be a quality in holy men and women—calmness, confidence, a presence which attracts attention, a glowing spirit within. Surely we all know someone with this wonderful 'something.' Mother Teresa, Nelson Mandela, and Barack Obama come to mind.

Maybe we could each acquire this laid back serenity if we were prepared to give enough energy and time to our Creator, a commitment to find the real source of love which comes with forgiveness, self-confidence, with no strings attached to those in every religion it seems. Why is it so easy to walk away?

Q. Think of the holiest person you know, they need not be a person of faith. List five of their qualities you admire about them.

Acts 4: 14-17

Seeing the man who was healed standing with them, they could say nothing against it. But when they had commanded them to go aside out of the council, they conferred among themselves, saying, 'What shall we do to these men? Because indeed a notable miracle has been done through them, as can be plainly seen by all who dwell in Jerusalem, and we can't deny it. But so that this spreads no further among the people, let's threaten them, that from now on they don't speak to anyone in this name.'

What greater temptation is there to pass on a story than to say, 'Don't tell anyone'? The authorities' tactic proved to be poor psychology, because the church grew in great numbers. To their acute discomfort, the leaders (Peter and John) were challenging the authority.

What a dilemma. Here was a crippled man leaping about. Surely the natural reaction would have been joy and wonder, but the authorities were frightened compassion or gladness was not in their minds. Blast him! Peter and John were making too great an impression on the people. The high priest, elders, and rulers of the temple were losing control.

Q. v 16-17: If you are in a position of authority and feel you are losing the attention or control of the situation—such as a classroom, committee, or speaking engagement—what would you do? There may be many interesting responses here. Play role for fun.

Acts 4: 18-22

They called them, and commanded them not to speak at all nor teach in the name of Jesus.

But Peter and John answered them, 'whether it is right in the sight of God to listen to you rather than to God, judge for yourselves, for we can't help telling the things which we saw and heard.'

When they had further threatened them, they let them go, finding no way to punish them, because of the people; for everyone glorified God for that which was done. For the man on whom this miracle of healing was performed was more than forty years old.

The apostles acknowledged that civic law has to be respected and is only to be challenged if it conflicts with the authority of God. Thousands of martyrs have died for this principle—no threat or torture can make them change their minds, even unto death.

How extraordinary that men and women will be persecuted and die for a mystical spirit they cannot see, physically talk to, or even hear—the Great 'Somebody' certainly passes any understanding.

From Ria: Again I think you should broaden the religions here—It reads again as if only Christians have this happen.
(Sorry Ria, but I did say 'the Great Somebody'.)

Q. Which other religions do you know have martyrs?

Acts 4: 23-26

Being let go, they came to their own company, and reported all that the chief priests and the elders had said to them. When they heard it, they lifted up their voice to God with one accord, and said, 'O Lord, you are God, who made the heaven, the earth, the sea, and all that is in them; who by the mouth of your servant, David, said,
'Why do the nations rage?
And the people plot a vain thing?'
The kings of the earth take a stand, and the rulers take council together, against the Lord, and against his Christ.

Peter and John, glad to be out of custody, report back to their growing community. The verse that begins 'Why do the nations . . .' is a quotation from Psalm 2: 1-2 and is generally believed to have been written by King David. David explores the same question that is often asked today: 'Why have politicians and leaders plotted evil, conflict, and war through all ages?'
Why do we humans constantly 'rage' against each other and against a Creator who made us? Why do we prefer to ignore, rather than listen? Why are we generally embarrassed and reluctant to talk about our creator?
People often rebel against religion and everyone else as well during teenage years.
When religion is hushed up, it will continue to be embarrassing. When church is associated with unpleasant memories from childhood, children will almost certainly 'rage against it.' and probably abandon looking for any spirituality altogether. We have much to learn from many indigenous people of the world, whose spirituality is as normal as breathing.

Q. Sean O'Casey said 'Politics has killed thousands, religion has killed ten thousands.'[7] Do you think this is true?

Acts 4: 27-31

'For truly, in this city against your holy servant, Jesus, whom you anointed, both Herod and Pontius Pilate, with the Gentiles and the people of Israel, were gathered together to do whatever your hand and your council foreordained to happen. Now, Lord, look at their threats, and grant to your servants to speak your word with all boldness, while you stretch out your hand to heal; and that signs and wonders may be done through the name of your holy Servant Jesus.' When they had prayed, the place was shaken where they were gathered together. They were all filled with the Holy Spirit, and they spoke the word of God with boldness.

Back in the meeting room, Peter and John prayed. Without any apparent reason the room shook inexplicably again, just as it did on the day of Pentecost. Was it a sign of spiritual encouragement, a symbol saying 'See, I am here with you, you are doing well'?

From Ria: Sorry, my mind immediately says the Arabian Plate probably moved and in those days the concept was unknown.

Maybe we all need a good shake sometimes to recognize that the deep inner voice is our enabler and encourager. Without it, we don't necessarily wither, although, as Ruth Abbey says, 'humans by their very nature have an orientation to transcendence.'[8] There is a part of the human make up that longs to be bonded with the Great Spirit—however mysterious this seems.

Q. Wincs, we need your help again here. What does your soul need and long for?

---

7   Richard Dawkins' quotes Sean O'Casey in his book *The God Delusion* chapter 7 page237.

8   Associate Professor Ruth Abbey, science department of Notre Dame University in the United States, speaking with presenter Margaret Coffey on Australian Broadcasting Corporation radio program *Encounter* October 2009.

From Ria: You could get a flood of stuff on this—e.g. why does one person recover well from an op which is done to many and others do not. Sometimes those who are not 'well' cope with an op, for example, when the very fit ones don't—the human body being an amazing organism.

Q2. What is the answer to Ria's interesting comments?

Acts 4: 32-33

The multitude believed, and was of one heart and soul. Not one of them claimed that anything of the things which he possessed was his own, but they had all things in common. With great power, the apostles gave their testimony of the resurrection of the Lord Jesus. Great grace was on them all.

The crucifixion of Jesus was enormously significant, but the central point to the apostles' story was the resurrection. The Christian gospel message is a story of pain and suffering, but the focus is the resurrection of Jesus as the narrative moves through fear and death to the hope, life, and joy that are to come. The Psalmist predicted *joy cometh in the morning,'* and it did on Easter morning.

Q. Wincs, please identify four principles you feel are the basis on which to live a 'good' life?
Sees, can you identify three or four fundamental principles that come out of the Gospels for you? Are you all able to prioritize and share them? I wonder if some answers from the Wincs and the Sees will be the same.

Acts 4: 34-35

For neither was there among them any who lacked, for as many as were owners of lands or houses sold them, and brought the proceeds of the things that were sold, and laid them at the apostles' feet, and distribution was made to each, according as anyone had need.

This is an interesting picture of community living, sharing, and caring as 'anyone had need.' We live in a modern society where the quality of our lives is not necessarily improving. The paragraph below describes the original Australians' way of life for many thousands of years. It could also be said to reflect the principles of Christianity or, indeed, the principles of most religions. The following passage is a quotation from the foreword of the book *Victors or Victims*:

'Imagine a society where every man achieves a position of status and respect . . . where authority is based on age, intellect and experience . . . that sharing of all material possessions is a cultural imperative, that every person is well nourished . . . economically independent and that the food quest leaves ample time for recreational, intellectual and spiritual pursuits.

Make this a religion which celebrates the communion of humanity and nature, which involves every family deeply . . . which provides a set of rules to live by, which shape both social and environmental harmony.'[9]

Reflect for a while on the value and quality of the events that fill our days; reflect on the values of the quotation. Here every person has a position of respect (no discrimination); possessions are shared, and everyone is nourished (no poverty); there is ample time to talk (quality time); and every family is deeply involved (strong community spirit). There is social and environmental harmony (no stress). What have we done to destroy such a perfect lifestyle? It sounds like heaven to me.

Q. Consider the five issues in this commentary—discrimination, poverty, quality time, community spirit, and stress. Write a sentence or two on each subject and how it relates to you, your family, your church, or your community. If there is anything you can do to alter the situation, write it in alongside the sentence.

Acts 4: 36-37

Joseph, who by the apostles was surnamed Barnabas (which is, being interpreted, Son of Encouragement), a Levite, a man of Cyprus by race, having a field, sold it, and brought the money and laid it at the apostles' feet.

---

[9] Excerpt from the introduction of Victims or Victors, The Story of the Victorian Aborigines Advancement League. Page xii.

What an honor to be given the nickname, 'Son of Encouragement.' Do we encourage each other enough? The new generation of parents is a group of much greater encouragers than the more severe disciplinarians of the past. Children need encouraging; (they need discipline too!)

Q. Encouragement is the greatest gift we can give to each other and our children. List by bullet point just ten occasions you can remember where you have encouraged someone or been encouraged. For example, Henry's homework, husband's kindness, etc.

Summary of Chapter 4

Peter and John were still in trouble with the Jewish authorities for preaching about the resurrection of Jesus Christ. To the increasing alarm of the Jews, the number of Christians grew dramatically. Peter and John are imprisoned to stem the flow.

During the court hearing the next day, Peter and John repeated the gospel theme. They remind the court that the coming of the Messiah was prophesied in the Old Testament. These prophecies foreshadowed the story of the life, death, and resurrection of Jesus Christ, who brought a message of God's forgiveness and love.

Peter and John were released and told not to preach any more. They rush out rejoicing and go straight back to the people to preach and teach again.

Barnabas, the encourager, enters the story. He and the believers sold their land and possessions to share among anyone who had need. 'There were no needy persons among them'.

Answer to word puzzle Acts 4:–: 1. Quiet full attention
2. Don't interrupt 3. Eye contact 4. Concentrate.
There are of course, many more, but these are a few for a start.

CHAPTER 5

Ananias and Sapphira Make a Big Mistake

Acts 5: 1-4

But a certain man named Ananias, with Sapphira, his wife, sold a possession, and kept back part of the price, his wife also being aware of it, and brought a certain part, and laid it at the apostles' feet. But Peter said, 'Ananias, why has Satan filled your heart to lie to the Holy Spirit, and to keep back part of the price of the land? While you kept it, didn't it remain your own? After it was sold, wasn't it in your power? How is it that you have conceived this thing in your heart? You haven't lied to men, but to God.'

Ananias made the mistake of pretending he and Sapphira were giving the *whole* amount from the sale of their property. They had every right to keep as much money as they wished, but their mistake was that they lied to Peter. Suddenly the money felt 'dirty.'

How did Peter know that Ananias was lying? Why tell a lie? Cheating, lying, and dishonesty are healthy signs of the devil or the dark side of our nature at work. Like a chip or crack in a beautiful vase, it spoils everything. The price for this lie will be high for Ananias and Sapphira.

Acts 5: 5-8

Ananias, hearing these words, fell down and died. Great fear came on all who heard these things. The young men arose and wrapped him up and they carried him out and buried him. About three hours later, his wife, not knowing what had happened, came in. Peter answered her, 'Tell me whether you sold the land for so much.' She said, 'Yes, for so much.'

The punishment seems a bit harsh, but a basic management problem was at stake here. If the lie had been allowed to go unnoticed, the new Christian movement would appear to have double standards—that lying was okay. It was important to set the record straight from the beginning to leave no doubt that hypocrisy, cheating, or lying would not be tolerated.

Poor Sapphira—supporting her husband's lie, trying to look good in Peter's eyes, unable to confess and ask for forgiveness, paid the ultimate price.

Q. When did you last tell a lie? Why? Does it need to be dealt with in some way or ceremoniously burned?

Acts 5: 9-11

But Peter asked her, 'How is it that you have agreed together to tempt the Spirit of the Lord? Behold, the feet of those who have buried your husband are at the door, and they will carry you out.'

She fell down immediately at his feet, and died. The young men came in and found her dead, and they carried her out and buried her by her husband. Great fear came on the whole assembly, and on all who heard these things.

Silly Sapphira literally dies of fright when she hears what has happened to Ananias. It is small wonder that the congregation was afraid and probably stunned into silence. The new gospel taught a new way of life, which placed an unfamiliar high standard of honesty, integrity, and truth on everyone.

Q. It was only the shock of being found out that killed them! Do you have a story of being caught out? I hope there are some funny ones here.

Acts 5: 12-14

By the hands of the apostles many signs and wonders were done among the people. They were all with one accord in Solomon's porch. None of the rest dared to join them, however the people honoured them. More believers were added to the Lord, multitudes of both men and women.

This sounds like a bit of a contradiction. Luke says that no one dared to join them, and yet their numbers grew so dramatically that the apostles had to move to larger premises. Solomon's Colonnade or Porch was a huge roofed porch on the inside of the outer court of the temple. Luke presumably means that many people, having heard the story of Ananias and Sapphira, were scared to join the apostles in case God, or the apostles, would spot their deceit too—then look out. They trembled at the possible consequence.

However, plenty of others took the risk to join them. Going to church is a risky business. Nobody ever said being a good and faithful Christian is easy. People change in mysterious, wonderful, loving ways as they explore, read, and listen to the whispering wind in their search for their spiritual home.

Q. Wincs and Sees, what are the hardest things about trying to be a good and faithful person, or a Christian? Can you identify three or more? Can I hear laughter? I hope you are having fun while you work.

Acts 5: 15-16

They even carried out the sick into the streets, and laid them on cots and mattresses, so that as Peter came by, at the least his shadow might overshadow some of them. Multitudes also came together from the cities around Jerusalem, bringing sick people, and those who were tormented by unclean spirits: and they were all healed.

We don't often hear of such miracles today except perhaps at Lourdes. God knows there are plenty of tormented spirits about. We need a Jesus or a Peter again, so the sick in mind and body can be healed as their shadows pass by.

Maybe it was these dramatic events, the healing miracles of Jesus, his resurrection, and the continued healing of the sick by the apostles, that were the catalyst to send the message of the gospel spinning off across the world in an amazingly short time. The miracles reinforced Jesus' teaching; the preaching alone may not have been enough.

Q. Richard Dawkins[10] says he suspects alleged miracles provide the strongest reason many believers have for their faith, and miracles, by definition, violate the principles of science. Wincs, do you agree with this statement? Sees, is your faith founded on miracles? If not, what is the reason for your faith?

Acts 5: 17-24

But the high priest rose up, and all those who were with him (which is the sect of the Sadducees), and they were filled with jealousy, and laid hands on the apostles, and put them in public custody. But an angel of the Lord opened the prison doors by night, and brought them out, and said, 'Go stand and speak in the temple to the people all the words of this life.'

When they heard this, they entered into the temple about daybreak, and taught. But the high priest came, and those who were with him, and called the council together, and all the senate of the children of Israel, and sent to the prison to have them brought. But the officers who came didn't find them in the prison. They returned and reported, 'We found the prison shut and locked, and the guards standing before the doors, but when we opened them, we found no one inside!'

Now when the high priest, the captain of the temple, and the chief priests heard these words, they were very perplexed about them and what might become of this.

Imagine these important men gathering in the Sanhedrin, responding to a call for an urgent committee meeting from the high priest. They waited for the prisoners to be brought in and waited and waited. This is such a dramatic part of the story.

The Sadducees were the temple guards. In chapter 4 they had arrested Peter and John and given them a stern warning to stop preaching the gospel before letting them go, but of course, they took no notice. Angry at being disobeyed, the guards again put Peter and John in jail, but the angel let them out.

The apostles and believers must have been overjoyed with excitement. Not even locked prison doors could stop God's message from spreading.

---

[10]   Richard Dawkins "The God Delusion" published by Bantam Press page 59.

We have our own prison doors that inhibit our growth and spoil precious relationships.

Q. Can you pause to find any personal 'prison doors' that are spoiling something? Share them if you can.

Acts 5: 25-26

One came and told them, 'Behold, the men whom you put in prison are in the temple, standing and teaching the people.' Then the captain went with the officers, and brought them without violence, for they were afraid that the people might stone them.

What an embarrassing moment for the high priest and elders. There is an interesting change of tactics by the chief priests and elders here. Their authority had been ignored and challenged again. They did not know how to handle the situation and were afraid of the people.

Peter and John had become high profile, popular people, so the authorities did not dare use force this time, although only a few days earlier they were quite happy to flog Peter and John and put them in jail for disobeying Jewish law. It was a tricky situation. The guards had the good sense to bring Peter and John along gently.

Q. 'Discretion is the better part of valor.' Can you think of an occasion when you had difficulty keeping quiet and discrete—but you did? Were you grateful you had been quiet afterwards? Is there a lesson here to share?

Acts 5: 27-32

When they had brought them, they set them before the council. The high priest questioned them, saying, 'Didn't we strictly command you not to teach in this name? Behold, you have filled Jerusalem with your teaching, and intend to bring this man's blood on us.'

But Peter and the apostles answered, 'We must obey God rather than men. The God of our fathers raised up Jesus, whom you killed, hanging him on a tree. God exalted him with his right hand to be a Prince and a Saviour, to give repentance to Israel, and remission of sins. We are His witnesses of these things; and so also is the Holy Spirit, whom God has given to those who obey him.'

Regardless of their safety, Peter and John boldly stood up to the Sanhedrin court. They spoke with the authority of this mystical newfound courage, accusing the authorities of murder, yet offering an 'olive branch' of peace, telling them that Jesus came to forgive them.

History may have been a different story if the priests had been able to think beyond their own precious ego, to sink their pride and ask Peter what he was talking about.

St. Theresa of Avila wrote, 'When I think of myself I feel like a bird with a broken wing, my mind cannot soar into higher things.'[11] The priests were certainly incapable of 'soaring into higher things.'

The authorities say '*you* . . . are determined to make us guilty of this man's blood' trying to lay the blame for their discomfort on Peter and John without taking responsibility for their own actions in crucifying an innocent man. There is something pathetic about their behavior.

Q. Difficult one here: Would you be prepared to break the law for any reason—faith or conscience? I am trying to think of an example but can't. Please remember the 'pass' rule is an option.

Acts 5: 33-39

But they, (the Sanhedrin) when they heard this, were cut to the heart, and determined to kill them. But one stood up in the council, a Pharisee named Gamaliel, a teacher of the law, honored by all the people, and commanded to put the apostles out for a little while. He said to them, 'You men of Israel, be careful concerning these men, what you are about to do. For before these days Theudas rose up, making himself out to be somebody; to whom a number of men, about four hundred, joined themselves: who was slain; and all, as many as obeyed him, were dispersed, and came to nothing.

After this man, Judas of Galilee rose up in the days of the enrollment, and drew away some people after him. He also perished, and all, as many

---

[11]   The Interior Castle by Teresa of Avila. Edited by Halcyon Backhouse.

as obeyed him, were scattered abroad. Now I tell you, withdraw from these men, and leave them alone. For if this counsel or this work is of men, it will be overthrown. But if it is of God, you will not be able to overthrow it, and you would be found even to be fighting against God!'

So at least one of the members of the Sanhedrin was listening. Gamaliel, a famous teacher of his time, reassured the others. By objectively looking at the situation he suggested caution by leaving the options open for another day. Gamaliel's diplomacy has to be admired.

Firstly, he respected his colleagues' dignity by asking the prisoners to wait outside so as not to embarrass them. Secondly, he gave the Sanhedrin members sound advice to hasten slowly, to wait and see what happens. Let it evolve and resolve. Thirdly, he pointed out the futility of fighting God.

Q. Can you remember an incident when you were *not* discrete this time, and blurted something out inappropriately, jumped the gun, and spilled the beans to finish up with a red face?

Acts 5: 40-42

They [the high priest and council] agreed with him [Gamaliel]. Summoning the apostles, they beat them and commanded them not to speak in the name of Jesus, and let them go. They therefore departed from the presence of the council, rejoicing that they were counted worthy to suffer dishonour for Jesus' name.

Every day, in the temple and at home, they never stopped teaching and preaching Jesus, the Christ.

The Jewish penalty of 'forty lashes minus one' would have been administered to them (2 Cor. 11: 24), and even so, the apostles were still able to rejoice. They were let out of prison with a warning but again took no notice. Their amazing courage was inviting trouble. Peter and John seem to be getting stronger and braver as time went by.

To say something important that we feel passionate about in a hostile environment takes courage to overcome the anxiety and the thumping pulse. But how extraordinary that as innocent men the authorities dared whip them and then let them go?

Q. It is not politically correct or Christian to support capital punishment, leave alone the whip, but are we too soft on the rapist, murderer, torturer, husband abuser, and child abuser? In John's or Peter's mother's shoes, charitable thoughts may have been stretched to the limit. My thoughts would be murderous if anyone seriously abused one of my children. What do you think? Are we too soft, or should I ask for forgiveness?

Summary of Chapter 5

A couple called Ananias and Sapphira sold a property to give the money to the church, saying they were giving the whole amount they had received, when in fact it was only part of the money. Peter chastises them for their deceit, and they die on the spot. A fear crept into the church. The authorities ordered Peter and John to stop preaching. They did not like the healing either. Peter and John were repeatedly put into jail.

This time the angel of the Lord unlocked the prison door and let them out to the anger of the authorities. They were warned and flogged again but bravely continued to preach and heal the sick.

Chapter 6

Saintly Stephen Speaks Out

Acts 6: 1-7

Now in those days, when the number of the disciples was multiplying, a complaint arose from the Hellenists against the Hebrews, because their widows were neglected in the daily service.

The twelve summoned the multitude of the disciples and said, 'It is not appropriate for us to forsake the word of God and serve tables. Therefore select from among you, brothers, seven men of good report, full of the Holy Spirit and of wisdom, whom we may appoint over this business. But we will continue steadfastly in prayer and in the ministry of the word.'

These words pleased the whole multitude. They chose Stephen, a man full of faith and of the Holy Spirit, Philip, Prochorus, Nicanor, Timon, Parmenas, and Nicolaus, a proselyte of Antioch; whom they set before the apostles. When they had prayed, they laid their hands on them. The word of God increased and the number of the disciples multiplied in Jerusalem exceedingly. A great company of the priests were obedient to the faith.

The job was getting too big-delegation was needed. From the very beginning, the church in Jerusalem attracted Greek-speaking Jews, born outside Palestine, as well as the local Aramaic—or Hebrew-speaking Jews, such as the apostles, born in Palestine.

Both congregations had their own Greek or Hebrew-speaking leaders and pastors. But Luke tells us that the local Jews looked after their poor and needy better than the Hellenists (the foreign Greek Jews).

Luke introduces Stephen and Philip for the first time. These two men were to have far greater roles than handing out food to the poorer community. The seven men chosen to wait at the table were picked from the Greek congregation, who had complained about the imbalance of services in the first place. The Greek noun for *deacon* means 'the one who waits on,' and this little episode resulted in the appointment of the first deacons to the church. Deacons no longer wait at the table but still wait on the needs of the congregation today.

Both congregations were apparently pleased with the decision, and the apostles laid hands on the seven men and commissioned Stephen and Philip to their new responsibilities.

Q. It is wonderful to hear about their numbers 'multiplying exceedingly.' Sees, suppose your church organized a Café Church each Sunday for a month with a lively local pop band of evangelists in the street, playing snappy, fun modern songs. Might your congregation multiply exceedingly?

Thinking of giving to the poor in the community—would it be appropriate to show the Whoopie Goldberg film, *Sister Act* or some other suitable film as an outreach to the community and also a fund raiser in the church hall or local cinema? It is a fun and profound film with a great message. Would it be worth putting on a charity screening of this film for everyone? Wincs, would you be willing to help sell the tickets? The event may even be a good moment to launch one of the dreams.

Acts 6: 8-10

Stephen, full of faith and power, performed great wonders and signs among the people. But some of those who were of the synagogue called 'The Libertines,' and of the Cyrenians, of the Alexandrians, and of those of Cilicia and Asia arose, disputing with Stephen. They weren't able to withstand the wisdom and the Spirit by which he spoke.

Some of the foreigners argued with Stephen—he was apparently far more intelligent and knowledgeable than they were.

Stephen was perhaps the first person who saw that division between the new Christian religion and the Jews was inevitable. The two groups had no hope of working together. Stephen was the trailblazer, followed shortly by Paul. The twelve apostles had kept the Jews' respect so far by attending the temple.

They appeared not to have changed greatly, apart from proclaiming that Jesus was the Messiah. But Stephen had no illusions about the changes that were taking place between the attitude of the Jews and the new Christian philosophy.

Q. Divisions. Divisions. Divisions. I hope your church, or community is not having a serious one. If there is a problem, will you discuss what action your small group may take to mend it—or maybe lending a voice to a community group would be helpful.

Acts 6: 11-15

Then they [the Libertines] secretly induced men to say, 'We have heard him speak blasphemous words against Moses and God.' They stirred up the people, the elders, and the scribes, and came against him [Stephen] and seized him, and brought him in to the council, and set up false witnesses who said, 'This man never stops speaking blasphemous words against this holy place and the law. For we have heard him say that this Jesus of Nazareth will destroy this place, and will change the customs which Moses delivered to us.' All who sat in the council, fastening their eyes on him, saw his face like it was the face of an angel.

To the Jews the temple was the most sacred place of worship, built to 'house' God. This belief went back about 1,500 years to the Exodus of the Israelites from Egypt, when Moses, the greatest leader in the Jews' history, led the Israelites out of bondage from Egypt to Canaan, through the desert, carrying the box-like Holy Ark of God before them.

They believed God dwelt in the Ark and was therefore with them all the way until they built the temple in Jerusalem.

The Ark was then housed in the temple, so obviously, God lived in the temple. To suggest otherwise was sacrilege and deserved the punishment of death. So although Stephen may not have said anything about destroying their temple, he was blaspheming in the eyes of the Jews by preaching that God was to be found throughout creation. He knew this would cause great concern to the Jews, but if the Jesus theory was to be believed and go beyond the city walls, Stephen had to say it. The price of breaking this news to the Jews would be very high for Stephen.

The rulers of the temple were no longer in a mood to listen and saw their chance to silence Stephen. By fabricating the facts a little, in the same way they had done so successfully at Jesus's trial a few months earlier, they imagined this growing troublesome new group could soon be silenced.

Filled with the Spirit of God, Luke says Stephen had the face of an angel. What a moving description.

There is a feeling in today's generation that we Christians still keep God in a 'box,' i.e. clinging to buildings, traditional doctrines, liturgies, rituals, many of which are wonderful and may be kept for special occasions, but for example, 'thou' and 'thee' are no longer words in general use, and although they are appropriate in many of the wonderful old hymns, they are certainly not comfortable in prayer.

This archaic performance disturbs so many people, not only the younger generation. People who long for spiritual nourishment are uncomfortable in this alien atmosphere, so leave it alone.

Q. Is this so in your area? What steps, however small, can you take to make church services more relevant to the mood of the twenty-first century? Wincs, atheist/agnostics, is this a reason why you are a Winc? Where do you find your spiritual nourishment?

Summary of Chapter 6

The chapter begins with the Greek half of the new Christian congregation in Jerusalem complaining about unfair and unequal treatment for their widows. The apostles ask the congregations to choose seven men to form a new committee to deal with the situation. The first church deacons were appointed with Stephen, a preacher of great skill and compassion, as their leader. The Libertines bring false accusations against Stephen. Trouble is looming for this saintly man.

CHAPTER 7

The Death of Stephen

Acts 7: 1-3

The high priest said, 'Are these things so?'

He said, 'Brothers and fathers listen. The God of glory appeared to our father Abraham, when he was in Mesopotamia, before he lived in Haran, and said to him, 'Get out of your land, and from your relatives, and come into a land which I will show you.''

It may be helpful to read Stephen's entire story in a block (Acts 7-8: 53) before returning here to read it slowly, bit by bit.

Having been arrested and brought before the Sanhedrin, the highest court in the land, Stephen begins his defense in the customary way by giving an historical overview. The two main points he was trying to get across were these:

1) Mesopotamia, which we call Turkey, had been the homeland of Abraham's nomadic tribe. God told Abraham to move to a new land, so God could not possibly have been contained in a temple or any other building, then or now. God does not suddenly change his mind where to live.

2) The Jews were nomadic and had constantly rebelled against God. Frequently they had reverted to worshiping idols, rejecting and mutinying against God's prophets. They had recently reacted in the same way by murdering Jesus.

The High Priest and members of the Sanhedrin refused to listen to God's message and certainly were not obeying it.

In summary, Stephen's message was that God is creator of the world, and it is impossible for him to be contained in any church, temple, synagogue, mosque, chapel, building, or box. It is only through religious tolerance that God's message of peace will be heard.

It would be so helpful if there were a Jewish or Muslim member of the group to tell about the level of tolerance or intolerance they feel from other faiths today.

Q. What does the rest of the group think about the level of religious tolerance or intolerance in your community? Share your attitudes as openly and honestly in this very special gathering.

Acts 7: 4-8

Stephen continues: Then he came out of the land of the Chaldaeans, and lived in Haran. From there, when his father was dead, God moved him into this land, where you are now living. He gave him no inheritance in it, no, not so much as to set his foot on. He promised that he would give it to him for a possession and to his seed after him, when he still had no child. God spoke in this way: that his seed would live as aliens in a strange land, and that they would be enslaved and mistreated for four hundred years. 'I will judge the nation to which they will be in bondage,' said God, 'and after that will they come out, and serve me in this place.' He gave him the covenant of circumcision.

So Abraham became the father of Isaac, and circumcised him the eighth day. Isaac became the father of Jacob, and Jacob became the father of the twelve patriarchs.

Although Abraham and his tribes were nomadic, God's predictions to him were not very encouraging. 'Your relatives will be enslaved and mistreated for four hundred years, but I'll punish the nation they serve. After they escape from bondage, I will give them their own country. In the meantime, as a sign of this contract, you are to circumcise all the boys at eight days old.'

What an extraordinary statement. It may have been a bit more heartening if God had said, '*Before you die*, I'll give you a land for your own children and future generations.'

The strange instruction to circumcision the boys has advantages; it decreases the incidence of infection, cancer of the penis, (and the contraction of AIDS), particularly in a hot climate, so this was a very practical request. It became a ceremonial event in the temple for eight-day-old baby boys. If the pledge was ignored by the parents (Gen. 17: 14), the punishment for disobedience was great for the child, who would 'be cut off from his people.' This was a serious matter, not to be taken lightly. Circumcision was soon to become a big issue for the young Christian church.

The baptismal service today is related to the Jews' covenant of the circumcision ceremony. It was, and still is, a pledge by parents and godparents to nurture the child and be responsible for the child's spiritual welfare to teach the child to know God as a friend, as one who will love and support the child faithfully throughout life.

Q. Has this pledge changed today? What do you all feel are the duties of a godparent?

Acts 7: 9-10

Stephen continues: 'The patriarchs, moved with jealousy against Joseph, sold him into Egypt. God was with him, and delivered him out of all his afflictions, and gave him favour and wisdom before Pharaoh, king of Egypt. He made him governor over Egypt and all his house.

Stephen reminds the assembled people that Abraham's son was Isaac. Isaac's son was Jacob. Jacob had twelve sons known as the Patriarchs (Gen. 35: 21-26), who were the founders of the twelve tribes of Israel. The youngest son, Joseph, was so favored and spoilt by his father that his brothers became jealous. To get rid of him, they dumped him down a well, where he was found and taken off as a slave to Egypt. The brothers' dreadful act caused their father much grief.

However, the end of the story had amazing benefits for them as Joseph later became a powerful leader and rescued them all (Gen.37:12-36).

There seem to be two main lessons here:

1) Favoritism, even perceived favoritism, is very dangerous. It is too often displayed by a parent, priest, teacher, or leader of any kind.

If a child or an adult is behaving in a particularly difficult way, perceived favoritism may be worth exploring.

2) God forgives us for whatever we have done, whenever we did it, and no matter how big or small the wrong may be. Prejudices, jealousies, anger, impatience, wrong deeds—all are forgiven and forgotten forever, after acknowledging them and repenting, the bible tells us.

Acts 7: 11-16

Stephen continues: Now a famine came over all the land of Egypt and Canaan, and great affliction. Our fathers found no food. But when Jacob heard that there was grain in Egypt, he sent out our fathers the first time. On the second time Joseph was made known to his brothers, and Joseph's race was revealed to Pharaoh. Joseph sent, and summoned Jacob, his father, and all his relatives, seventy-five souls. Jacob went down into Egypt, and he died, himself and our fathers, and they brought him back to Shechem, and laid in the tomb that Abraham bought for a price in silver from the children of Hamor of Shechem.

Can you visualize this scene in Egypt? The brothers had sold their younger brother to get rid of him, because he was such a spoilt brat.

Then years later they were confronted by this very important and powerful politician on whom they would depend for food. Joseph tells them that he is the one whom they mistreated so vilely years ago. The story has a lovely end, as the brothers are able to forgive each other.

The Sanhedrin was familiar with this story and would understand the significance of returning Jacob's body to their homeland.

The Jews were no longer a nomadic people, but had become an insular nation with great traditional values, which included a strong bonding to their clan and their land. This national pride has sustained them through persecution and prejudice. Their single-minded support for each other and their success has caused much hatred and jealousy around the world. Their deep love of their land has become a passion, almost an obsession.

Many indigenous people feel this same strong bond to the earth, which is the very foundation of their spirituality. Perhaps it would be useful if the rest of us looked for this bond with creation afresh.

Dr. Rachael Kohn writes in her book *The New Believers—re-imaging God*, ' . . . believing in the earth comes at a time when some people are willing to turn their gaze away from a total preoccupation with the self, . . . The time has come to turn toward the silent partner *(the planet earth)* who has been there for us all along.'[1]

Q. What procedures do you take regularly to help preserve this precious world? Can you name at least three and share them around?

Acts 7: 17-22

Stephen continues: 'But as the time of the promise came close which God had sworn to Abraham, the people grew and multiplied in Egypt, until there arose a different king, who didn't know Joseph. The same took advantage of our race, and mistreated our fathers, and forced them to throw out their babies, so that they wouldn't stay alive. At that time Moses was born, and was exceedingly handsome. He was nourished three months in his father's house. When he was thrown out, Pharaoh's daughter took him up, and reared him as her own son. Moses was instructed in all the wisdom of the Egyptians. He was mighty in his words and works.

Stephen probably refers to a verse from Exodus (1: 8) when the treacherous new 'different' King Ahmose tried to rid the world of the Jewish race by killing their baby boys. But Moses slipped through the net to eventually and dramatically change the course of Jewish history by leading them back to Israel.

When the Jews were slaves in Egypt, the king tried to kill the Israelite's baby boys. So without Moses and the Exodus, the Jews may have become extinct, in which case Jesus Christ may never have been born. It was a carefully God-planned coincidence that Pharaoh's daughter found Moses in the basket that day.

Nobody could have imagined that small desperate act to save a baby would have had such far-reaching consequences for the human race.

Acts 7: 23-29

Stephen continues: But when he [Moses] was forty years old, it came into his heart to visit his brothers, the children of Israel. Seeing one of them suffer wrong, he defended him, and avenged him who was oppressed, striking the Egyptian. He supposed that his brothers understood that God, by his hand, was giving them deliverance; but they didn't understand.

'The day following, he [Moses] appeared to them as they fought, and urged them to be at peace again, saying, 'Sirs, you are brothers. Why do you wrong one another?' But he who did his neighbor wrong pushed him away, saying, 'Who made you a ruler and a judge over us? Do you want to kill me, as you killed the Egyptian yesterday?' Moses fled at this saying, and became a stranger in the land of Midian, where he became the father of two sons.

The downtrodden Hebrew community in Egypt would have known that Moses, the favored son who lived in a palace, was also a Jew. It is hardly surprising they resented his privileged life while they were being beaten and ill-treated as slaves. Yet Moses was amazed at their attitude and rejection.

Fearing they would inform on him to the Egyptian authorities, Moses fled. Stephen points out that Moses came to the quarrelsome Jewish slaves as a peacemaker, to try to help them, but they rejected him—like 'guess who?'

Acts 7: 30-34

Stephen continues: 'When forty years were fulfilled, an angel of the Lord appeared to him in the wilderness of Mount Sinai, in a flame of fire in a bush. When Moses saw it, he wondered at the sight. As he came close to see, a voice of the Lord came to him, 'I am the God of your fathers, the God of Abraham, the God of Isaac, and the God of Jacob.' Moses trembled, and dared not look. The Lord said to him, 'Take your sandals off your feet, for the place where you stand is holy ground. I have surely seen the affliction of my people that is in Egypt, and have heard their groaning. I have come down to deliver them. Now come, I will send you into Egypt.'

There is a species of bush that grows in the Middle Eastern desert, I am told, which looks as though it's on fire in certain light. God often works his miracles through natural circumstances—the wind and storm, the sunsets and vegetation—which many people find more comfortable. The fact is says Stephen, that Moses saw a bush burning, and God spoke to him clearly.

A feeling of calm came over the Sanhedrin as Stephen recounted this old and much loved story—calm before the storm. Stephen reminds the

Sanhedrin that God was not found in the temple but instead, in a desert bush. God sent two great messengers to them, Moses and Jesus, both of whom had been rejected.

Q. There are too many rejected, afflicted, and groaning people in the world today. Too many people—full stop. Why doesn't God rescue them? Is there anything, as a group, you would like to do to help the world's 'groaning' people?

Acts 7: 35-40

Stephen continues: 'This Moses, whom they refused, saying, 'Who made you a ruler and a judge?'—God has sent him as both a ruler and a deliverer by the hand of the angel who appeared to him in the bush. This man led them out; having worked wonders and signs in Egypt, in the Red Sea, and in the wilderness for forty years. This is that Moses, who said to the children of Israel, 'The Lord our God will raise up a prophet for you from among your brothers, like me.

This is he who was in the assembly in the wilderness with the angel that spoke to him on Mount Sinai, and with our fathers, who received living oracles to give to us, to whom our fathers wouldn't be obedient, but rejected him, and turned back in their hearts to Egypt, saying to Aaron, 'Make us gods that will go before us, for as for this Moses, who led us out of the land of Egypt, we don't know what has become of him.'

Stephen hammers home his point again, highlighting the fact that the Jews rejected their revered Moses as a ruler. By telling the court this story, Stephen was building a legal case, subtly pointing out the similarities of the Jesus story with the Moses story. This fact would not have been missed by the Jews.

For example, Moses was in danger when the Egyptians killed all the male babies, just as Jesus was in danger from King Herod. Moses and Jesus clearly had been sent by God, demonstrated by their ability to do miracles and heal the sick.

Moses and Jesus were both Jews, and both were rejected by the Jewish people. Moses rescued his people from slavery and their separation from God, as did Jesus for all mankind.

Stephen tried to tell the court Jesus came with the same message as their beloved Moses.

I am trying to imagine what I would be feeling, at the moment, as a Jewish member of this group, and hope that two thousand years later we can talk about it together in friendship, without feeling uncomfortable.

Acts 7: 41-43

Stephen continues: They made a calf in those days, and brought a sacrifice to the idol, and rejoiced in the works of their hands. But God turned, and gave them up to serve the army of the sky, as it is written in the book of the prophets,

'Did you offer to me slain animals and sacrifices for forty years in the wilderness, O house of Israel?

You took up the tabernacle of Moloch, the star of your god Rephan, the figures which you made to worship.

I will carry you away* beyond Babylon.'

The Israelites in the desert began to hanker for the life they had left in Egypt. 'Okay,' God said, 'do what you like, worship your idols, and see what happens.' God allowed them to stew as an act of judgment, and then later on, off to Babylon in exile they went.

As a parent, one of the hardest parts of seeing our children grow up was curbing the temptation to interfere. I'm not sure I succeeded very well. If this is hard to do for imperfect humans, it must be a thousand times harder for God to stand back when we mess things up.

People often say, 'How can there be a God when there is so much evil and misery in the world?' Maybe he has to stand aside and leave things in our own hands until, often painfully; we come back to our senses.

Q. What do you all think are three main reasons for suffering and turmoil in the world today?

Acts 7: 44-50

Stephen continues: 'Our fathers had the tabernacle of the testimony in the wilderness, even as he who spoke to Moses commanded him to make it according to the pattern that he had seen; which also our fathers, in their turn, brought in with Joshua when they entered into the possession of the nations, whom God drove out before the face of our fathers, to the days of David, who found favor in the sight of God, and asked to find a habitation for the God of Jacob. But Solomon built him a house. However, the Most High doesn't dwell in temples made with hands, as the prophet says,

'heaven is my throne, and the earth a footstool for my feet.
What kind of house will you build me?' says the Lord;
'or what is the place of my rest?
Didn't my hand make all these things?'

The tabernacle of testimony was the ark the Israelites carried with them through the desert when they escaped from Egypt. It symbolized the throne of God wherever they were. God cannot be contained in any building. Charles Roderick, in his book *Listen to the Wind*, says, 'for can you control the wind and say to it 'Here shall you blow, not there?' Of course you cannot. Nor can you control the Spirit of God or confine it . . . We erect walls and barriers and articles of faith. We love to build walls to keep some in and to shut others out. But God has a way of stepping over them.'[12]

Stephen pours his soul into the climax of his story by saying God had created the world, which is his own beautiful temple. 'What kind of house will you build me? Or where will my resting place be?'

This comment was intolerable to the Jews, because it attacked their most cherished center of religious life—the temple. The Jews in the Sanhedrin stubbornly refused to accept the clear picture that Stephen had drawn for them.

Acts 7: 51-53

Stephen finishes: 'You stiff-necked and uncircumcised in heart and ears, you always resist the Holy Spirit! As your fathers did, so you do. Which of the prophets didn't your fathers persecute? They killed those who foretold the coming of the Righteous One, of whom you have now become

---

[12] The late Rev. Charles Roderick, taken from his book of sermons "Listen to the Wind" page 2.

betrayers and murderers. You received the law as it was ordained by angels, and didn't keep it!'

Something must have caused this sudden outburst and change in Stephen's mood—maybe a heckler or a murmur among the listeners. Whatever it was, Stephen was obviously very angry as he accuses the Jewish leaders of behaving in a deliberately stupid way.

God's command, mentioned in chapter 7 referring to Genesis 17: 14, instructed Moses to circumcise the babies or be cut off from God.

Stephen tells them they, too, had spiritually cut themselves off by their egotism and lack of serious commitment by pedantically dotting every *I* and crossing every *T* of God's law while persecuting the messengers of God. They had received the Law of Moses but had not kept it. Now they had betrayed and murdered the very son of God, Jesus the messenger. Brave and courageous Stephen risked his life for the Savior, in whom he passionately believed.

Q. Phew—that was a long speech. Have the days of the 'hell and damnation' preacher gone? Has the fear of God been diluted and overdone? Has the respect for God diminished in the twenty-first century compared to days gone by? What are the barriers which need to be overcome to make church services more comfortable for a newcomer? Wincs please help here.

Acts 7: 54-8: 1

Now when they heard these things, they were cut to the heart, and they gnashed at him with their teeth. But he, being full of the Holy Spirit, looked up steadfastly into heaven, and saw the glory of God, and Jesus standing on the right hand of God, and said, 'Behold, I see the heavens opened, and the Son of Man standing at the right hand of God!'

But they cried out with a loud voice, and stopped their ears, and rushed at him with one accord. They threw him out of the city, and stoned him. The witnesses placed their garments at the feet of a young man named Saul. They stoned Stephen as he called out, saying, 'Lord Jesus, receive my spirit!' He kneeled down, and cried with a loud voice, 'Lord, don't hold this sin against them!' When he had said this, he fell asleep.

Saul was consenting to his death. A great persecution arose against the assembly which was in Jerusalem in that day. They were all scattered abroad throughout the regions of Judea and Samaria, except for the apostles.

The court scene burst into chaos and fury; they wanted to hear no more from this man. Stephen stood calmly, seeing a vision of Jesus standing in Heaven, just as though Jesus were standing there as his advocate and support. Jesus had been through this same hideous process only a little while before.

During his trial, Jesus had said, '*You will see the Son of Man sitting at the right hand of the Mighty One*' (Mark 14: 62; a quote from Psalm 101). In turn, Stephen sees it too. Two very brave men, bore witness to their faith against bitter odds. Jesus' words, '*that whoever acknowledges me before man, I will acknowledge before God*' (Luke 12: 8), would surely have inspired and comforted Stephen. The crowd dragged Stephen out to die.

The witnesses presumably took their garments off to prepare for the physical exercise of hurling stones. The accusers were privileged, if that word could be used, to cast the first stones at someone they had condemned to death. Saul, the main character in the second half of this story of Acts, appears for the first time as a persecutor of Christians; the accusers gave their coats to him, rolled up their sleeves, and got on with the job of stoning a man to death—while Saul watched on.

Q. Have our senses become dull to the suffering of others—such as abused children in our community? Is it all too big to tackle?

Will you share any of the things you do to help make the world a better place? However big or small that may be, list your contributions. Please do not be humble, and share them.

Summary of Chapter 7

The chapter begins with Stephen being accused of repeating Jesus's prophesy that the Jews' precious temple would be destroyed. 'Are these charges true?' the high priest asked. Stephen presented his case by comparing Jesus to their much-revered mentor, Moses. In strong terms, Stephen accused them of murder and hypocrisy. So the brave, passionate Stephen, with a face like an angel, was stoned to death. Saul, later Paul the apostle, is first mentioned.

CHAPTER 8

Second Explosion of the Gospel

Acts 8: 1b-3

They were all scattered abroad throughout the regions of Judea and Samaria, except for the apostles. Devout men buried Stephen, and lamented greatly over him. But Saul ravaged the assembly, entering into every house, and dragged both men and women off to prison.

Saul was on the rampage. A scene of grief and fear spread as another, even more furious campaign of persecution broke out. As Stephen had come from the Greek congregation, it was these Christians who suffered most and were dragged out and thrown into prison. The church went underground.

The apostles were not immediately identified with Stephen, so they were able to stay in Jerusalem to be near their colleagues in prison. They became the contact point for the scattered believers.

The plight and flight of these early believers caused a dramatic explosion—another spread of the gospel over a large region of the Middle East—as Christians took their message home to many lands around the Mediterranean.

Q. Perhaps leaving the Holocaust out of this question, can you think of another such explosive, religious persecution in history? Write a paragraph or two in your journal to bring to the group about the incident and what happened, or what is happening.

Acts 8: 4-8

Therefore those who were scattered abroad went around preaching the word. Philip went down to the city of Samaria, and proclaimed to them the Christ. The multitudes listened with one accord to the things that were spoken by Philip, when they heard and saw the signs which he did. For unclean spirits came out of many of those who had them. They came out, crying with a loud voice. Many who had been paralyzed and lame were healed. There was great joy in that city.

These early Christians were amazingly brave. Having fled from persecution in Jerusalem after Stephen's death, they took off immediately to preach again in new areas. The strong, compelling drive of the Holy Spirit to tell the Good News, against dangerous odds, was being carried out fearlessly.

During recent times, we have seen, and are still seeing, great numbers of people fleeing persecution or hardship from their homelands. Many have fled to England, North America, Canada, Australia, New Zealand, and other host countries.

These countries have benefited from their culture in the variety of food, language, and customs they brought with them.

Q. Share two or three introductions of ethnic origin from which your community benefits.

Acts 8: 9-10

But there was a certain man, Simon by name, who used to practice sorcery in the city, and amazed the people of Samaria, making himself out to be some great one, to whom they all listened, from the least to the greatest, saying, 'This man *is that* (or has the) great power of God.'

In early Christian writings, it is recorded that a man named Simon Magnus visited Rome and other parts, where he is said to have gathered many followers. He was a clever sorcerer who claimed to be God's chief messenger. The Simonians are known to have survived for at least another three centuries.

When Simon met Philip, he recognized the integrity of the apostles' work versus his own sorcery. He may also have realized that these men were about to spoil his trade.

Q. Under the heading of sorcerer, Roget's Thesaurus names 'the reading of palms, horoscopes, hypnotism, astrology, clairvoyants, and soothsayers.' What do you feel about these activities?

Acts 8: 11-13

They listened to him, because for a long time he had amazed them with his sorceries. But when they believed Philip preaching good news concerning the Kingdom of God and the name of Jesus Christ, they were baptized, both men and women. Simon himself also believed. Seeing signs and great miracles occurring, he was amazed.

It is not easy to see how genuine Simon's feelings were at the time of his baptism, but he was fascinated by the healing strength that was demonstrated by the apostles, through the name of Jesus. Was it magic?

It is amazing to see dramatic changes in people who have suddenly searched and found Jesus. It is one of the great mysteries we encounter on earth. Philip was not keen to allow Simon to join the brothers for some reason. The apostles did not trust him.

Q. Do you have a good story about a 'hunch' you have had? Will you share what happened with the group?

Acts 8: 14-17

Now when the apostles who were at Jerusalem heard that Samaria had received the word of God, they sent Peter and John to them, who, when they had come down, prayed for them, that they might receive the Holy Spirit; for as yet he had fallen on none of them. They had only been baptized in the name of Christ Jesus. Then they laid their hands on them, and they received the Holy Spirit.

Philip, the new recruit, was doing well in Samaria. The apostles had stayed in Jerusalem to set up headquarters so they would be near those who had been thrown into prison by Saul. But they felt responsible for the newly converted Christians too, so Peter and John were sent to consecrate the new Samarian group, laying their hands on their heads.

The lovely tradition of laying on of hands, which has lasted through the ages, is the physical sign of receiving and accepting the Holy Spirit.

These ceremonies seem important to affirm our commitment publicly and to set landmarks on our journey.

Q. Many people say they don't need the structure and discipline of the church to find their way to God; they find the doctrines, language, and rituals a barrier. But they find God in the hills, the sea, or somebody's smile.

Will you share your thoughts about the need or the lack of need for the church? Wincs, (remembering that Wincs are everyone who is not a professed Christian) we need your input please? You are so valuable.

Acts 8: 18-23

Now when Simon saw that the Holy Spirit was given through the laying on of the apostles' hands, he offered them money, saying, 'Give me also this power, that whomever I lay my hands on may receive the Holy Spirit.' But Peter said to him, 'May your silver perish with you, because you thought you could obtain the gift of God with money! You have neither part nor lot in this matter, for your heart isn't right before God. Repent therefore of this, your wickedness, and ask God if perhaps the thought of your heart may be forgiven you. For I see that you are in the gall of bitterness and in the bondage of iniquity.'

Peter may have regretted baptizing Simon. But, in all conscience, can a priest or apostle refuse to baptize anyone? To the apostles' fury, Simon hoped he could buy the power of God. Peter could see that Simon's motive was to make money and try to add another trick to his collection.

Q. It must be one of the most painful duties for a priest to refuse to administer the sacraments or dismiss someone from a church who they see is 'in the gall of bitterness and in bondage.' Can this happen today? Have you experienced any such eruptions? What happened and how did you feel about it? Wincs, have you had any such experience? I hope this is not why you are a Winc.

Acts 8: 24-25

Simon answered, 'Pray for me to the Lord, that none of the things which you have spoken happen to me.'

They therefore, when they had testified and spoken the word of the Lord, returned to Jerusalem, and preached the Good News to many villages of the Samaritans.

Simon had seen Peter do great things, and therefore realized Peter's pronouncement, '*may your silver perish with you*' was no idle threat. Simon is mentioned again later in Christian literature as the father of all heresies, adding the word 'simony' to the English language.

So we leave sinful Simon behind, while Peter and John return to Jerusalem and Philip travels on to preach.

Acts 8: 26-29

But an angel of the Lord spoke to Philip, saying, 'Arise, and go toward the south to the way that goes down from Jerusalem to Gaza. This is a desert.'

He arose and went; and behold, there was a man of Ethiopia, a eunuch of great authority under Candace, queen of the Ethiopians, who was over all her treasure, who had come to Jerusalem to worship. He was returning and sitting in his chariot, and was reading the prophet Isaiah.

The Spirit said to Philip, 'Go near, and join yourself to this chariot.'

Maybe these spiritual messages are delivered in spontaneous moments when you feel a surging conviction to do something. Who knows? Whatever it is, this was the first recorded historic moment when a Jew began to explain the Christian religion to a Gentile.

The Ethiopian was a 'God-fearing' man from the region between Aswan and Khartoum around the Upper Nile. He had an important job looking after the treasury for the Queen Mother, Candace, who was responsible for the routine civil duties of the king. The king was deified as a child of the sun god and therefore considered too sacred to do secular duties himself.

The Ethiopian had been on a pilgrimage to Jerusalem when Philip was impelled to *'Go near, and join yourself to this chariot.'* God's great plan of spreading his message beyond the Jews to the Gentiles began in this little incident.

Q. Breaking new ground is usually exciting. What 'new ground' in any direction have you broken lately—a holiday—an adventure—a project?

Acts 8: 30-31

Philip ran to him, and heard him reading Isaiah the prophet, and said, 'Do you understand what you are reading?'

He said, 'How can I, unless someone explains it to me?' He begged Philip to come up and sit with him.

The Ethiopian had probably obtained a scroll of Isaiah while he was in Jerusalem, and reading aloud was the custom at that time. Apparently he was not alarmed as this stranger came bounding up to him with such a strange question, *'Do you understand what you are reading?'* He invited Philip to hop in and he probably gave him a lift along his seventy-five kilometer walk.

Acts 8: 32-35

Now the passage of the Scripture which he was reading was this,
'He was led as a sheep to the slaughter.
As a lamb before his shearer is silent, so he doesn't open his mouth.
In his humiliation, his judgment was taken away.
Who will declare His generation?
For his life is taken from the earth.
The eunuch answered Philip, 'Who is the prophet talking about? About himself or about someone else?'

Philip opened his mouth, and beginning from this Scripture, preached to him Jesus.

Philip told the Ethiopian that these verses were an accurate description of Jesus at his trial. He eagerly explained the story of Jesus, God's slaughtered lamb; the story of Jesus's humiliation and death, which had been prophesied by Isaiah about seven hundred years earlier.

The sentence 'he was led like a sheep to the slaughter, and as a lamb before the shearer is silent,' speaks of a helpless victim. A lamb does not know what is going to happen as it is led off to be killed; it only feels fear. Yet Jesus, the lamb, was led out of Gethsemane, knowing exactly what was going to happen to him.

Helpless in earthly terms, yet demonstrating such strength and compassion that it changed the history of the world when he said, 'Father, forgive them, for they know not what they do.'

'Tell me about it please,' the Ethiopian said.

We are asked to tell people about God, too, when the opportunity arises, with sensitivity at an appropriate moment. Philip sensed the opportunity and took it. Christianity began to spread, at this moment, and nobody realized it, except God.

Evangelism is such a delicate thing. Powerful overbearing views are so destructive. The sanctimonious 'I know my faith is the only one' attitude has caused, and is causing, such conflict.

Q. Philip was willing to go and talk to a complete stranger, an Ethiopian, from a very different background to his own. When did you go up to a total stranger and start a conversation? What happened? Please share everything you can—always.

Acts 8: 36-40

As they went on the way, they came to some water, and the eunuch said, 'Behold, here is water. What is keeping me from being baptized.

He commanded the chariot to stand still, and they both went down into the water, both Philip and the eunuch, and he baptized him. When they came up out of the water, the Spirit of the Lord caught Philip away, and the eunuch didn't see him anymore, for he went on his way rejoicing. But Philip was found at Azotus. Passing through, he preached the Good News to all the cities, until he came to Caesarea.

Philip may have just slipped away to leave the preoccupied and excited eunuch to marvel at his spiritual rebirth. How strange that Philip should disappear like that. But nothing else mattered; the Ethiopian was filled with the extraordinary joy of the Spirit.

Philip now slips away from the Acts story (it is thought that he settled down locally and brought up a family) until he is mentioned again about twenty years later in Acts 21: 8 still working in the same area.

Summary of Chapter 8

The chapter begins in grief and fear, as Stephen is buried after being stoned to death. Saul begins to persecute the Christians who scatter all over the Middle East; Philip is in Samaria where the apostles arrive from Jerusalem to visit the new followers. They come across the trickster magician Simon, who asks to buy the God-given power of the apostles to the fury of the apostles. 'May your money perish with you,' Peter says. 'Perhaps God will forgive you.'

The apostles leave for Jerusalem. Philip is sent to Gaza. On the way he meets an Ethiopian eunuch, who is reading the book of Isaiah. Philip converts him to Christianity and later baptizes him in the river. This is the first recorded seed of Christianity sown to the Gentiles. The Ethiopian heads home to spread the Good News in Africa.

CHAPTER 9

Enter—Saul of Tarsus

Acts 9: 1-9

But Saul, still breathing threats and slaughter against the disciples of the Lord, went to the high priest, and asked for letters from him to the synagogues of Damascus, that if he found any who were of the Way, whether men or women, he might bring them bound to Jerusalem. As he traveled, it happened that he got close to Damascus, and suddenly a light from the sky shone around him. He fell on the earth, and heard a voice saying to him, 'Saul, Saul, why do you persecute me?'

He said, 'Who are you, Lord?' The Lord said, 'I am Jesus, whom you are persecuting. But rise up, and enter into the city, and you will be told what you must do.'

The men who traveled with him stood speechless, hearing the sound, but seeing no one. Saul arose from the ground, and when his eyes were opened, he saw no one. They led him by the hand, and brought him into Damascus. He was without sight for three days, and neither ate nor drank.

The high priest and the Jewish leaders had been delighted to have Saul, the leader of the persecuting campaign, on side to stamp out these pestilent Christians . . .

Saul was born a Roman citizen in the Greek city of Tarsus, but his parents were Jews, 'a Hebrew born of Hebrews' (Phil. 3: 5). He was educated in Jerusalem by the great teacher Gamaliel, the moderate leader of the Pharisees, whom we met during Peter and John's trial.

Saul, like Stephen, was clever enough to see the old Jewish order and the new Christian doctrine were never going to mix; separation was inevitable.

However, Saul, unlike Stephen, set out to vigorously protect the traditions of his Jewish people—resolved to stamp out the new Christian movement before it divided his nation.

Saul sought permission from the high priest to go to the next city to root out and destroy the Christians there. The word of the high priest was highly respected in the synagogues throughout the empire. The Romans acknowledged his authority in Jewish religious matters.

Saul was on the road to create further havoc when he had his encounter with Jesus whose very authority he was determined to crush. In the words of Lord George Lyttelton, the eighteenth century statesman, Saul's conversion 'was of itself a demonstration sufficient to prove Christianity to be of divine revelation.'[13]

As predicted by Stephen, Luke realized the significance of the conversion of Saul, repeats the story three times in Acts, here and again in chapters 22 and 26. Saul's conversion was the end of Christianity remaining under the umbrella of the Jewish faith,

Undeniably, something happened on that road to Damascus, and whatever happened, it changed the thinking of one very strong-minded man forever.

Acts 9: 10-14

Now there was a certain disciple at Damascus named Ananias. The Lord said to him in a vision, 'Ananias!'

He said, 'Behold, it's me, Lord.'

The Lord said to him, 'Arise, and go to the street which is called Straight, and inquire in the house of Judah for one named Saul, a man of Tarsus. For behold, he is praying, and in a vision he has seen a man named Ananias coming in, and laying his hands on him, that he might receive his sight.'

But Ananias answered, 'Lord, I have heard from many about this man, how much evil he did to your saints at Jerusalem. Here he has authority from the chief priests to bind all who call on your name.'

---

[13] Eighteenth-century statesman George, Lord Lyttelton. The New Bible Commentary Revised published by Inter-Varsity Press page 983.

Although Ananias' dream understandably made him fearful, God, the great arranger, was preparing the way for Saul to be accepted by the Christians in Damascus. Ananias' enormous faith enabled him to not only trust God enough to go to the arch-persecutor Saul but also to have the confidence to be sure that he had the correct message. Imagine God said to you, 'Go and see President Robert Magabe in Zimbabwe or General Gaddafi in Lybia; he is my chosen instrument. Trust me.'

Q. How would you react? Be brave ☺.

Acts 9: 15-16

But the Lord said to him, 'Go your way, for he is my chosen vessel to bear my name before the nations and kings, and the children of Israel. For I will show him how many things he must suffer for my name's sake.'

God's description of Saul as his 'chosen vessel' is a name that has stuck to him ever since. Although he didn't realize it at the time, in later years Saul recognized his 'chosenness.' The advantages he received from being born and educated a Jew, doubled with the privilege of Roman citizenship, would open many doors for him in his future missionary work.

Q. List the advantages you have gained from your 'chosenness'?

Acts 9: 17-19

Ananias departed, and entered into the house. Laying his hands on him, he said, 'Brother Saul, the Lord, who appeared to you on the road by which you came, has sent me that you may receive your sight, and be filled with the Holy Spirit.' immediately something like scales fell from his eyes, and he received his sight. He arose and was baptized. He took food and was strengthened. Saul stayed several days with the disciples who were at Damascus.

The new Christians were in a predicament. Saul, the instrumental in stoning Stephen to death, persecuting and killing, many others, was committed to stamping out Christianity. God had picked this villain as his chosen spokesperson. Ananias was anxious but obedient; God was not joking. Apparently nothing was going to stop God's plan to spread Christianity across the world.

It would have been tempting for Saul to rush out to tell the world about his new conversion, his meeting with Jesus on the road, his blindness, and his newfound reason for living. But he didn't; he waited.

If God wants a particular villain to do his work, that villain must change—perhaps that sums us all up.

Acts 9: 20-22

Immediately in the synagogues he proclaimed the Christ, that he is the Son of God. All who heard him were amazed, and said, 'Isn't this he who in Jerusalem made havoc of those who called on this name? And he had come here intending to bring them bound before the chief priests!'

But Saul increased more in strength, and confounded the Jews who lived at Damascus, proving that this is the Christ.

No wonder the Jews were amazed (and everyone else, too—Romans, priests, Christians, Jews, and Gentiles). Saul was the talk of the town, a powerful news story in Damascus, which is at the crossroads of the vast Middle Eastern trade route, which is another example of God's precise planning of time and place to spread his message in a busy center where many people are traveling every which way.

We are not told who baptized Saul (probably Ananias), but we know that he got straight down to business. Being a good Jew, he would have had a sound knowledge of the Old Testament and was, therefore, able to preach about Jesus in context as the long-awaited Messiah.

Paul had changed. He was on fire.

Q. Can you recall a moment when you were spiritually or passionately 'on fire'? Please share it.

Acts 9: 23-25

When many days were fulfilled, the Jews conspired together to kill him, but their plot became known to Saul. They watched the gates both day and night that they might kill him, but his disciples took him by night, and let him down through the wall, lowering him in a basket.

Luke records the lovely picture of Saul's escape as he was lowered down the city wall in a basket. This would have been an ideal moment to drop him if they had wanted to get rid of him.

Saul had apparently managed to allay the fears of the Damascus followers after many days. Now he had to leave Damascus and again find the energy and enthusiasm to convince a new group of fearful Christians in Jerusalem they had nothing to fear from him. He faced a hard road ahead.

Q. Saul scaled down that wall with unprecedented courage, knowing an arrow may pierce him any. Can you think of a similar modern-day example of such courage?

Acts 9: 26-27

When Saul had come to Jerusalem, he tried to join himself to the disciples; but they were all afraid of him, not believing that he was a disciple. But Barnabas took him, and brought him to the apostles, and declared to them how he had seen the Lord in the way, and that he had spoken to him, and how at Damascus he had preached boldly in the name of Jesus.

Saul stayed with Peter in Jerusalem for about two weeks, where he met James, the brother of Jesus (Gal. 1: 18-19). Apparently, the other apostles were away, making Peter and James feel vulnerable.

Then dear Barnabas, the encourager, came to the rescue. To Peter and James' relief, Barnabas had heard Saul's story from Ananias. His arrival in Jerusalem at the right moment was another coincidence, or God-incidence. Barnabas was able to smooth things over for the rejected Saul, paving the way for him to begin his life's work—becoming the greatest missionary of all time to spread the Christian gospel.

Saul was swept along, completely trusting God's plan for him.

Q. Do you know what rejection feels like? Saul did nothing except wait and trust God to solve his rejection, which proved to be a good idea. Do you have a rejection story to tell?

Acts 9: 28-30

He was with them entering into Jerusalem, preaching boldly in the name of the Lord Jesus. He spoke and disputed against the Hellenists, but they were seeking to kill him. When the brothers knew it, they brought him down to Caesarea, and sent him off to Tarsus.

Saul had overcome the suspicion and fear of the elders in Jerusalem and now enjoyed their friendship, but he failed to convince the suspicious Christian Greek Jews that he was a reformed character. After all, he had caused so much trouble and watched on as their dear Stephen was stoned to death—they didn't trust him—they wanted to kill him. But now at last Paul had Christian friends to help him.

Q. Sees, have you ever preached boldly in the name of Jesus? When? What happened?

Wincs, have you ever stood up and proclaimed, talked, or lectured on a contentious issue in which you believe strongly? Will you share it with the group?

Acts 9: 31

So the assemblies throughout all Judea and Galilee and Samaria had peace, and were built up. They were multiplied, walking in the fear of the Lord and in the comfort of the Holy Spirit.

We are told Saul and the apostles were given a time to rest and recover from their turmoil, to be strengthened before continuing their mission.

Acts 9: 32-35

It happened, as Peter went throughout all those parts, he came down also to the saints who lived at Lydda. There he found a certain man named Aeneas, who had been bedridden for eight years, because he was paralysed. Peter said to him, 'Aeneas, Jesus Christ heals you. Get up and make your bed!' Immediately he arose. All who lived at Lydda and in Sharon saw him, and they turned to the Lord.

Aeneas was probably outside the temple on his mat, maybe begging for money. Healing seems to have been Peter's particular ministry. This is another amazing story which is difficult to visualize today for this lucky man.

The story leaves Saul in Tarsus for a while, preaching in his home town, while Peter travels around the countryside healing, preaching, and bringing people to Christianity in droves.

Sankara Saranam says 'a definition of miracles would be events that have not yet been explained.' And from a broader perspective, all of life is miraculous. '[14] Amen to that.

Richard Swinburne says 'he (God) can make planets move in quite different ways, and chemical substances explode or not explode under quite different conditions . . . God is not limited by the laws of nature; he makes them and he can change or suspend them—if he chooses.'[15] Therefore, we may happily believe that healing a leg or two is not a huge problem to him.

Q. You are all newspaper reporters. The challenge is that you have been asked to write an account of this miraculous event for your local paper next week, in one or two paragraphs. Please all share.

Acts 9: 36-38

Now there was at Joppa a certain disciple named Tabitha, which when translated, means Dorcas. This woman was full of good works and acts of mercy which she did. It happened in those days that she fell sick, and died. When they had washed her, they laid her in an upper room. As Lydda was near Joppa, the disciples, hearing that Peter was there, sent two men to him, imploring him not to delay in coming to them.

Joppa, a suburb of Tel Aviv, is called Jaffa today. If Dorcas had died in Jerusalem, by law her body would have to be buried on the day she died.

---

14   Sankara Saranam "God without Religion-questioning centuries of accepted truths."

15   Richard Swinburne "Is there a God?" published by Oxford University Press. Pages 32-33.

However, there was a three-day delay limit outside Jerusalem, so the body was allowed to remain upstairs.

The disciples expressed their faith in Peter by sending him a message to come quickly. By the time the messenger reached Peter, there was little time to travel the twelve miles back again to get from Lydda to Joppa in time for the burial. The three days must have been nearly up. It was a big ask for the disciples to send for Peter to come and heal a woman who had been dead for nearly three days. Why should he bother? We shall see.

Acts 9: 39-43

Peter got up and went with them. When he had come, they brought him into the upper room. All the widows stood by him weeping, and showing the coats and garments which Dorcas had made while she was with them. Peter put them all out, and kneeled down and prayed. Turning to the body, he said, 'Tabitha, get up!' She opened her eyes, and when she saw Peter, she sat up. He gave her his hand, and raised her up. Calling the saints and widows, he presented her alive. And it became known throughout all Joppa, and many believed in the Lord. It happened that he stayed many days in Joppa with one Simon, a tanner.

Luke describes the vivid scene of the customary wailing for the dead, and in this case, it was obviously filled with personal grief for the cherished dressmaker Tabitha. Through their tears, they show Peter the clothes their friend Dorcas had made for them. It is unlikely that Peter, the fisherman, was very interested in their clothes, but he would surely have been gentle and patient with the mourners.

As far as we know, Peter had not raised anyone from the dead before Tabitha, but he had been with Jesus on all three occasions when Jesus had brought a person back to life—Jairus' daughter, his friend Lazarus, and the ruler who asked Jesus to come to lay his hand on his dead daughter in Matthew 9: 2.

Jesus had asked the crowd to leave when he was with Jairus' daughter; Peter does the same. Unlike Jesus, Peter knelt down, prayed, and then, in the strength of the miraculous spiritual energy of the Holy Spirit, said, 'Tabitha, get up,' and apparently she did.

However confident Peter was, and however strong his faith, it must have been a huge relief when Tabitha opened her eyes. What astounding faith, but then Peter had been with Jesus.

Q. If you read an account of these supernatural and miraculous episodes in a newspaper today, would you accept them unconditionally as easily as if you were reading them in the Bible, or would you feel skeptical? Similarly today, how hard is it for new young Christians to accept the miracles from the first century?

Try to focus on the three episodes in this context. Let's change Saul's name to make it feel more realistic.

1) Henry Smith *heard* Jesus talking to him on Wednesday while he was walking the dog down the lane. Jesus told him to stop doing the dreadful things he was up to and to go into the city and he would be told what to do.
2) Henry subsequently lost his sight during his conversation with Jesus last week, but he received it again a few days later.
3) Angus McCubbins met a man on Sunday who had been paralyzed from the waist down all his life. Angus healed him instantly by telling him to get up and walk in the name of Jesus, which he did.
4) Bert Doolittle, the tent maker, was called to see Diana Jones this week. Diana had been dead for three days. He told her to get up; she opened her eyes and got up!

We may laugh now, but the smile may disappear quite soon if Jesus told you, as he did to Paul, go and tell everyone to believe these stories today.

How difficult was it for the apostles to get their story across? Of course they needed the miracles to back them up, and luckily all these events had witnesses.

Today, Henry, Angus, and Bert would be locked up in the lunatic asylum for life or imprisoned for fraud without witnesses to substantiate their claims.

Q. How difficult do you feel it would be for the apostles to spread the Jesus's dramatically different message, with or without the miracles? Draft an advertisement for the paper advertising for someone to fill the post as one of Jesus' apostles—list the qualities of the applicant you would be looking for. Be sure to share your advertisements.

Summary of Chapter 9

Saul of Tarsus, 'breathing out murderous threats' against the Christians, is struck down on the way to Damascus. He hears the voice of Jesus challenging him. Saul is blinded temporarily and led into Damascus. Ananias comes to heal him, and Saul begins to preach the gospel of Jesus Christ. The Christians overcome their suspicion of him and rescue him from the Greek Jews' plots to kill him. He finds himself in his birthplace of Tarsus where he continues to preach, away from trouble.

While Peter was traveling around the countryside, he receives an urgent message from the disciples in Jaffa to come quickly, as a popular lady, Tabitha, had died. Peter prays and tells Tabitha to get up. She does, and Peter presents her to her friends. This is the first time in the Bible that we hear Peter has brought someone back to life.

The spread of the gospel had had three enormous bursts of energy so far:

1) The Holy Spirit descended onto the apostles at Pentecost in a busy cosmopolitan market place in Jerusalem.

2) Saul's vicious persecution of the churches in Jerusalem caused new Christians to scatter far and wide over the Middle East, spreading the gospel story as they went.

3) Saul's dramatic encounter with Jesus at the crossroads of world trade routes changed him into the first great Christian evangelist.

CHAPTER 10

Conversion of the First Gentile, Cornelius

Acts 10: 1-4

Now there was a certain man in Caesarea, Cornelius by name, a centurion of what was called the Italian Regiment, a devout man, and one who feared God with all his house, who gave gifts for the needy generously to the people, and always prayed to God. At about the ninth hour of the day, he clearly saw in a vision an angel of God coming to him, and saying to him, 'Cornelius!'

He, fastening his eyes on him, and being frightened, said, 'What is it, Lord?'

He said to him, 'Your prayers and your gifts to the needy have gone up for a memorial before God.

A memorial, or a remembrance offering, was usually a portion of grain that was burned on the altar as an offering to God. This was a less gruesome sacrifice than the previous custom of slaughtering a sanctified animal.

Caesarea was the Roman army headquarters, about thirty miles north of Joppa. A Roman legion was made up of about six thousand men. The centurions were carefully chosen officers of good standing and were in charge of about one hundred men each within the regiment. Each regiment had its own name, as they do today; this one was called the Italian Regiment.

Cornelius, the Roman centurion, was a God-fearing man, a term used for a non-Jewish person who believed and practiced the teaching of the Jews.

As Cornelius prayed, he had a vision of the angel calling him by name. Apparently it was not a dream or a trance but a great moment of revelation for this good man. This was another meticulous event to spread the gospel message to the Gentiles through the Roman army.

Q. This is a big request. If you were God (forgive me, but I believe we all are in part) which group of people would you choose in your community that has most need to hear the Good News or some really helpful, encouraging, positive news which will change their lives? Is there something that needs doing about it?

Acts 10: 5-8

Now send men to Joppa, and get Simon, who is surnamed Peter. He lodges with one Simon, a tanner, whose house is by the seaside.

When the angel who spoke to him had departed, Cornelius called two of his household servants and a devout soldier of those who waited on him continually. Having explained everything to them, he sent them to Joppa.

Cornelius must have been on comfortable and familiar terms with his servants to tell them about this very personal experience. He gave the servants detailed instructions where to find Simon Peter and thoughtfully sent a soldier with them to protect them on the journey.

Acts 10: 9-12

Now on the next day as they were on their journey, and got close to the city, Peter went up on the housetop to pray at about noon. He became hungry and desired to eat, but while they were preparing, he fell into a trance. He saw heaven opened and a certain container descending to him, like a great sheet let down by four corners on the earth, in which were all kinds of four-footed animals of the earth, wild animals, reptiles, and birds of the sky.

Peter was having a perfectly normal prayer time on the flat roof, waiting for lunch. While he prayed, the NIV Study bible says his 'consciousness was heightened' to receive the vision from God. As with Cornelius' experience, this was not Peter's imagination or even a dream.

Most of us are not given to having visions or hearing God speak to us audibly, but occasionally there may be moments, perhaps in prayer or during meditation, when we feel our state of mind is sharpened to communicate with a 'something' that is beyond our understanding.

For Christians it has been said that the cross is the meeting place of God and man. At the moment of taking the bread and wine, the symbol of the body and blood of Christ's sacrifice, God metaphorically opens a pathway from heaven to earth, enabling us to receive that holy moment and receive a touch from heaven.

Q. You can probably explain this better than I. Would you like to jot down and share your experience of a holy moment, or Wincs, a spiritual or magical moment? Try to list the emotions which are similar in the different stories?

Acts 10: 13-16

A voice came to him, 'Rise, Peter, kill and eat!'

But Peter said, 'Not so, Lord; for I have never eaten anything that is common or unclean.'

A voice came to him again the second time, 'What God has cleansed, you must not call unclean.' This was done three times, and immediately the vessel was received up into heaven.

The Jewish law was so deeply ingrained in Peter that the idea of eating pork, for instance, could have initially made him feel sick and cause him to refuse to do as God asked. The eating rules of the Jews had been introduced by the rabbis five hundred years earlier, as they chose to reinterpret the laws of Moses.

Jesus had already established a statement about clean and unclean food when he made that wonderful remark to the Pharisees in Matthew 15: 11, 'What goes into a man's mouth does not make him 'unclean' but what comes out of his mouth.'

Luke attaches great importance to this story, in which God emphasizes that nothing he has made is to be called unclean or unworthy, for Luke repeats it three times in the Acts.

Q. Peter's message suggested that God was trying to cut through unhelpful practices in the Jewish law. Do you feel there are pedantic words and out of date traditions in your church today? If the answer is 'yes', please do something about it.

Acts 10: 17-20

Now while Peter was very perplexed in himself what the vision which he had seen might mean, behold, the men who were sent by Cornelius, having made inquiry for Simon's house, stood before the gate, and called and asked whether Simon, who was surnamed Peter, was lodging there. While Peter was pondering the vision, the Spirit said to him, 'Behold, three men seek you. But arise, get down, and go with them, doubting nothing; for I have sent them.'

The Great Planner's perfect timing is evident again. Peter had no time to stop and question this strange intrusion to his day. A new door had just opened for him, and Peter went through it obediently.

The communication is different here. The spirit spoke to Peter this time, not an angel. One can only wonder what the difference is, but that deep still small voice instructed him, and with complete confidence, Peter somehow knows it is the will of his Lord.

Q. When did your deep inner voice/conscience direct you in an act which was quite contrary to your belief, culture or religion? How hard was it to take notice of the deep inner voice? Did you? Will you share what happened?

Acts 10: 21-23

Peter went down to the men, and said, 'Behold, I am he whom you seek. Why have you come?'

They said, 'Cornelius, a centurion, a righteous man and one who fears God, and well-spoken of by all the nation of the Jews, was directed by a holy angel to invite you to his house, and to listen to what you say.' So he called them in and lodged them. On the next day Peter arose and went out with them, and some of the brothers from Joppa accompanied him.

Peter wondered what on earth was going on when he was called down to meet the Romans. Peter still did not understand the meaning of his vision of the sheet descending from heaven, carrying all those animals. By Jewish law, the Jews were not supposed to associate with Gentiles, so for Peter to welcome these Gentiles and teach them the gospel would be revolutionary stuff.

It is refreshing to feel the gentle pace of life for the people in this story. Simon's wife or servants just accepted three extra guests dropping in for lunch, dinner, bed and breakfast with no apparent fuss.

Q. A total stranger knocks on your door and asks you to go and witness your passionate belief to an unknown man's boss some distance away, right now. How would you react?

Acts 10: 24-26

On the next day they entered into Caesarea. Cornelius was waiting for them, having called together his relatives and his near friends. When it happened that Peter entered, Cornelius met him, fell down at his feet, and worshipped him. But Peter raised him up, saying, 'Stand up! I myself am also a man.'

By the next day, Peter had collected six other 'brothers' to come with him (Acts 11: 12). Interestingly, all these people were able to drop everything and go off to Caesarea for an unknown length of time, at a moment's notice. Cornelius did not really know why Peter was coming. He'd called his friends in to support him. Peter didn't know why the messengers had come either. In fact, nobody except God knew what was going on.

From Ria: (bet the women were at home looking after the children!)

They probably were too! Being a Roman in charge of Israel, Cornelius was supposed to be in the senior position, and yet it was he who fell at Peter's feet intending to honor him with respect as a messenger from God. However, he was met with a sharp response from Peter, highlighting the tension between these two men.

Caroline A. Westerhoff, in her book *Calling*, talks about the need for healthy conflict and tension to enable us to grow. 'Healthy bodies—and communities—are in constant tension regarding change.'[16] Conflict can be

---

[16]   Caroline A Westerhoff's "Calling—A song for the Baptized" published by Cowley Publications. Page 67.

a challenge that often leads to a stronger relationship. Peter and Cornelius were about to grow in leaps and bounds.

Q. When did you last 'grow', mentally or spiritually in leaps and bounds, in any direction?

Acts 10: 27-29

As he [Cornelius] talked with him, Peter went in and found many gathered together. He said to them, 'You yourselves know how it is an unlawful thing for a man who is a Jew to join himself or come to one of another nation, but God has shown me that I shouldn't call any man unholy or unclean. Therefore also I came without complaint when I was sent for. I ask therefore, why did you send for me?'

Peter reinforces Jesus's clear teaching that it is the words, thoughts, and actions that come out of a man that make him acceptable or unacceptable, not his social or cultural background. God's plan was working beautifully. Cornelius, a well-respected officer, and an excellent spokesman was about to spread the gospel through the Roman community.

Q. Where do you go in this noisy, frantic world to meditate on your problems and look for solutions?

Acts 10: 30-33

Cornelius said, 'Four days ago, I was fasting until this hour, and at the ninth hour, I prayed in my house, and behold, a man stood before me in bright clothing, and said, 'Cornelius, your prayer is heard, and your gifts to the needy are remembered in the sight of God. Send therefore to Joppa, and summon Simon, who is surnamed Peter. He lodges in the house of Simon a tanner, by the seaside. When he comes, he will speak to you.' Therefore I sent to you at once, and it was good of you to come. Now therefore we are all here present in the sight of God to hear all things that have been commanded you by God.'

Cornelius acknowledged Peter's faithfulness, recognizing the difficult situation he was in (being a Jew visiting a Gentile), by thanking him for coming.

Cornelius had obviously repeated the story about the man in shining clothes to the Romans gathered in his house. He had asked them to come and listen to an unknown Jew from Joppa for a reason he knew not. All this happened over four days.

First day: The man in shining clothes appeared to Cornelius.
Second day: The messengers arrived in Joppa to look for Peter, while Peter had a vision on the rooftop.
Third day: The messengers set off for Caesarea with Peter.
Fourth day: They all arrived at Cornelius' house.

In summary, it had to be a very strong message to convince a Roman to seek enlightenment from a Jew or for a Jew to travel a day's journey to give it to him. That still small voice in Peter's energetic spiritual mind was whispering to him again.

Acts 10: 34-38

Peter opened his mouth and said, 'Truly I perceive that God doesn't show favouritism; but in every nation he who fears him and works righteousness is acceptable to him. The word which he sent to the children of Israel, preaching good news of peace by Jesus Christ—he is Lord of all—you yourselves know what happened, which was proclaimed throughout all Judea, beginning from Galilee, after the baptism which John preached; even Jesus of Nazareth, how God anointed him with the Holy Spirit and with power, who went about doing good and healing all who were oppressed by the devil, for God was with him.

At this moment it dawned on Peter the importance of this meeting; God had set it up to enable Jews and Gentiles to accept each other unconditionally. We are told that Cornelius was a God-fearing man, and therefore, he would have been familiar with the passage Peter quotes from Isaiah.

Peter pointed out the connection between the Jewish faith and the coming of the 'anointed one' predicted in Isaiah. Jesus was this Messiah,

Isaiah's promised one, whom God had chosen to change the thinking of the world.

Jesus himself refers to the same passage in Luke 4: 16-21, referring to himself as the anointed servant whose ministry is to bring gladness instead of misery and beauty instead of ashes, to be liberated from sin and all its consequences.

The price is too high for some. The price is the willingness to trust and believe in an invisible God.

Karen Armstrong, the British writer on comparative religion and a former nun, says, 'We need God to grasp the wonder of our existence. Religion was not supposed to provide explanations that lay within the competence of reason, but to help us live creatively with realities, for which there are no easy solutions and find an interior haven of peace.' [17]

Q. Wincs, what do you say to Karen Armstrong? As we live on the border of the known and the unknown, from where or from whom do you 'grasp the wonder of your existence?' Wincs and Sees, is the price of believing in an invisible unknown God becoming too high? How can the price be reduced?

Acts 10: 39-43

We are witnesses of everything he did both in the country of the Jews, and in Jerusalem; whom they also killed, hanging him on a tree. God raised him up the third day, and gave him to be revealed, not to all the people, but to witnesses who were chosen before by God, to us, who ate and drank with him after he rose from the dead.

He commanded us to preach to the people and to testify that this is he who is appointed by God as the Judge of the living and the dead. All the prophets testify about him, that through his name everyone who believes in him will receive remission of sins.'

---

[17] Karen Armstrong, former nun and British author wrote a newspaper article in the "Inquirer" section of the *Weekend Australian* newspaper 19-20 September 2009 called "Nothing beyond belief" page 6.

Peter was chosen by Jesus from a *chance* meeting on the beach. God had a very specific ministry for Peter—to faithfully carry on teaching after Jesus's death. The gospel story has been repeated against dangerous odds and still manages to survive the passage of time. Having faith was, and still is, a hugely difficult message to get across.

Q. Wincs, in whom do you have faith? How about three suggestions? And Sees, how about some more?

Acts 10: 44-46

While Peter was still speaking these words, the Holy Spirit fell on all those who heard the word. They of the circumcision who believed were amazed, as many as came with Peter, because the gift of the Holy Spirit was also poured out on the Gentiles. For they heard them speaking in other languages and magnifying God.

Sometimes, from our home on a crisp autumn morning, we can see mist floating down the estuary, on the water. The change from water to mist is invisible, which is similar to the invitation God 'pours out' at our baptism. While the sprinkling of baptismal water is the physical sign of the spiritual invitation from God, the statement 'the Holy Spirit poured out on them' expresses the process of invisible change.

One day, perhaps much later on, when we say 'yes' to God, in a split second, we change again invisibly. Some people change into steaming geysers like Peter, Paul, Martin Luther, Martin Luther King Jr., and Billy Graham. Others gently find their interior haven of peace, like the mist on the water this morning. Sadly, sometime later the haven evaporates from neglect.

The Jews were amazed that the Holy Spirit should be "poured out" onto the Gentiles. After all, in their thinking, they were/are the only chosen race. There is no doubt that the gospel would never have been passed to the Gentiles without a *huge* dramatic and divine push.

Q. Write yourself a note from God, or Wincs and A&A's, from a much loved person who has died, telling you how much the effort you make in the service to others is appreciated. Be quite specific and try not to be humble. God or your beloved relative or friend wouldn't be humble in their words to you.

Acts 10: 47-48

Then Peter answered, 'Can any man forbid the water, that these who have received the Holy Spirit as well as we should not be baptized?' He commanded them to be baptized in the name of Jesus Christ. Then they asked him to stay some days.

The unimaginable had happened. The Gentiles had been given the same gift as the Jews. The NIV Study Bible says, 'This was unavoidable evidence that the invitation to the Kingdom of God was open to Gentiles as well as to Jews.'[18] Peter did not try to hide this astounding fact but obediently organized baptism for the new Gentile Christians.

Generous, honest Peter accepted God's decision without further fuss, although it was certainly a huge surprise and contrary to everything he had ever been taught. Peter recognized how vulnerable these new Christians were feeling. It is all very well to take on a new project, but the test is to get over the obstacles, stick to it, and see it through.

Q. Is there a very special project you would like to complete, or have completed? Will you share your story?

---

[18]   NIV Bible Acts 10:47 page 1666

Summary of Chapter 10

This chapter has enormous historic significance.

1. Peter has a vision and is called by God to go to Caesarea and to talk to a Roman, non-Jewish, 'God-fearing' army officer named Cornelius. This breaks a long tradition of Jews never mixing with Gentiles. Peter tells the Gentiles the gospel story, and the Holy Spirit comes to them. Peter is astonished.
2. The explosion of Christianity flew from Pentecost—the Holy Spirit descended on the apostles in the marketplace, where a crowd from many different countries was gathered. This was followed by the little incident when Philip was sent to explain the reading in Isaiah to the Ethiopian in the chariot. The Ethiopian took the message back to Africa.
3. Saul's persecution of the early Christians forced the believers to scatter all over the Middle East, until Saul's conversion—his encounter with Jesus on his way to Damascus gave him the zeal to spread the Good News throughout Asia Minor. And finally, so far, in a vision God instructed Peter to include Gentiles in his teaching.

The conversion of these new Christians opened a massive channel of evangelism through the Roman Army and around the Mediterranean Sea and the Middle East.

There were still three hundred years of persecution ahead, until the Roman Emperor Constantine proclaimed tolerance for the Christian religion AD 313 AD. Christianity continued to spread and become recognized across Europe; at last, in AD 800, the name of the Roman Empire was later changed to the *Holy* Roman Empire.

CHAPTER 11

The First Gentile Church Is
Established in Antioch

Acts 11: 1-3

Now the apostles and the brothers who were in Judea heard that the
Gentiles had also received the word of God. When Peter had come up
to Jerusalem, those who were of the circumcision contended with him,
saying, 'You went in to uncircumcised men, and ate with them!'

The news traveled quickly ahead of Peter to the apostles in Jerusalem.
They were appalled that Peter should fraternize with an uncircumcised
Roman centurion, Cornelius, and his friends.

In matters of deep concern, the leaders of the church in Jerusalem did
not act alone but sought the opinion of the whole church. God and Peter
had taken a shortcut here, and the church leaders didn't like it. It suggested
more change.

Q. Can any of you think of a significant policy change, or law, to which
you have been asked to adjust? Explain how you felt about it?

Acts 11: 4-18

But Peter began, and explained to them in order, saying, 'I was in the
city of Joppa praying, and in a trance I saw a vision: a certain container
descending, like it was a great sheet let down from heaven by four corners.
It came as far as me. When I had looked intently at it, I considered, and

saw the four-footed animals of the earth, wild animals, creeping things, and birds of the sky. I also heard a voice saying to me, 'Rise, Peter, kill and eat!' But I said, 'Not so, Lord, for nothing unholy or unclean has ever entered into my mouth.' But a voice answered me the second time out of heaven, 'What God has cleansed, don't you call unclean.' This was done three times, and all were drawn up again into heaven. Behold, immediately three men stood before the house where I was, having been sent from Caesarea to me. The Spirit told me to go with them, without discriminating.

These six brothers also accompanied me, and we entered into the man's house. He told us how he had seen the angel standing in his house, and saying to him, 'Send to Joppa, and get Simon, whose surname is Peter, who will speak to you words by which you will be saved, you and all your house.'

As I began to speak, the Holy Spirit fell on them, even as on us at the beginning. I remembered the word of the Lord, how he said, 'John indeed baptized in water, but you will be baptized in the Holy Spirit.' If then God gave to them the same gift as us, when we believed in the Lord Jesus Christ, who was I, that I could withstand God?'

When they heard these things, they held their peace, and glorified God, saying, 'Then God has also granted to the Gentiles repentance to life!'

The disciples and their church leaders in Jerusalem were hard and fast Jews. They had suffered enough lately from emerging new ideas. Stephen had started by suggesting that Christianity should be passed on to the Gentiles, and look what happened to him. It was outrageous to think that their beloved leader Peter would agree.

Peter told the disciples of the two visions, his own and Cornelius', and told them how the Gentiles reacted when they heard the gospel, proving that apparently God had new plans for them.

Astounding though it was, they were convinced that Peter had acted wisely.

Q. Sees, can you think of an incident when you felt God's direction clearly? Or Wincs, when you felt your conscience clearly giving you direction, but you wanted to say, 'No, thank you'? Can you say what happened? Or have we done it? Pass.

Acts 11: 19-21

They therefore who were scattered abroad by the oppression that arose about Stephen traveled as far as Phoenicia, Cyprus, and Antioch, speaking the word to no one except to Jews only. But there were some of them, men of Cyprus and Cyrene, who, when they had come to Antioch, spoke to the Hellenists, preaching the Lord Jesus. The hand of the Lord was with them, and a great number believed and turned to the Lord.

At about the same time as Peter began to preach to the Gentiles in Caesarea, other apostles began to preach and teach to the Gentiles in Antioch in the north. Antioch was the third largest city in the Roman Empire after Rome and Alexandria.

There were more Gentiles than Jews in Antioch, so the religious differences seemed less important. God's business plan was still on track, targeting key spots to spread the gospel.

The number of Christians grew rapidly. The second Christian church was established in Antioch, with a large proportion of Gentiles among them and *'the Lord's hand was with them,'* showing divine approval and blessing. What a lovely phrase.

Q. Sees, what are the signs that the Lord's hand is upon your congregation? It could be a wonderful, happy time to research this question.

Wincs, if you are working with a team for a good cause, do feel at times that (you are blessed/sorry Ria) or that something very special is happening?

Ria commented: I would be very irritated as a Winc to be told to accept that I was blessed.

I am being patronizing again, sorry Ria and Wincs. Perhaps Christians need to look more sensitively at how we hand out blessings.

But thank you Ria for highlighting another point. As Christians in the 21st century I believe we need to be far more thoughtful about our language. We sing, pray and confess constantly that Jesus is the one and only true Savior of the world.

Because we were born in a certain place is usually the only reason we follow a certain faith. Could we be accused of being possessively arrogant to suggest that every other religion is wrong? Do we believe Christians

are superior species? Will this attitude help to promote world peace and
harmony? What do you all think? I hope there is a mixed group of A&A's
and different faiths here.

Acts 11: 22-24

The report concerning them came to the ears of the assembly which
was in Jerusalem. They sent out Barnabas to go as far as Antioch, who,
when he had come, and had seen the grace of God, was glad. He exhorted
them all, that with purpose of heart they should remain near to the Lord.
For he was a good man, and full of the Holy Spirit and of faith, and many
people were added to the Lord.

The headquarters of the church in Jerusalem continued its practice of
sending one of its own members to supervise and guide a newly established
church. Barnabas was the obvious choice, as Antioch was his hometown.
He arrived to find the new group working well together, encouraged
to see the harmony, goodwill, and excitement the Christians had found in
their new faith. It is interesting to reflect on the churches today and which
of them are alive, for to be part of a vibrant, caring church family is one of
the greatest treasures that may be found this side of the grave.

Q. Sees, where or when do you feel the joy and excitement of being
spiritually alive?
   Wincs, what gives you a similar sense of joy and excitement? Please
write your feelings about this important point to share.

Acts 11: 25-26

Barnabas went out to Tarsus to look for Saul. When he had found
him, he brought him to Antioch. It happened, that for a whole year they
were gathered together with the assembly, and taught many people. The
disciples were first called Christians in Antioch.

Saul had been working in his hometown, Tarsus, and as a citizen of that
city, he was automatically a Roman citizen. Tarsus was situated ten miles
upstream from the sea, on the Cydnis River. A deep gorge through the

mountains made Tarsus *'no ordinary city'* (Acts 21: 39). It was a university city and along with Damascus and Antioch, was a commercial crossroads for trade from east to west.

Barnabas went to look for Saul and brought him back to help with the new church in Antioch.

The new believers were named Christians, which could have come from the Gentiles, meaning 'Christ's people.' Christ was only a personal name like Sam or Harry to the Gentiles, while to the Jews it meant 'the Messiah.'

The Jews, who were initially uncertain and unhappy about this new Christian group, would certainly not have called them 'the Messiah's people.' Nobody is quite sure whether the word *Christian* was a derogatory nickname that stuck or one adopted by the church members themselves. The Christians in Antioch were in for a year of dynamic leadership with Saul and Barnabas to lead them.

Q. (a) Sees, are there many young people in your church? Do they share the leadership in your services? Is there a good balance, or could they be encouraged even more?

(b) Wincs, (for those of other traditions) are young people encouraged to develop leadership skills in your place of worship?

(c) A&A's are there any ways young people in your community, could receive more help to 'stay on the rails' or be helped to find their potential?

(d) Was there any common ground in these three answers?

Acts 11: 27-30

Now in these days, prophets came down from Jerusalem to Antioch. One of them named Agabus stood up, and indicated by the Spirit that there should be a great famine all over the world, which also happened in the days of Claudius. As many of the disciples had plenty, each determined to send relief to the brothers who lived in Judea; which they also did, sending it to the elders by the hands of Barnabas and Saul.

Apparently the practice of prophesy was strong in Jerusalem. The church took it very seriously, so to prepare for the predicted drought, the Antioch Christians set aside money regularly for the time of need. We will hear of Agabus again in chapter 21, as he predicts Paul's imprisonment.

Claudius was emperor from 41-54 AD. The contemporary writer at the time, Josephus, tells us that in about AD 46 Palestine was hard hit by famine—the Queen Mother Adiabenein in northeastern Mesopotamia had to buy her corn in Egypt and figs in Cyprus to relieve the hungry Palestinians. Claudius' reign was apparently marked by '*constant seasons of unfruitfulness*' (NIV Study Bible).

Q. Who are our prophets today—and to whom do 'we', being the church or individuals, 'send relief'?

Summary of Chapter 11

The Jewish followers of Christ are astounded that God intended to give his gift of the Holy Spirit to non-Jews. Peter, having started the ball rolling when asked by God in a vision to visit a Roman centurion in Caesarea, is then criticized by the Jews in Jerusalem for doing so. However, they all seem to come to terms with the idea and continue with the great task of spreading the gospel. The terms *Christian* and *the gift of prophesy*, are recorded in this chapter for the first time in the Bible.

CHAPTER 12

Herod Is Too Big for His Boots

Acts 12: 1-4

Now about that time, King Herod stretched out his hands to oppress some of the assembly. He killed James, the brother of John, with the sword. When he saw that it pleased the Jews, he proceeded to seize Peter also. This was during the days of unleavened bread. When he had arrested him, he put him in prison, and delivered him to four squads of four soldiers each to guard him, intending to bring him out to the people after the Passover.

These Herod's were a fearsome lot. This Herod was the grandson of Herod the Great, the villain of the Christmas story, and his uncle, Herod Antipas, beheaded John the Baptist on the whim of a pretty woman.

Now this fellow calmly kills James and plans to kill Peter to please the Jews—a political vote catcher. But God had had enough of these Herods; to the relief of the Christians, this one died the following year,

As he was thrown into jail again, Peter must have wondered if his time had come. God must wonder why he ever bothered to create humans when we do such dreadful, vindictive things to each other.

'Father, forgive them, for they know not what they do,' Jesus said on the Cross.

Thought: If there is someone up there, please forgive us for every spiteful thing we do or say.

Acts 12: 5-10

Peter therefore was kept in the prison, but constant prayer was made by the assembly to God for him. The same night when Herod was about to bring him out, Peter was sleeping between two soldiers, bound with two chains. Guards in front of the door kept the prison.

And behold, an angel of the Lord stood by him, and a light shone in the cell. He struck Peter on the side, and woke him up, saying, 'Stand up quickly!' His chains fell off from his hands. The angel said to him, 'Get dressed and put on your sandals.' He did so. He said to him, 'Put on your cloak, and follow me.' And he went out and followed him. He didn't know that what was being done by the angel was real, but thought he saw a vision. When they were past the first and the second guard, they came to the iron gate that leads into the city, which opened to them by itself. They went out, and went down one street, and immediately the angel departed from him.

What a vivid description. Old Herod didn't want to be caught out with a red face with Peter slipping through his fingers, as Peter had done with the Sanhedrin. Herod must have had a healthy respect for Peter's ability to escape to order such a heavy guard for him.

Of course, the apostles were fearful. James had been killed, surely not Peter, too. We are given these lovely details of this practical angel waking Peter, remembering to tell him to put on his cloak and shoes. Peter, in a sleepy daze, followed obediently. Locked chains fell off, prison doors opened, and at the end of the street, the angel was gone.

What a good thing the angel saw to it that he had his warm cloak and shoes on. Keeping warm would alleviate the shock of this amazing experience. I wonder who the angel was. He had a key, anyway, which was the important thing.

It is a beautiful story.

Q. At certain times, the Great Arranger seems to organize someone to be in the right place at the right time to be an angel, to help someone else. It could be any one of us, and we don't even know it.

I am not sure about the white feathered variety of angels, but who knows?

What do you think about angels? Are some angels human? Could this angel have been a human one? What do you think about spiritual beings, Wincs?

From Ria: While I was reading these paragraphs I kept thinking if it happened as indicated, why could it not have been a human being or beings and their names suppressed for their safety, then the angel bit suited the storytelling better and there was your last question.

Ria *agreed.* What fun, I love having Ria with us; I hope you are enjoying her company too.

Acts 12: 11-14

When Peter had come to himself, he said, 'Now I truly know that the Lord has sent out his angel and delivered me out of the hand of Herod, and from everything the Jewish people were expecting.' Thinking about that, he came to the house of Mary, the mother of John whose surname was Mark, where many were gathered together and were praying. When Peter knocked at the door of the gate, a maid named Rhoda came to answer. When she recognized Peter's voice, she didn't open the gate for joy, but ran in, and reported that Peter was standing in front of the gate.

Imagine poor Peter, stunned, shocked, and possibly shivering. He bolts quickly off to Mary's house. It must have been early morning by now, probably chilly too. God's perfect plan fitted in with prison routine and the guards' alertness. Rhoda, the silly girl, leaves Peter standing outside the door in her excitement to tell the others. She may have even slammed the door in his face. He just kept knocking.

Q. Have you ever had a wonderful and sudden shocking surprise? Have fun sharing them.

Acts 12: 15-17

They said to her, 'You are crazy!' But she insisted that it was so. They said, 'It is his angel.' But Peter continued knocking. When they had opened, they saw him, and were amazed. But he, beckoning to them with his hand to be silent, declared to them how the Lord had brought him out of the prison. He said, 'Tell these things to James, and to the brothers.' Then he departed, and went to another place.

Poor Peter stood there wrapped in his cloak, terrified of being caught again. His friends thought that Rhoda is crazy, and although they were praying for Peter's release, they were amazed when their prayer was answered! Let's hope they gave him a hearty breakfast before he departed.

Q. Sees, do you pray truly believing that your prayer will be answered, or like the apostles, are you surprised when it is?
   Wincs, do you find you sneak in a prayer in moments of crisis? ☺
   (I am surprised, there is no comment from Ria.)

Acts 12: 18-19

Now as soon as it was day, there was no small stir among the soldiers about what had become of Peter. When Herod had sought for him, and didn't find him, he examined the guards, and commanded that they should be put to death. He went down from Judea to Caesarea, and stayed there.

Luckily, Peter had a good hiding place. Herod who was in a rage, probably thought the guards were in a plot to rescue Peter. They might have been, too; we don't exactly know what happened.
   Herod, no doubt, felt very foolish, so he blames the guards—no trial and no justice, orders them to be killed in anger and humiliation. Herod presumably ran away to save face; his authority had been flouted, and the carefully guarded prisoner had walked away *again*.

Q. It is a human reaction to put the blame on somebody else if we do something wrong. Can you relate to Herod's gross injustice? Do you have any stories to share here?

Acts 12: 20-23

Now Herod was very angry with the people of Tyre and Sidon. They came with one accord to him, and, having made Blastus, the king's personal aide, their friend, they asked for peace, because their country depended on the king's country for food. On an appointed day, Herod dressed himself in royal clothing, sat on the throne, and gave a speech to them. The people shouted, 'The voice of a god, and not of a man!' Immediately an angel of the Lord struck him, because he didn't give God the glory, and he was eaten by worms and died.

The Herods seemed to quarrel a lot. The people on the coast in the north needed grain, which grew in Herod's province of Judaea in the south. They had to try and keep the peace, or they'd get no grain.

According to the historian Josephus in his writings *Antiquities,*[19] Herod, celebrating to honor of Claudius Caesar dressed up like Elvis Presley, was wallowing in the crowds flattery, when he was seized with violent pains, he was carried out to die five days later.

'Eaten by worms' may mean he had some infestation of worms that killed him. Whatever the cause of death, it seems that God was not impressed by his boasting and conceit.

Q. Have you ever been troubled by someone's conceit and boastfulness? How did you, or do you, react to it? Perhaps you have some amusing stories to tell, because boastful pomposity is often very funny—or very boring.

---

[19] Josephus was a Jewish priest with royal relations. He was a Jewish military leader against the Romans in the first Jewish Roman war in 66-73 AD. A historian of note, he was accused of "shocking duplicity" by changing his allegiance to Rome. He ended up comfortably retired in the Roman camp. His major works, which give crucial information on Pontius Pilate, Herod the Great, and many leaders of the time, were the history of the Jewish revolt. In "Jewish War," later called "Antiquities," he writes about Jesus "of Nazareth, a man who was a prophet mighty in deed and word before God and all the people . . . " quoted from the Wikipedia Web site on the historian Josephus.

Acts 12:24-25

But the word of God grew and multiplied.

When Barnabas and Saul had finished this mission, they returned from Jerusalem, taking with them John, also called Mark.

Despite the considerable pressure to try and suppress the spread of Christianity, the message was going off like a rocket. These three men, Barnabas, Saul, and Mark had become a strong team.

Mark was to accompany Saul and Barnabas again on their next mission. Now that the unscrupulous Herod was dead, they were able to finish their mission in peace—a well-earned respite in the dangerous work they had been called to do.

Summary of Chapter 12

Peter is in jail and in grave danger from King Herod, who had killed James and was thinking about doing the same to Peter. However, an angel takes Peter out of prison, past the guards, and through locked gates. Peter wisely leaves the area. Herod dresses himself up in fancy clothes for a festival day, collapses, and dies suddenly, enabling Barnabas, Saul, and Mark to thankfully carry on their mission in peace.

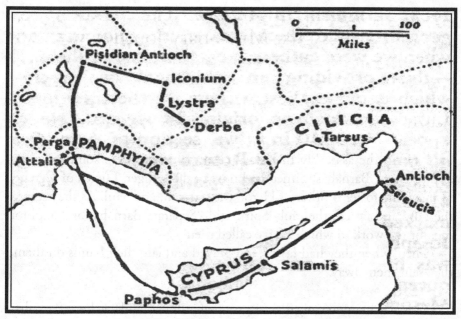

Map of Paul's First Missionary Journey

Taken from *New Bible Commentary*
edited by Gordon J. Wenham, J. Alec Motyer and others. Copyright© 1970
InterVarsity Press, PO box 1400 Downers Grove, IL 605 15 www.ivpress.com
Printed with permission.

CHAPTER 13

Paul's First Missionary Journey

Acts 13: 1-3

Now in the assembly that was at Antioch there were some prophets and teachers: Barnabas, Simeon who was called Niger, Lucius of Cyrene, Manaen the foster brother of Herod the tetrarch, and Saul. As they served the Lord and fasted, the Holy Spirit said, 'Separate Barnabas and Saul for me, for the work to which I have called them.'

Then, when they had fasted and prayed and laid their hands on them, they sent them away.

This was an interesting diverse group of prophets and teachers. Barnabas and Saul had connections in Antioch. There was

- Simeon, nicknamed Niger (no prizes for guessing that Niger is Latin for black, indicating his dark-skin) he probably came from Africa;
- Lucius, a Latin name from Cyrene on the north coast of Africa;
- Manaen, a Hebrew name. Manaen was Herod's foster brother, so he would know the king well and understand his quirks;
- John, called Mark, was Barnabas' cousin was probably there, too.

While they were praying, one or some of them received a conviction that Barnabas and Saul had special evangelical skills and were wasting time sitting about in Antioch. As happens today, they laid hands on them to bless them on their way.

The laying on of hands in prayer is another mystical symbol—a moment when the soul can soar to meet God, a similar feeling to the moment of receiving bread and wine in Communion.

St. Teresa of Avila says, 'The soul which gives itself to prayer . . . must absolutely not have limits set on it. Since God has given it such dignity, it must be free to roam . . . But like a bee making honey in the hive, humility must constantly be at work. However, the bee also leaves the hive to fly from flower to flower. So the soul must come out from self-knowledge and soar up high to meditate upon God's greatness and Majesty.' [20]

Q. Can you relate to St Teresa's prayer of 'soaring up high to meditate upon God's (or whoever's) greatness'? '

Sees and Wincs, please tell each other about your soaring up high moments.

From Ria: I have been asked this question before (or something like) and when I say words to the effect that I can understand it may be the same feeling, i.e. beautiful music, scenery etc., I am told that of course it is all God's work and it infuriates me as of course I don't have the same 'take' on it and find this sort of response exceedingly 'off' when I do not accept, let alone believe, that some invisible thing has done it. It would put me right off taking any further involvement in the discussion.

A sincere thank you, Ria. Please don't run away Wincs. Do you sometimes 'soar on high' to ponder and wonder on some beautiful happening?

Acts 13: 4-5

So, being sent out by the Holy Spirit, they went down to Seleucia. From there they sailed to Cyprus. When they were at Salamis, they proclaimed the word of God in the Jewish synagogues. They had also John as their attendant.

Imagine the scene as they left the apostles in Antioch. Maybe the friends traveled down the sixteen miles to Seleuca, on the banks of the Orantes River, to see them off.

---

[20] St. Teresa of Avila, "The Interior Castle" edited by Halcyon Backhouse.

How did Barnabas and Saul know where to go? It was possibly another of those 'casting lots' decisions to allow God to choose. Anyway, Cyprus was to be the destination.

As many Jews lived in Cyprus, and with Barnabas' family connections, they could be sure of a friendly welcome. They found a boat and set off. What an adventure; what amazing faith, courage, and commitment. They just took off into the blue, for better or for worse.

Q. Maybe one or two of you have or are going to 'take off into the blue' at some time, perhaps after school to see the world. For those who have done it, what did it feel like? Can you jot down your adventure to share briefly?

Acts 13: 6-7

When they had gone through the island to Paphos, they found a certain sorcerer, a false prophet, a Jew, whose name was Bar-Jesus, who was with the proconsul, Sergius Paulus, a man of understanding. This man summoned Barnabas and Saul, and sought to hear the word of God.

They traveled nearly one hundred miles from Salamis to Paphos, through Cyprus, through olive groves, and along rocky roads. Maybe they borrowed a donkey, for there were, and still are, plenty of them on the island. Barnabas and Saul would have met Bar-Jesus through their Jewish community.

Bar is Aramaic for 'Son of' and *Jesus* is derived from the Greek word for Joshua. This son of Joshua worked for the Roman Proconsul of this Roman province.

Bar-Jesus must have told his boss, the intelligent Sergius Paulus, there were two visitors in town. Bar-Jesus was impressed with the power he saw in Barnabas and Saul, but his motive may not have been any more honorable than the last fellow, Simon the magician in chapter 8 who wanted to 'buy' the power of God for his magic tricks.

Sergius Paulus was interested to know what was going on in his province, so he called a meeting. It looked as though the Great Planner was about to spread the gospel message further through the Roman diplomatic service.

Acts 13: 8-12

But Elymas the sorcerer (for so is his name by interpretation) withstood them, seeking to turn aside the proconsul from the faith. But Saul, who is also called Paul, filled with the Holy Spirit, fastened his eyes on him, and said, 'Full of all deceit and all cunning, you son of the devil, you enemy of all righteousness, will you not cease to pervert the right ways of the Lord? Now, behold, the hand of the Lord is on you, and you will be blind, not seeing the sun for a season!'

Immediately a mist and darkness fell on him. He went around seeking someone to lead him by the hand. Then the proconsul, when he saw what was done, believed, being astonished at the teaching of the Lord.

Whoops—Elymas! I think this is called learning a lesson the hard way.

There are subtle changes in Saul's ministry here. The name Saul (of Hebrew origin) was changed to Paul (of Roman/Greek origins) making his new job easier when he introduced himself to the Romans and Gentiles.

The other subtle change occurred as Luke began to put Paul before Barnabas in his script, suggesting that the leadership roles had been reversed. Saul's apprenticeship was over. Paul began work in earnest, and he certainly was not afraid to pull some punches.

This poignant story of deceitful Elymas portrays Paul as a perceptive leader. It is interesting that Elymas lost his sight in the same way as Paul had done on the road to Damascus.

Q. List the qualities that you think made Paul so outstanding.—

Acts 13: 13-15

Now Paul and his company set sail from Paphos, and came to Perga in Pamphylia. John departed from them and returned to Jerusalem. But they, passing on from Perga, came to Antioch of Pisidia. They went into the synagogue on the Sabbath day, and sat down. After the reading of the law and the prophets, the rulers of the synagogue sent to them, saying, 'Brothers, if you have any word of exhortation for the people, speak.'

Paul was apparently recognized as a rabbi in his new leadership role. It was customary for visiting rabbis to preach in the synagogue where many Gentiles worshipped.

Paul was not happy about John pushing off just now. John may have been homesick for Jerusalem, or an illness could have necessitated a change of plan, or most likely the change of leadership from Cousin Barnabas to Paul was not comfortable for John.

We all know a change in leadership can be unsettling, and here we see friction even among the saints. However, the placid, encouraging Barnabas who didn't seem to mind the leadership change enabled the work to go on.

Q. Dear Barnabas, the peace maker. When did you last have the privilege of being a peace maker? Please share your stories.

Acts 13: 16-19

Paul stood up, and beckoning with his hand said, 'Men of Israel, and you who fear God, listen. The God of this people chose our fathers, and exalted the people when they stayed as aliens in the land of Egypt, and with an uplifted arm, he led them out of it. For a period of about forty years he put up with them in the wilderness. When he had destroyed seven nations in the land of Canaan, he gave them their land for an inheritance, for about four hundred fifty years.

Perhaps Luke had a smile on his face as he wrote about God having to patiently put up with that tiresome lot in the wilderness for forty years. He gives us another small personal detail here, as Paul 'with an uplifted arm' began to lay the foundation of his message to the congregation. Paul followed Stephen's example, earlier in chapter 7, by beginning his talk with the Jews' history, explaining where the story came from before launching into new ground, although this may not have been so important to this mainly gentile congregation.

Acts 13: 20-25

After these things (giving the land of Canaan to the Israelites) he gave them judges until Samuel the prophet. Afterward they asked for a king, and God gave to them Saul the son of Kish, a man of the tribe of Benjamin, for forty years. When he had removed him, he raised up David to be their king, to whom he also testified, 'I have found David the son of Jesse, a man after my heart, who will do all my will.' From this man's seed, God has brought salvation to Israel according to his promise, before his coming, when John had first preached the baptism of repentance to Israel. As John was fulfilling his course, he said, 'What do you suppose that I am? I am not he. But behold, one comes after me the sandals of whose feet I am not worthy to untie.

Paul developed his theme with John the Baptist, preparing the way for Jesus' ministry, before coming to the central point of his talk, which was the love and forgiveness of God.

John the Baptist was brave enough to point out the king's injustice and immoral behavior. John was to die for his outspokenness, followed by Jesus, Stephen, James, and so many others.

God seems to choose amazingly strong, fearless men and women to do his work.

Q. Is anything more important to you than life itself? Why?

From Ria: I am reminded here the incredible bravery for example of the search and rescue teams which are so much in the headlines right now (March 2011 Japanese earthquake and tsumami). People who go in and risk their lives for others, people of all nationalities and creeds—I am reacting to your paragraphs above and the apparent assumption that it is only 'God' who 'chooses amazingly strong men and women' . . . etc.

Q. Any thoughts on Ria's comment?

Acts 13: 26-27

Brothers, children of the stock of Abraham, and those among you who fear God, the word of this salvation is sent out to you. For those who dwell in Jerusalem, and their rulers, because they didn't know him, nor the voices of the prophets which are read every Sabbath, fulfilled them by condemning him.

The question is sometimes asked that if God knows everything, and if nothing is impossible for him, how is it that he allows such dreadful things to happen in the world?

This question may not be completely answered this side of the grave. Could it be, as we are not robots, that although God is all-powerful, he does not interfere with our doings? If we wish to behave in a certain way, God will not stop us but instead will allow us to learn from our mistakes—just as parents try to do.

God gave the vision of the Jesus story to the prophets to prepare people for the event when Jesus arrived, but those in authority did not recognize Jesus when he came.

Q. To be honest, if Jesus arrived this week in the supermarket, the marketplace, or even the pulpit, do you think he would be recognized? Can you feel and understand the skepticism that the Jesus story created for the Jews? How easy it is for us to be wise after the event.

From Ria: My reaction to this question is that he would probably be held to be suffering from a mental illness. After all you can reverse the question and say what would happen if you suddenly appeared in the time of the Bible and said that men had landed on the moon for example, or that HIVaids existed.

Q. Any answers or discussion on this interesting thought?

Acts 13: 28-31

Though they found no cause for death, they still asked Pilate to have him killed. When they had fulfilled all things that were written about him, they took him down from the tree, and laid him in a tomb. But God raised him from the dead, and he was seen for many days by those who came up with him from Galilee to Jerusalem, who are his witnesses to the people.

People often think the idea of the resurrection is crazy. Perhaps this is the reason why there were many physical healing miracles at this time; a visible sign of the supernatural to reinforce the unlikely story that there is life after death—an almost impossible message the apostles were bravely trying to bring to the world.

The resurrection is the central point of the Christian faith, with its message of hope, love, and forgiveness. Is the resurrection a stumbling block for many in this modern scientific age?

Q. What do you all think, Wincs and Sees?

Acts 13: 32-37

We bring you good news of the promise made to the fathers, 13: 33 that God has fulfilled the same to us, their children, in that he raised up Jesus. As it is also written in the second psalm,

'You are my Son. Today I have become your father.'

'Concerning that he raised him up from the dead, now no more to return to corruption, he has spoken thus: 'I will give you the holy and sure blessings of David.' Therefore he says also in another psalm, 'You will not allow your Holy One to see decay.' For David, after he had in his own generation served the counsel of God, fell asleep, and was laid with his fathers, and saw decay. But he whom God raised up saw no decay.

It would be interesting to compare these verses with other versions of the bible. Paul was a scholar and able to quote from the Torah, the Jewish Bible, with confidence. The quotation '*You are my Son; today I have become your Father*' is worth reading in context in Psalms 2: 7-9. It establishes the bonding relationship between God and Jesus, which God offers so generously and eagerly to us.

Secondly, 'I will give you the holy and sure blessings promised to David.' is a promise that God the Father will send his blessing to you.

Thirdly, 'You will not let your Holy One see decay' emphasizing that God will not allow us to snuff out, although we humans physically decay, there is a promise the spirit within us will live forever. These standards do not vary (unlike humans) and offer unconditional friendship, support and a future life to look forward—a recipe for helping to live in harmony and balance.

Q. Close your eyes for a moment or two, and ask your inner voice what it is that most helps you live in harmony and balance. Write it down in case you forget. It may have something to do with your talents.

From Ria: Can it not seem the case that to 'live personally' etc. (i.e. in balance and harmony) is often dependent on what other people do, and do to you as well?

Q.2 Has Ria answered the question? Please share your thoughts?

Acts 13: 38-39

Be it known to you therefore, brothers, that through this man is proclaimed to you remission of sins, and by him everyone who believes is justified from all things, from which you could not be justified by the law of Moses.

Faith in Christ enables the debt for all wrongdoing to be obliterated, a situation which was impossible through Moses' law or any other law. This is another very difficult message the apostles had to try and explain.

Do you remember the bishop in the wonderful musical *Les Miserable*[21]? Valjean, released from prison, visited the Bishop of Digne and stole the bishop's silver. Later he broke his parole. He was caught; the bishop was called as a witness to identify the stolen silver. But the bishop graciously defended him and said he *gave* Valjean the silver, and here was some more that he left behind. This wonderful gesture enabled Valjean to start his life again with no recriminations, a free man.

We too are free again, like Valjean, without any recrimination. It seems too good to be true. It seems strange that everyone in the world is not clambering for the privilege.

---

[21]   The musical show based on Victor Hugo's novel "Les Miserables" 1862, lyric by Herbert Kretzner.

Acts 13: 40-41

Beware therefore, lest that come on you which is spoken in the prophets:
'Behold, you scoffers, wonder, and perish; for I work a work in your days, a work which you will in no way believe, if one declares it to you.'

There are plenty of scoffers about today. Paul is referring to the Old Testament prophet Isaiah 29: 14-15, which tells us 'the wisdom of the wise will perish; the intelligence of the intelligent will vanish. Woe to those who go to great depths to hide their plans from the Lord.' So look out any scoffers!

When people scoff and say the whole God idea is nonsense, is it helpful to remember religion is a part of our very being, our soul, and millions of people have died rather than deny it?

From Ria: It is interesting here that you are specifically pointing your statement to 'religion' being 'Christianity'—do you think you should be more specific because not all 'religions' believe in the same God.

Q 2. Do they or don't they?

From another point of view, Professor Brett Lee from Dundee University said "We need religion as a useful structure for getting along with people better and behaving better. Religion promotes peace and harmony."

Australian Broadcasting Corp. National Radio program, *Philosophers.* June 5th 2011.

Q. Is this food for the scoffers or fodder for the faithful?

Acts 13: 42-43

So when the Jews went out of the synagogue, the Gentiles begged that these words might be preached to them the next Sabbath. Now when the synagogue broke up, many of the Jews and of the devout proselytes followed Paul and Barnabas; who, speaking to them, urged them to continue in the grace of God.

Imagine the buzzing scene outside church after this excellent sermon. The excited people crowd around the speaker—and they want more. How wonderful it is to see that fresh, joyful wonder in the shining face of a new Christian, like falling in love. Their infectious happiness radiates to everyone.

Q. Sees, can you remember a time when you felt the overwhelming joy and happiness of your first real encounter with God? Was there a special moment or a gradual exploration? Record your last spiritual excitement.

Wincs, do you have a similar amazing moment of discovery about something, perhaps an unexpected talent, or an amazing love or friendship?

Acts 13: 44-45

The next Sabbath almost the whole city was gathered together to hear the word of God. But when the Jews saw the multitudes, they were filled with jealousy, and contradicted the things which were spoken by Paul, and blasphemed.

Well, the whole city seemed to be clamoring to hear the word of God, for five minutes anyway.

News had sspread through the town quickly. 'You must go and hear these new preachers' was the buzz of the week. But the joy of yesterday looked as though it may be short lived. Trouble was brewing in jealous hearts, but the seed had been sown, and nothing can take that away. It was too late to stop it, as '*almost the whole city gathered to hear the word of the Lord.*'

Q. Many non-Christians have attended enormous Christian gatherings, such as a Billy Graham Crusade or perhaps a huge concert. Can you describe the emotional impact it had on you? Will you write your experience down for a future reminder and share with others?

Acts 13: 46-47

Paul and Barnabas spoke out boldly, and said, 'It was necessary that God's word should be spoken to you first. Since indeed you thrust it from you, and judge yourselves unworthy of eternal life, behold, we turn to the Gentiles. For so has the Lord commanded us, saying,

'I have set you as a light for the Gentiles, that you should bring salvation to the uttermost parts of the earth."

Paul, passionate about his people and his religion, quotes from Isaiah 49: 6b to substantiate his mission to the gentiles. However, he says, the Jews need to be told first.

Q. Sees, is your church bringing 'salvation to the uttermost parts' of your parish? Is there anything you can to do help a gentle outreach? Perhaps you can jot down a plan and discuss some possibilities.

Wincs, do you have a special, precious project you would like to promote? Is there a way people in the group could help you?

Acts 13: 48

As the Gentiles heard this [that they would receive salvation from God], they were glad, and glorified the word of God. As many as were appointed to eternal life believed.

When the Gentiles heard from Paul and Barnabas that they, too, were to be included in this exclusive Christian club, they felt honored.

Sometime ago a group of us visited a synagogue as part of the Education for Ministry course. The Jews in the congregation were very welcoming. After the service, I asked a Jewish lady, 'If I wanted to join the Jewish faith, would I be welcome?' Kindly she said, 'Good gracious! No! You would have to go through years of instruction before that would be allowed.'

It was only a decade ago that a prominent Melbourne citizen was refused membership to an exclusive Melbourne club, because he was a Jew. But in the above text, it was the other way around. It was the Jews being 'toffee nosed' while the Gentiles wanted to join the Jewish Club, exhibiting that both Jew and Gentile are just as prejudiced as each other. Perhaps it is called just being a human being. God says, 'Stop it,' for there is no place for prejudice.

Acts 13: 49-52

The Lord's word was spread abroad throughout all the region. But the Jews stirred up the devout and prominent women and the chief men of the city, and stirred up a persecution against Paul and Barnabas, and threw them out of their borders. But they shook off the dust of their feet against them, and came to Iconium. The disciples were filled with joy with the Holy Spirit.

Off again, expelled from the region, rejected, and driven away. Yet they were happy and confident and really didn't seem to care. They shook the dust from their feet in protest.

In Galatians 5: 22, the fruits of the Spirit help to develop our Christian ethic of love, joy, peace, patience, kindness, goodness, faithfulness, gentleness, and self-control which seemingly has the added bonus of promoting self-confidence.

Q. At a literary lunch recently, our excellent guest speaker talked about the trials of arriving at a self-confident place, in her case, as an author. She said there was a need to go through three stages, persistence, the need to experience and accept failure, which brings one to the third stage—humility.

Do any of you have another recipe for arriving at a place of self-confidence and humility in your school, work, career, or life?

Summary of Chapter 13

Barnabas and Saul are 'set apart' for a ministry of traveling evangelism. They go to Cyprus first and convert the Roman Proconsul to Christianity. Saul changes his Hebrew-sounding name to the Roman Greek—sounding name of Paul. There appears to be a leadership change as Barnabas and Saul become Paul and Barnabas and also a name change as Saul becomes Paul. John goes back to Jerusalem to Paul's displeasure. Paul preaches in Antioch, where the whole city gathers to hear him. The Jews become jealous and expel Paul and Barnabas from their region. The disciples shake off the dust of Antioch from their sandals and move on, unperturbed, to Iconium.

CHAPTER 14

Paul Struggles to Preach above the Noise

Acts 14: 1-3

It happened in Iconium that they entered together into the synagogue of the Jews, and so spoke that a great multitude both of Jews and of Greeks believed. But the disbelieving Jews stirred up and embittered the souls of the Gentiles against the brothers. Therefore they stayed there a long time, speaking boldly in the Lord, who testified to the word of his grace, granting signs and wonders to be done by their hands.

A pattern has emerged. In each new place Paul and Barnabas had great success until the authorities felt threatened, and tried to get rid of them. But it was always too late; the seed was sown. Inspired Paul and Barnabas never tired of preaching the gospel. What a team—Paul the preacher and scholar, with Barnabas the encourager, driven on fearlessly by this incredible spiritual energy.

Have you ever thought how much easier it may have been to be an early Christian, forgetting the persecution aspect for a moment? There was one single stream of allegiance with no denominations, no choices with in it, and not too many church leaders all thinking they were right.

Have we watered down the original strong current of faith of the first saints with too many denominations that the Christian church has almost diluted into a stagnant puddle? The word *renewal* is constantly mentioned today, yet only a few seem be to experiencing it.

Q. Sees, has the time come to unite—to dialogue with other denominations—to work together to combat the current religious apathy, and go back to being just Christians? What do you think?

Would one church in each village be enough, or would it start World War III?

Write a paragraph or two about your vision for the future of the church.

Wincs what do you think about the future of the church? Would you like it to disappear altogether or change it? How would you change it?

From Ria: The divisions are not as bad as in my childhood, but scratch a bit and they are there.

Q 2. Would you agree with Ria's statement? Are the divisions today political, only theoretical, or in attitude?

Acts 14: 4-7

But the multitude of the city was divided. Part sided with the Jews and part with the apostles. When some of both the Gentiles and the Jews, with their rulers, made a violent attempt to mistreat and stone them, they became aware of it, and fled to the cities of Lycaonia, Lystra, Derbe, and the surrounding region. There they preached the Good News.

Neither Paul nor Barnabas was one of the twelve apostles, but they may have witnessed the crucifixion. They were now in grave danger of being stoned to death. This time, instead of the Jews stoning a Jew to death like Stephen, it was the Gentiles who joined the Jews in their persecution. Paul and Barnabas were cautious but not afraid.

Pontius Pilate had asked Jesus, *'Are you the Christ? The Son of the Blessed One?'* Jesus said, 'I am.' The reason the Jews wanted to stamp out any suggestion that Jesus, the local boy from Nazareth, was more than a preacher was because his teaching of freedom and forgiveness threatened the very foundation of their authoritarian Jewish faith. The Jewish leaders in Lystra and Derbe seemed to be just as afraid of them as those in Antioch. Christianity was a dangerous business.

Q. Religious wars have raged for centuries in the West. There have been very few religious wars in the East-India, China, and Asia—who have not seen conflict on the same scale. Can you give any reasons why this should be? Could Christians benefit from learning more about meditation, karma, and enlightenment from Eastern religions? Can the Wincs add anything to explain the benefit of learning from Eastern religions?

Acts 14:8-10:

At Lystra a certain man sat, impotent in his feet, a cripple from his mother's womb, who never had walked. He was listening to Paul speaking, who, fastening eyes on him, and seeing that he had faith to be made whole, said with a loud voice, 'Stand upright on your feet!' He leaped up and walked.

This wonderful story has two 'mountain top' moments. Luke sensitively notices the eye contact moment again—an instance of transcendence as Paul 'fastened eyes on him'.

The dictionary says 'transcendent' means 'visionary', beyond the normal limits of understanding, communication with another at a deep spiritual level. This was surely such a moment.

The precious moment passed—and then Paul said, 'Stand up!' and he did. What a wonderful day for them both.

Q: Have you experienced a moment of transcendence—a moment maybe with a total stranger, or another person, when there was unspoken communication? Can you share it with the group?

Acts 14: 11-13

When the multitude saw what Paul had done, they lifted up their voice, saying in the language of Lycaonia, 'The gods have come down to us in the likeness of men!' They called Barnabas 'Jupiter,' and Paul 'Mercury,' because he was the chief speaker. The priest of Jupiter, whose temple was in front of their city, brought oxen and garlands to the gates, and would have made a sacrifice along with the multitudes.

An ancient legend had it that the gods Zeus and Hermes had once visited the city of Lystra, but had not been recognized by anyone except an elderly couple. The people of Lystra were anxious this should never happen again. Zeus was the patron god of the city and a pagan god to whom the people brought sacrifices.

As Paul and Barnabas did not speak the Lycaonian language they may not have understood what was happening. It is suggested that Barnabas was more imposing-looking than Paul, so the adoration was directed mainly towards him.

Professor James McEvoy said, 'I was presenting this picture of religion . . . to the staff of a large Catholic school . . . one very talented and also very committed teacher said some of my students turn to Madonna for spiritual nourishment and they are not thinking about the mother of Jesus. I wonder how you would respond to her.'[22]

Q. As the world is changing dramatically, do you think this adoration and hero worship of pop singers is filling a form of 'spiritual nourishment'? Does it matter, or is there a way to convert this hero worship into something more spiritually constructive? I believe dream No.2 and 3 could help re-direct some of this passion.

From Ria: I would comment, 'Good Luck'.

Acts 14: 14-18

But when the apostles, Barnabas and Paul, heard of it, they tore their clothes, and sprang into the multitude, crying out, 'Men, why are you doing these things? We also are men of like passions with you, and bring you good news, that you should turn from these vain things to the living God, who made the sky and the earth and the sea, and all that is in them; who in the generations gone by allowed all the nations to walk in their own ways. Yet he didn't leave himself without witness, in that he did good and gave you rains from the sky and fruitful seasons, filling our hearts with food and gladness.'

Even saying these things, they hardly stopped the multitudes from making a sacrifice to them.

---

[22] Rev. Dr. James McEnvoy, theologian at Adelaide's Catholic Theological College and Flinders University. Montreal.

Panic-stricken and appalled, Paul and Barnabas rushed in to deny any such adoration.

Suddenly realizing what was happening, Paul and Barnabas tore their clothes in the Jewish custom of anguish. They may have wondered what on earth they had said or done to give the Lystrans the impression they were gods. They tried to put it right quickly.

Q. Do you know, or can you understand, how uncomfortable this 'hero worship' must have felt? Any stories to share? No need for false humility.

Acts 14: 19-20

But some Jews from Antioch and Iconium came there, and having persuaded the multitudes, they stoned Paul, and dragged him out of the city, supposing that he was dead.

But as the disciples stood around him, he rose up, and entered into the city. On the next day he went out with Barnabas to Derbe.

Here we go again. News from the previous trouble spots had not taken long to catch them up. They were staying in the cities of Lystra and Derbe, where a short time ago the crowds had thought Paul and Barnabas were gods. A few evil men quickly changed the minds of the crowd. How fickle and ungrateful can people be, after so many wonderful healing miracles?

We can only admire the amazing faithfulness of the apostles to keep going. Their lives resembled an emotional sauna, running hot and cold, acclaimed and applauded, then stoned and driven out of town. How incredible that they did not get sick of it and give up and go home. If someone today tried to persuade the church we love, for all its frailties, that we had it all wrong, I don't think we'd stone them. Shoot them maybe.

A modern day version of this story would be the death of Martin Luther King Jr. 'I have a dream that one day . . . the sons of former slaves will be able to sit down together at the table in brotherhood with slave owners.

From every mountainside, let freedom ring'[23] he said before he was shot on 4 April 1968.

Q. Had he lived longer, Dr King's dream may well have expanded to encompass Christians, Muslims, Hindus and Buddhists, and people of any other religion, who will sit down at the table together in brotherhood. What say you? Where can we begin? Find one new idea *please,* and be sure to tell the world about it.

Mine are in the dreams. Dream on please.

Acts 14: 21-25

When they had preached the Good News to that city, and had made many disciples, they returned to Lystra, Iconium, and Antioch, confirming the souls of the disciples, exhorting them to continue in the faith, and that through many afflictions we must enter into the Kingdom of God. When they had appointed elders for them in every assembly, and had prayed with fasting, they commended them to the Lord, on whom they had believed.

They passed through Pisidia, and came to Pamphylia. When they had spoken the word in Perga, they went down to Attalia.

Paul and Barnabas went back again to areas where they encountered hostility, with unbelievable courage, to encourage the new Christians and their leaders. They'd been nearly killed in Lystra and driven out of Antioch. They were not only brave, but had great administration skills too. In an efficient flash, they organized an assembly and appoint elders, stressing that being a follower of the Way, as it was called at the time, demanded hardship but reaped great reward.

Q. Without strong support, the work load for any leader falls heavily on their shoulders. Are there areas where you could help your boss or minister by offering to do a task, however small? Perhaps drop them a line to offer and see what comes. At least they will be encouraged.

---

[23]   Dr. Martin Luther King Jr. American clergyman, activist, and prominent leader of the African American civil rights movement. He was shot on April 4, 1968 aged 39.

Acts 14: 26-28

From there they sailed to Antioch, from where they had been committed to the grace of God for the work which they had fulfilled. When they had arrived, and had gathered the assembly together, they reported all the things that God had done with them, and that he had opened a door of faith to the nations. They stayed there with the disciples for a long time.

What a relief to get on that boat with nothing to bother them, except storms. What a joy it must have been to have this rest before meeting their friends in Antioch. Paul and Barnabas were to stay 'a long time' here, probably more than a year (NIV Study Bible) to establish the first largely Gentile church. Well done, good and faithful servants.

Q. Who are the good and faithful servants in your church family and/or your workplace? Is there some way you can tell them, and show your appreciation?

Summary of Chapter 14

Paul and Barnabas travel to Iconium and Lystra. In the beginning, they are received with great applause before news of the riots in the previous town arrives. The anxiety of the Jewish authorities is enough to make the locals panic and drive both Paul and Barnabas out of town. Paul just escapes with his life but still bravely returns to the trouble spots to check all the new churches again before leaving by boat for Antioch in Syria—a mission which took about two years from AD 46-48. In Antioch they settled down for about a year to a peaceful ministry.

CHAPTER 15

Second Missionary Journey

Acts 15: 1-4

Some men came down from Judea and taught the brothers, 'Unless you are circumcised after the custom of Moses, you can't be saved.' Therefore when Paul and Barnabas had no small discord and discussion with them, they appointed Paul and Barnabas, and some others of them, to go up to Jerusalem to the apostles and elders about this question. They, being sent on their way by the assembly, passed through both Phoenicia and Samaria, declaring the conversion of the Gentiles. They caused great joy to all the brothers. When they had come to Jerusalem, they were received by the assembly and the apostles and the elders, and they reported all things that God had done with them.

A policy change was looming here—an interfaith issue. Should the Gentiles, like the Jews since Moses' time, be circumcised before being accepted? Paul and Barnabas, with some of the congregation, came to Jerusalem for a council meeting to avert a potentially dangerous split in the church between Jews and Gentiles. To resolve the issue, Paul and Barnabas went straight to the Committee of Management which was made up of Peter and the elders.

After the initial welcome home and hearing about their adventures, the focus of the discussion began in earnest. Some men from Judea in the northern part of Israel, probably Pharisees, insisted that all Christians should follow the Jewish tradition of circumcision before they became 'proper' followers of the Way.

Similarly, the current female circumcision issue has been a stumbling block, and a source of concern and conflict between the Christian and

Islamic worlds for centuries. Mercifully, it is being discouraged. At an International Conference in Egypt in 2006 attended by many Muslim scholars, there was an appeal to all Muslims to stop this practice 'to adhere to Islamic teaching of not inflicting harm on anyone.'[24]

How strange that we humans get into such muddles. An inter-space visitor could be forgiven for wondering what kind of a world this could be, to create so much anxiety and fear over a small, perfectly created, human organ.

From Ria: Some years ago I was involved in assisting in drafting a NSW Act on this issue—it didn't appear on the legislative books until the 1980s and it still happens.

I'd use something stronger than a 'muddle' when you are talking about female circumcision. Is there a question about what you would do if you found it was happening to a girl in an Australian community?

Thank you Ria. Q. What would you all do if you discovered a girl in this situation?

Acts 15: 5

But some of the sect of the Pharisees who believed rose up, saying, 'It is necessary to circumcise them, and to command them to keep the Law of Moses.'

---

[24] A conference on Female Genital Mutilation in Cairo, Egypt on 24 November, 2006 TARGET attended by Muslim scholars from many nations, passed a statement: "The conference appeals to all Muslims to stop practicing this habit, according to Islam's teachings which prohibit inflicting harm on any human being . . . The conference reminds all teaching and media institutions of their role to explain to the people the harmful effects of this habit in order to eliminate it . . . The conference calls on judicial institutions to issue laws that prohibit and criminalize this habit . . . which appeared in several societies and was adopted by some Muslims although it is not sanctioned by the Qur'an or the Sunna." From http://www.religioustolerance.org/fem.cirm.htm

The leaders of this new Christian community came from the ordered stable background of the Jewish faith and were severely shaken each time a change threatened their established centuries-old customs. Already they had had to cope with the resurrection of Jesus, which was difficult to swallow. Then, heaven forbid, Peter and Paul had gone off and preached to the Gentiles. Having come to terms with these changes, now circumcision was to go out of the window. They were being asked to do a huge, dramatic rethink. How we fear change.

Q. Have you been asked to dramatically rethink an attitude or principle lately? Can you share the episode? If this has been covered before, just pass.

Acts 15: 6-7

The apostles and the elders were gathered together to see about this matter [circumcision]. When there had been much discussion, Peter rose up and said to them, 'Brothers, you know that a good while ago God made a choice among you, that by my mouth the nations should hear the word of the Good News, and believe.

The die-hard Pharisees found it difficult to contemplate radical change from tradition. The question of change had to be dealt with. It would have made evangelism profoundly inhibiting for Gentiles to have to be circumcised before becoming Christians.

Listening to Paul's situation, Peter confidently got up to support Paul's statement with the irrefutable conviction that God expects change.

We too have experienced great change in the church in the last fifty years, which has mainly, and sadly, left the last two generations outside. According to David Tacey, 'The down-beat, dismal or negative tone of much youth culture derives from the sense that the skies have fallen (Lawence), . . ., where everything is meaningless, broken and profoundly out of joint.'[25] Tacey goes on to say that the rubbish dump will compost into beautiful earth, and there is an emerging sense of hope.

---

25   Associate Professor David Tacey, Reader in Arts at La Trobe University,
      Victoria, Australia. "The Spirituality Revolution—emergence of contemporary

Q. If you agree with David Tacey, where is this emerging sense of hope appearing? How can it be fostered and encouraged in your area?

Acts 15: 8-9:

God, who knows the heart, testified about them, giving them the Holy Spirit, just like he did to us. He made no distinction between us and them, cleansing their hearts by faith.

The phrase 'God who knows the heart' paints a picture of a God who knows our minds—every detail of our lives; every naughty deed and action; and every joy, expectation, and hope. God also knows the tools needed to purify the things that bring us pain, hurt, and negative thoughts. God, the parent, knows his children and tries to direct them.

Hillsong is a church in Sydney that has more than six thousand young people jumping for joy in their worship every Sunday. A very religious Christian acquaintance said to me one day, referring to the Hillsong congregation, 'but they are dreadful people!'

From Ria: What about the discoveries over time of the Hillsong type movements in the US and how the leaders turn out to have 'feet of clay'?

Q. Hillsong, for all the criticism that is heaped against it, has become a spiritual Pied Piper. What do you feel about spiritual renewal? Is it all just wishful thinking or is it a reality? Do you encourage or resent those joyful, noisy youngsters—those 'dreadful people'—who make such a happy noise?

Sadly we come back to Ria's bad apple in every bucket syndrome, but stand up the perfect church, law court, police station, or medical practice, etc. They all have their own specimen of rotten apples, but what a great job these 'imperfect' services do in the Community—we couldn't do without them.

---

spirituality" Published by HarperCollins Publishers, page 181.

Q. Would some of the group Google churches like Planetshakers, Paradise Community Church, Emerging Church, City Life, Bridgeman Downs, for an interesting 'moment of Wow' for the next session.

Thanks again for your input Ria.

Acts 15: 10-11

Now therefore why do you tempt God, that you should put a yoke on the neck of the disciples which neither our fathers nor we were able to bear? But we believe that we are saved through the grace of the Lord Jesus, just as they are.'

"Take my yoke upon you and learn . . ." Jesus said in Matthew 11:29-30. Learn—not rebel or rubbish God. 'Why do you [or we] test or tempt God . . . ?' Peter asks. Can you explain what Peter means?

Q. Tacey's young people, 'where everything is meaningless, broken and profoundly out of joint,'[26] have largely deserted the traditional church. Have drugs or pop stars become an easier escape?

The late Bishop John Wilson, in his book *Christianity Alongside Islam*, says, ' . . . the public significance of the Christian faith needs to be demonstrated in fresh and creative ways.'

Q. If the group decides to "demonstrate the Christian faith in fresh and creative ways," how about trying one of the dreams? Could it happen in your area?

Acts 15: 12

All the multitude kept silence, and they listened to Barnabas and Paul reporting what signs and wonders God had done among the nations through them.

---

26   Associate Professor David Tacey, Reader in Arts at La Trobe University, Victoria, Australia. "The Spirituality Revolution—emergence of contemporary spirituality" Published by HarperCollins Publishers, page 181.

The Paul and Barnabas sequence has done a switch again to Barnabas and Paul, indicating the senior role Barnabas held among the leaders in Jerusalem. It sounds petty, but it tells us something of the human side of the men in the story. The media keeps us well aware of people's rights these days. The author Luke ensures that by naming the apostles in order of seniority, he will not offend.

Imagine the scene; the people chattering away in the assembly as they wait for the elders to finish their meeting. Then a hushed silence, the meeting begins and they listen to the amazing things God had performed through Barnabas and Paul. They would have marveled at the courage of these two men, who had repeatedly been welcomed in each city and then abused, stoned, even left for dead, and yet miraculously escaped without serious injury. They had carried on their mission of spreading the gospel, inspired by the joy of seeing the Holy Spirit poured out to the new Christians.

Q. Surely we each have a purpose for being on earth. What is yours? If it is the same as your piece of the jigsaw puzzle in Ch. 2: 29 just pass. Maybe you can think of other contributions you are making.

Acts 15: 13-18

After they were silent, James answered, 'Brothers, listen to me. Simeon has reported how God first visited the nations, to take out of them a people for his name. This agrees with the words of the prophets. As it is written,

'After these things I will return.
I will again build the tabernacle of David, which has fallen.
I will again build its ruins.
I will set it up,
That the rest of men may seek after the Lord;
All the Gentiles who are called by my name,
Says the Lord, who does all these things.
All his works are known to God from eternity.'

Peter's Hebrew name was Simeon bar Jonah (Simeon son of Jonah). Jesus seemed to have given his beloved Peter a nickname of Petros, or perhaps Petra, a Greek word for rock. However, James uses his brother's family name, Simeon, to speak to the assembly.

We do not know what happened to Jesus's other brothers and sisters, but James was still there, and confirmed Jesus' story firsthand.

James had apparently become the leader of the disciples in Jerusalem. 'Listen to me,' he says. God spoke through the prophets, "my word is for *all* people and nations." Amose 9:12

Q. Who are 'the rest of men and all nations who call on my name'? Can anyone doubt that includes Hindus, Sunnis, Shi'ites, Jehovah's Witnesses, and the other faiths?

The Parliament of World Religions is worth looking up on the web, to see the great work they are doing. A paragraph in your journal summarizing their activities would be a useful source of information.

Acts 15: 19-21

Therefore my judgment is that we don't trouble those from among the Gentiles who turn to God, but that we write to them that they abstain from the pollution of idols, from sexual immorality, from what is strangled, and from blood. For Moses from generations of old, have in every city those who preach him, being read in the synagogues every Sabbath.

It took the weight of Peter's authority, with confirmation by Paul and Barnabas, and finally their leader James, to sway the Council to drop the circumcision issue for Gentiles. This very important decision enabled the gospel to spread comfortably to the Gentiles.

As Jewish author Amy-Jill Levine suggests, 'Had the (Christian) church remained a Jewish sect, it would not have achieved its universal mission. Had Judaism given up its particularistic practices, it would have vanished from history. That the two movements eventually separated made possible the preservation of each.'[27]

This decision to allow Gentiles to be Followers of the Way without being circumcised landed the final blow to any integration of the new

---

[27] Amy-Jill Levine is University Professor of New Testament and Jewish Studies, E. Rhodes and Leona B. Carpenter Professor of New Testament Studies, and Professor of Jewish Studies at Vanderbilt University Divinity School and College of Arts and Sciences.Nashville, Tennessee.

Christian religion with the Jewish tradition. Amy-Jill Levine says the Jews would have been lost to the world had Judaism and Christianity become one. (Or maybe the other way around Amy.)

It is interesting to wonder what Palestine and Israel would look like today, and World War II may have been a different story had there been no Jewish nation.

We can safely say this decision to allow the new followers of the Way to remain uncircumcised changed the course of history.

But I deviate from the text. Forgive me.

From Ria: I once mediated for twelve months between a group of Jewish women and Muslim women . . . I was chosen because I had no religious background/faith etc. It was astounding, and not just to me, but to the women on both sides of the table (this was after the first Gulf War) that their practices throughout life—we went from birth to death and excluded religion—were virtually identical.

Interesting observation Ria, thank you. Now back to Peter.

Q. 'Therefore my judgment is . . .' said Peter assertively. Sees, can you explain to the Wincs, what happened to the old hot-headed, yet fearful Peter who has turned into this brave, calm man of authority?

Wincs, can you give your version of what you think may have happened to him and why?

From Ria: My response would be he 'grew up' and probably about time. ☺

Acts 15: 22-23

Then it seemed good to the apostles and the elders, with the whole assembly, to choose men out of their company, and send them to Antioch with Paul and Barnabas: Judas called Barsabbas, and Silas, chief men among the brothers. They wrote these things by their hand:

'The apostles, the elders, and the brothers, to the brothers who are of the Gentiles in Antioch, Syria, and Cilicia: greetings.

The council made a unanimous decision to send Silas and Judas to Antioch with Paul and Barnabas. Silas, a church leader, was a prophet and a Roman citizen, which made him a good choice to send to work with the Roman Gentiles. Antioch was the main city in the provinces of Syria and Cilicia, which had the largest Gentile Christian church so far. The first big split in the new fledgling religion had been averted. More preachers were needed to cement the foundations of the new church.

Q. Are more preachers or different teachers needed today—to open the windows for a fresh draft of sincere, modern, joyful worship to the Creator? Remembering your recent 'Googling' session, is there any way of introducing such groups at your local level?

A&A, would you be any more accepting of the Church if it had a fresh approach, a modern theme, and . . . what else would you like? Wouldn't it be wonderful if the Wincs took a service one day? Please invite me—or at least tell me what happens.

Acts 15: 24-32

Because we have heard that some who went out from us have troubled you with words, unsettling your souls, saying, 'You must be circumcised and keep the law,' to whom we gave no commandment; it seemed good to us, having come to one accord, to choose out men and send them to you with our beloved Barnabas and Paul, men who have risked their lives for the name of our Lord Jesus Christ.

We have sent therefore Judas and Silas, who themselves will also tell you the same things by word of mouth. For it seemed good to the Holy Spirit, and to us, to lay no greater burden on you than these necessary things: that you abstain from things sacrificed to idols, from blood, from things strangled, and from sexual immorality, from which if you keep yourselves, it will be well with you. Farewell.'

So, when they were sent off, they came to Antioch. Having gathered the multitude together, they delivered the letter. When they had read it, they rejoiced over the encouragement. Judas and Silas, also being prophets themselves, encouraged the brothers with many words, and strengthened them.

The letter had been written, the elders were in agreement, everyone was pleased, and the matter was settled. The Gentile men in the congregation were thankful and more than happy to settle for dietary restrictions.

Acts 15: 33-35

After they had spent some time there, they were sent back with greetings from the brothers to the apostles. But Paul and Barnabas stayed in Antioch, teaching and preaching the word of the Lord, with many others also.

So Judas and Silas were sent back to Jerusalem with the good news that the decision was welcomed in Antioch. The circumcision issue was thankfully over.

Acts 15: 36-41

After some days Paul said to Barnabas, 'Let's return now and visit our brothers in every city in which we proclaimed the word of the Lord, to see how they are doing.' Barnabas planned to take John, who was called Mark, with them also. But Paul didn't think that it was a good idea to take with them someone who had withdrawn from them in Pamphylia, and didn't go with them to do the work.

Then the contention grew so sharp that they separated from each other. Barnabas took Mark with him, and sailed away to Cyprus, but Paul chose Silas, and went out, being commended by the brothers to the grace of God. He went through Syria and Cilicia, strengthening the assemblies.

Oh, dear. After their great letter of solidarity had been sent with 'our beloved Barnabas and Paul,' there is sharp contention already. What a pity.

Paul wanted to follow up the towns from his first missionary journey, so he went off with Silas and sailed away. Mark had left Paul and Barnabas in a huff over the leadership issue in the middle of their first journey (Acts 13: 13); he had apparently got over by now, and he worked well with Barnabas.

To avoid any more friction, the whispering spirit had very good reason to split them up just now.

Barnabas and Mark do not appear again in Acts, although they are mentioned in Paul's letters to the Corinthians and Galatians. By the end of his life, Paul had a change of heart. He became so fond of Mark that he asked him to be with him for his last days.

What an interesting example of the fragility of human relationships and how imperative it is, that to survive breakups, we can choose to rely heavily on the teaching of Jesus—with large generous doses of forgiveness.

Summary of Chapter 15

There are two sharp disputes in this Chapter between Paul and Barnabas. Firstly, the vital issue of whether gentiles, like the Jews, should be circumcised before being allowed to become Christians. Secondly, there was controversy as to whether Mark should accompany Paul and Barnabas on a follow-up visit to newly established churches.

The Antioch Church sent Paul and Barnabas down to the council in Jerusalem to settle the circumcision issue, and they returned with the problem solved. Men need not be circumcised to become Christians, although there were certain dietary restrictions. Any other decision would certainly have altered the history books. Everyone is pleased with this result.

Barnabas and Mark go off to Cyprus while Paul and Silas revisit the churches from Paul's first missionary journey.

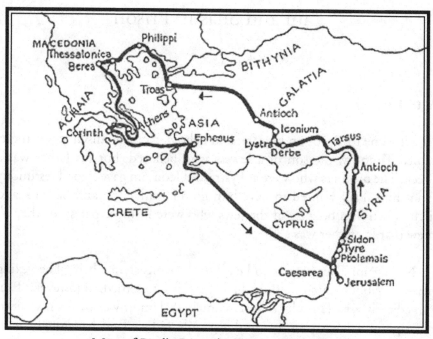

Map of Paul's Second Missionary Journey

Taken from *New Bible Commentary*
edited by Gordon J. Wenham, J.Alec Motyer and others. Copyright© 1970
InterVarsity Press, PO box 1400 Downers Grove, IL 605 15 www.ivpress.com
Printed with permission.

CHAPTER 16

Paul and Silas in Prison

Acts 16: 1-3

He came to Derbe and Lystra: and behold, a certain disciple was there, named Timothy, the son of a Jewess who believed; but his father was a Greek. The brothers who were at Lystra and Iconium gave a good testimony about him. Paul wanted to have him go out with him, and he took and circumcised him because of the Jews who were in those parts; for they all knew that his father was a Greek.

Not again! There seems to be a bit of inconsistency here. The vexing question about circumcision had just been settled. However, Paul immediately asks Timothy to be circumcised. Timothy came from a mixed marriage of a Jewish mother and a gentile father. Paul had fought hard against any suggestion that gentiles should be circumcised; however, Paul was a seriously practicing Jew, and Timothy was only half and half. In order to establish Timothy's identity as a practicing Jew, Paul advised him, in this case, to be circumcised.

One wonders who would really have known whether Timothy was or wasn't circumcised, but it was obviously important to Paul. Apparently, men of that time exercised in a gymnasium naked, so that did it.

The end of this drama of circumcision seemed to have a 'they lived happily ever after' ending. What a fuss. But the question may fairly be asked, did it really matter? As things stood, yes, enormously. But if God made men the way he did in the first place, it seems strange that people should start snipping away at his handy work for religious reasons.

Q. Can you recall an issue that seemed so hugely important in your life time? Will you each name the change that has been most important to you?

Acts 16: 4-5

As they went on their way through the cities, they delivered the decrees to them to keep which had been ordained by the apostles and elders who were at Jerusalem. So the assemblies were strengthened in the faith, and increased in number daily.

The decrees delivered in this verse were the list of "do and don't"s established by the recent council meeting in Jerusalem. They included the dreaded circumcision issue, the need to abstain from food polluted by idols, from sexual immorality, and eating meat or blood from strangled animals. Paul and Timothy took the guidelines around to the earlier established churches to keep them informed. The rules had been laid down.

An old Spanish proverb says 'Mas claridad, mas amistad,' which means, 'More clarity, more friendship.' How true. With a sigh of relief, the congregations received the happy news, and the numbers grew rapidly.

Acts 16: 6-7

When they had gone through the region of Phrygia and Galatia, they were forbidden by the Holy Spirit to speak the word in Asia. When they had come opposite Mysia, they tried to go into Bithynia, but the Spirit didn't allow them.

We are not told how the Spirit told them they were not allowed to go on. Throughout the New Testament the expressions the Holy Spirit, the Spirit, and the Spirit of Jesus are used interchangeably with God at times. The Spirit had advised the missionaries what to do in a number of ways through visions, trances, dreams and the use of prophesy. This time the rather bossy message came some other way.

Acts 16: 8-10

Passing by Mysia, they came down to Troas. A vision appeared to Paul in the night. There was a man of Macedonia standing, begging him, and saying, 'Come over into Macedonia and help us.' When he had seen the vision, immediately we sought to go out to Macedonia, concluding that the Lord had called us to preach the Good News to them.

Suddenly, the script talks about 'us,' indicating that Paul, Silas, and Timothy were joined by the writer of this Gospel, Luke. Now Paul has a vision calling them to take the gospel to Europe, instead of Asia.

What is a vision? Does something happen in that quiet, still trying-not-to-think-of-anyone-or-anything-else time? Is it in moments of meditation that an image can appear in the mind? In his novel *Sylvia*, the highly acclaimed author Bryce Courtenay paints an interesting picture. 'Well, a vision is what is known as an out-of-body experience. We see it and we are immersed in it, but we are not necessarily a physical part of it, experiencing it not with our body, but in our hearts and minds.'[28]

Paul's vision was so clear that it sent four men spinning off in another direction.

Q. Will you share your visions? Or what may have seemed an extraordinary supernatural incident? Or if you have already done this earlier, just pass, or perhaps you have another to tell.

Acts 16: 11-13

Setting sail therefore from Troas, we made a straight course to Samothrace, and the day following to Neapolis; and from there to Philippi, which is a city of Macedonia, the foremost of the district, a Roman colony. We were staying some days in this city.

On the Sabbath day we went forth outside of the city by a riverside, where we supposed there was a place of prayer, and we sat down, and spoke to the women who had come together.

---

[28]   Novelist author Bryce Courtenay "Sylvia." Published by Viking an imprint of the Penguin Group. Page 194.

The residents of Philippi were mainly Roman; ten Jewish men in a congregation was the requirement to qualify for a synagogue. Presumably, in Philippi there were not enough Jewish men, so the women gathered for their worship by the Gangrites River instead.

It was a hard life for these early missionaries, particularly in places where there were no synagogues to help them meet people. It is difficult to imagine how they managed for food, accommodation, or even to have enough money for shoe repairs with so much trampling about.

This is a pleasant scene as our four men wander down to the riverbanks outside the city and begin to talk to the women at their place of prayer.

Acts 16: 14-15

A certain woman named Lydia, a seller of purple, of the city of Thyatira, one who worshiped God, heard us; whose heart the Lord opened to listen to the things which were spoken by Paul. When she and her household were baptized, she begged us, saying, 'If you have judged me to be faithful to the Lord, come into my house, and stay.' So she persuaded us.

Lydia was a businesswoman from Thyatira, which was famous for its dyeing works. Although Lydia was a gentile, she believed in God and the teachings of the scriptures. Initially, Lydia would have hesitated to invite four Jews to her house, knowing how uncomfortable Jews would be in the home of a gentile.

However, the women were obviously inspired by Paul's message. They were baptized in the river—there and then—and Lydia settled the accommodation question for a while by persuading them to stay.

Well, what do you think about that? The story becomes stranger by the minute.

Q. What would your reaction be if your mother, or daughter, came home and told you she was having a lovely time with her friends by the river when four men came along, complete strangers, who began to chat to them? They made such an impression she'd invited them all home to stay for a while, and what's more their clothes were dripping wet? This is what happened here!

Acts 16: 16-18

It happened, as we were going to prayer that a certain girl having a spirit of divination met us, who brought her masters much gain by fortune telling. Following Paul and us, she cried out, 'These men are servants of the Most High God, who proclaim to us a way of salvation!' She was doing this for many days.

But Paul, becoming greatly annoyed, turned and said to the spirit, 'I command you in the name of Jesus Christ to come out of her!' It came out that very hour.

Imagine the difficulty of trying to preach with this poor girl shouting at them. Paul managed well to control himself not to bellow, 'Be quiet will you?' He didn't even challenge her with fortune-telling as an evil practice, but when his patience was tried to the limit, he asked the Spirit to deal with her. Well done, Paul.

But this healing was to have unfortunate consequences for Paul and Silas.

Q. Why do you imagine Paul waited so long before he dealt with such tiresome interruptions?

How may you have dealt with it differently?

Acts 16: 19-22

But when her masters saw that the hope of their gain was gone, they seized Paul and Silas, and dragged them into the marketplace before the rulers. When they had brought them to the magistrates, they said, 'These men, being Jews, are agitating our city, and set forth customs which it is not lawful for us to accept or to observe, being Romans.'

The multitude rose up together against them, and the magistrates tore their clothes off.

A religion that failed to be approved by Roman law was considered 'religio illicita,' or illegal. The Jewish faith was accepted by the Romans, but the new Christian doctrine was not accepted for another three centuries.

The owners of this unfortunate girl, with the help of others, grabbed Paul and Silas and took their clothes off! Paul and Silas were and looked

Jewish. Timothy and Luke, who were from Greek descent and probably clinging to their clothes, got away with it. Oh, dear; the stripping of clothes began another session of whipping.

The owners accused Paul and Silas of 'religio illicita,' so as Jews they were fair game for punishment without trial. How strange that they did not tell the authorities that they were Roman citizens. If the two magistrates had only done their homework properly, they would have discovered they had no right to order them to be beaten. Paul and Silas may have had another reason for their silence.

Q. Paul and Silas could have told the magistrates they were Roman citizens, but chose not to. Have you been in a situation when you were bursting to take the risk of telling an important piece of information that would make a significant difference to the outcome? That was the position Paul and Silas found themselves in. Did you keep quiet? Please share your experience.

Acts 16: 23-24

When they had laid many stripes on them, they threw them into prison, charging the jailer to keep them safely, who, having received such a command, threw them into the inner prison, and secured their feet in the stocks.

Rods for flogging were carried in bundles by the magistrates, as a sign of their office. Maybe the magistrates handed the rods to the guards to use when necessary. In 2 Corinthians 11: 24 Paul writes that he had been given the recognized forty lashes minus one five times, beaten with rods three times, and stoned once, being left for dead on that occasion. Many died after this treatment. I tremble to think what Paul's back looked like.

The stocks were in the inner cell, not only for security but also to be used as a torture chamber. The stocks had many holes for the legs, which were forced far apart, causing great pain.

The great second century Christian thinker and lawyer Tertullian said, 'The legs feel no pain in the stocks when the heart is in heaven.' Well, what do you feel about that? I wonder if he'd tried it himself.

Thought: If there is anyone up there, please show us when we torture each other, maybe not in obvious ways like the stocks, but in subtle critical, abusive, and negligent ways.

Acts 16: 25-28

But about midnight Paul and Silas were praying and singing hymns to God, and the prisoners were listening to them. Suddenly there was a great earthquake, so that the foundations of the prison were shaken; and immediately all the doors were opened, and everyone's bonds were loosened. The jailer, being roused out of sleep and seeing the prison doors open, drew his sword and was about to kill himself, supposing that the prisoners had escaped. But Paul cried with a loud voice, saying, 'Don't harm yourself, for we are all here!'

If a prisoner escaped from prison, the jailer was killed for his negligence, this is a repeat of the mysterious event that released Peter from prison in Acts 12: 19whose jailers were executed by Herod. This jailer, silhouetted against his lantern would be clearly seen by the prisoners, but the sleepy jailer, unable to see into the dark, could only see to his horror the prisoner's cell door was wide open.
Shock, horror, pit in stomach—then relief and joy—as Paul called out from his dark pit, 'It's okay. All is well; put your sword away.'
The jailer had no business to be asleep on duty anyway.

Q. Have you ever been in an earthquake? Where and what happened? Will you share the experience?

Acts 16: 29-34

He called for lights and sprang in, and, fell down trembling before Paul and Silas, and brought them out and said, 'Sirs, what must I do to be saved?'
They said, 'Believe in the Lord Jesus Christ, and you will be saved, you and your household.' They spoke the word of the Lord to him, and to all who were in his house.

He took them the same hour of the night, and washed their stripes, and was immediately baptized, he and all his household. 16: 34 He brought them up into his house, and set food before them, and rejoiced greatly, with all his household, having believed in God.

The jailer would have had some idea why these prisoners were so heavily guarded. These men were not only preachers of a new religion but had also wrecked the business of some traders.

After the shock he'd just had, and a near scrape with suicide, the jailer wanted to know what it was that had kept these men in their cells when they had had such a golden opportunity to escape—making the jailer a dead man.

'As he washed their wounds, so he himself was washed from sin and his entire household with him,'[29] said the early church youth educator John Chrysostom. He may have felt that warm glow of joy, the hallmark of the Holy Spirit, the mysterious feeling of utter bliss.

Do you think that after the baptism Paul and Silas climbed back into the stocks again for the sake of the jailer? I bet he didn't make them so tight this time. What a night to remember.

Acts 16: 35-37

But when it was day, the magistrates sent the sergeants, saying, 'Let those men go.'

The jailer reported these words to Paul, saying, 'The magistrates have sent to let you go; now therefore come out, and go in peace.'

But Paul said to them, 'They have beaten us publicly, without a trial, men who are Romans, and have cast us into prison! Do they now release us secretly? No, most certainly, but let them come themselves and bring us out!'

Cheeky? The magistrates discover the gaffe they had made by ordering a public beating for two Roman citizens. The public beating was

---

[29] St. John Chrysostom, 347-407 AD, "The Divine Liturgy of St. John Chrystostom." Greek preacher, theologian, and liturgist. Wikipedia.

misdemeanor enough, let alone a beating without a trial. The magistrates were in trouble and suddenly anxious to get rid of the prisoners.

Paul and Silas did not ask to be escorted out of prison to save their injured pride, but to establish their innocence. This must be the reason they did not tell the magistrates they were Roman citizens before the flogging with rods. They realized it would suit the purpose for the church to remain silent—making the authorities more careful how they treated Christians in future.

Brave, committed, unselfish Paul and Silas had given the authorities a hefty scare.

Q. Spare a thought for those who suffered in the Holocaust or were beaten and starved on the Burma railway.

Paul and Silas stayed calm, despite their very painful backs. Have you stood up against some law or authority? What happened?

Acts 16: 38-40

The sergeants reported these words to the magistrates, and they were afraid when they heard that they were Romans, and they came and begged them. When they had brought them out, they asked them to depart from the city. They went out of the prison, and entered into Lydia's house. When they had seen the brothers, they encouraged them, and departed.

Well. Well. Well. Lesson learned the hard way, magistrates.

Summary of Chapter 16

Paul has a vision of a man calling them to cross over from Asia Minor to Europe to preach. This provides another leap for the spread of the gospel. They go to Philippi where they meet and convert Lydia, an influential business woman. After this, they convert a fortune-telling slave girl. Beaten and flogged, Paul and Silas are thrown into prison for spoiling the fortune-teller's wage-earning skills. A sudden earthquake opens all the prison doors, but the prisoners did not run away. The jailer's family was subsequently converted, as the prisoners saved the jailer's life by returning to their cell.

Three very different people are converted to Christianity in this chapter, showing the message of the gospel is able to affect the most diverse people and to reach every level of society.

It is interesting that the two main incidences recorded in the book of Acts, referring to gentiles objecting to the behavior of Jewish Christians, are related to money and loss of income. Here the slave girl loses her fortune-telling skill and, therefore, a loss of income for her employers.

The other incident occurred in Ephesus (Acts 19: 23-27). The traders were annoyed when the Christians discouraged the gentiles from buying silver idols, causing heavy loss of sales. The hip pocket was always thus—and still is, says Ria.

CHAPTER 17

Paul Gathers a Harvest of Enemies

Acts 17: 1-4

Now when they had passed through Amphipolis and Apollonia, they came to Thessalonica, where there was a Jewish synagogue. Paul, as was his custom, went in to them, and for three Sabbath days reasoned with them from the Scriptures, explaining and demonstrating that the Christ had to suffer and rise again from the dead, and saying, 'This Jesus, whom I proclaim to you, is the Christ.'

Some of them were persuaded, and joined Paul and Silas, of the devout Greeks a great multitude, and not a few of the chief women.

The great highway joining East and West was called the Egnatian Way; the Roman roads were a boon to all who wanted to travel. This road crossed the whole of northern Greece, including the towns mentioned here. In several locations, the road is still visible. Thessalonica, the Macedonian capital, had a colony of Jews and was therefore eligible for a synagogue. The 'chief' women may have been the wives of important men in town or even businesswomen, like Lydia. Paul speaks of the role women with respect, devoid of superiority, which diverts my mind to the 2009 Parliament of World Religions.

Sister Joan Chittester[30]was one of the many speakers. She asked some hundred men in her lecture room to put up their hands and then to stand

---

[30] Sr Joan Chittester, OSB a noted national and international lecturer who focuses on women in church and society, human rights, peace and justice, and contemporary religious life and spirituality. Former nun and author of

up. She challenged them to look after the women in the workforce, to ensure they had equal pay and conditions for doing the same job as the men. 'We need you to look after us,' she said. And most of us love it when they do.

From Ria: I hope Sister Chittester's quote does not look as it does to me, as it is of course taken out of a much larger commentary. The 'look after' seems quite patronizing, should they not be able to—of their own volition—make equality the norm!

Good point—probably my inadequate reporting—but in their time there seemed to be surprisingly little discrimination. The women seem well-adjusted and confidently play important roles in this story. Have any of you come across any such discrimination? Can you share your experience?

From Ria: Now I think it depends on whether you are talking to men and women together, or from women on their own—you would get far more response. For most women it would be 'where do I start'.

Q 2. Do any of the women in the group feel like this? Would you like to share your experience? Remember there is always the 'pass' option.

My tears.
    I weep for the women in Afghanistan, Somalia, Sudan, Iran, and Iraq—for those anywhere who are beaten mercilessly for showing an ankle or not wearing the correct veil—for the women whose hands are cut off at the whim of a man. For children, at the age of twelve, being sent off to marry a sixty-year-old man in exchange for some barter. For the young ones sent to prison at their fathers' pleasure for falling in love with the 'wrong' man. The girls who are brave enough to go to school at the risk of their lives are to be honored. I pray that their voices will be heard, like a great wave in protest against the brutality many have to endure.
    Of course, most Muslim men have decent hearts and minds, but courage is needed to challenge the cruel suppressive cultural habits being practiced in too many countries. These practices are neither the ways of a

---

twenty-two books. Executive director of Benetvision, a center for contemporary spirituality in Erie, Pennsylmania.

loving God or Allah, nor are they following the teaching of Mohammed or Jesus, and neither is this practice the policy of their leaders (see reference: Ch. 15: 5)—it is slavery, and dishonors their manhood.

Please, 'someone up there', may we see a great revival in these countries and see men throughout the Muslim world stand up to advocate protection and education for their women and children—to cherish and nurture them in a loving, manly way—allowing their women a voice at last.

To Muslim men, whether living in western countries in safe havens or in Muslim dominated countries around the world, your women and children need you—we all need you—to rescue your sisters still in bondage and to stand up for fairness, honor, and peace on earth.

Q. I wonder what you are all thinking. Will you go around the group and share your thoughts?

Acts 17: 5-9

But the unpersuaded Jews took along some wicked men from the marketplace, and gathering a crowd, set the city in an uproar. Assaulting the house of Jason, they sought to bring them out to the people. When they didn't find them, they dragged Jason and certain brothers before the rulers of the city, crying, 'These who have turned the world upside down have come here also, whom Jason has received. These all act contrary to the decrees of Caesar, saying that there is another king, Jesus!' The multitude and the rulers of the city were troubled when they heard these things. When they had taken security from Jason and the rest, they let them go.

The traditional Jews, jealous of this sudden interest and response to Paul's ministry by so many of their people, collected the rabble and persuaded them to tell dreadful lies to the magistrates. General turmoil reigned. The mob rampaged about noisily, looking for Paul and Silas.

A Roman citizen's worst crime was to support any rivalry to Caesar. This was treason, which could lead to confiscation of property or even death. Jason let out on bail as long as he guaranteed a peaceful community with no more rampaging from the Christians. This meant Paul and Silas obviously had to go, so they moved off down the Egnatian Way to the next town.

Acts 17: 10-12

The brothers immediately sent Paul and Silas away by night to Beroea. When they arrived, they went into the Jewish synagogue.

Now these were more noble than those in Thessalonica, in that they received the word with all readiness of the mind, examining the Scriptures daily to see whether these things were so. Many of them therefore believed; also of the prominent Greek women, and not a few men.

Paul and his companions had to escape from the city at night again, with no idea where they would find their next bed. Off they went at the dead of night for a long fifty-mile walk. What enormous energy was driving Paul. These men must have been very fit—again it would have been so tempting to go home, settle down, and get away from all this friction. However, on they went to Berea. Everything looked promising for a while.

Q. Wincs, A&A's and Sees, have you ever had to escape from a perilous situation? Will you share it?

Acts 17: 13-15:

But when the Jews of Thessalonica had knowledge that the word of God was proclaimed by Paul at Beroea also, they came there likewise, agitating the multitudes. Then the brothers immediately sent out Paul to go as far as to the sea, and Silas and Timothy still stayed there. But those who escorted Paul brought him as far as Athens. Receiving a commandment to Silas and Timothy that they should come to him very quickly, they departed.

Paul's story is like a wall of dominoes—touch the first and the others follow. Some of the Thessalonians were even more fanatically opposed to Paul than the Bereans. Paul was only in Thessalonica for a short time, but he still managed to start a new church. In his letter to the Thessalonians he tells of his cherished wish to be with them, and he expresses his joy at their faithfulness (1 Thess. 2: 17-38). Paul apparently made good friends easily and very quickly. What a gift; it brought him great pleasure.

Q. Some people say friends are more important to them than family. Have you experienced this? Who would you like to have nearby in a crisis? Do they know it?

Acts 17: 16-18

Now while Paul waited for them at Athens, his spirit was provoked within him as he saw the city full of idols. So he reasoned in the synagogue with the Jews and the devout persons and in the marketplace every day with those who met him. Some of the Epicurean and Stoic philosophers also were conversing with him. Some said, 'What does this babbler want to say?'

Others said, 'He seems to be advocating foreign deities,' because he preached Jesus and the resurrection.

Athens had been a great center for art, literature, and philosophy for the previous five centuries, with a reputation for its fine university. The two leading schools of philosophy were the Epicureans and the Stoics, who pursued contentment and learning as their highest priority, but over time, the ideals had degenerated into a more sensual way of life—life was meant to be fun.

Paul arrived in beautiful Athens, with the Acropolis, the lovely harbor, and magnificent architecture and sculptures. He probably hoped for a break from trouble here, with time to enjoy like-minded academics—then they called him a 'babbler'—how patronizing. Paul's spirit was understandably 'provoked'.

Q. How would you react to being called a 'babbler'? While sharing together make an agreed list of suggestions to help overcome irritations and suggestive 'proddings.' Keeping it on the fridge door as a reminder may be useful. Laminate it if necessary.

Acts 17: 19-21

They took hold of him, and brought him to the Areopagus, saying, 'May we know what this new teaching is, which is spoken by you? For you bring certain strange things to our ears. We want to know therefore what these things mean.' Now all the Athenians and the strangers living there spent their time in nothing else, but either to tell or to hear some new thing.

The Areopagus was not a place, but a group of men. The Court of Areopagus met in the Agora, or marketplace. The court felt responsible for any new religious or teaching or the introduction of new idols or gods. Always hungry for a new theme to debate, the Epicureans and Stoics pounced on Paul's teaching of a resurrection after life. The Greeks accepted immortality, but resurrection of the body was not acceptable.

So the court members took him to the Agora to enable them to think through this new theory at their next meeting.

Q. Put yourselves in the shoes of the inquisitive Agora, and explore any new religious ideas you may have to stimulate interest in the church. Maybe the A&A's, Wincs, Jewish, Muslim friends will have some inspirations.

Acts 17: 22-28

Paul stood in the middle of the Areopagus, and said, 'You men of Athens, I perceive that you are very religious in all things. For as I passed along, and observed the objects of your worship, I found also an altar with this inscription: 'TO AN UNKNOWN GOD.' What therefore you worship in ignorance, this I announce to you. The God who made the world and all things in it, he, being Lord of heaven and earth, doesn't dwell in temples made with hands, neither is he served by men's hands, as though he needed anything, seeing he himself gives to all life and breath, and all things. He made from one blood every nation of men to dwell on all the surface of the earth, having determined appointed seasons, and the boundaries of their dwellings, that they should seek the Lord, if perhaps they might reach out for him and find him, though he is not far from each one of us. 'For in him we live, and move, and have our being.' As some of your own poets have said, 'For we are also his offspring.'

Paul started off by complimenting the men of Athens for being 'very religious' and cleverly picked on a theme that was familiar to them, the altar to an unknown god. To cover any possible offense to a forgotten deity, they erected this altar to an unknown God.

Paul explained that this unknown God was the designer of the world, who leaves nothing to chance (unlike the laid-back gods of the Epicureans). This God is the designer of nations, who even decides when they should rise and fall, but this God was also a very personal God.

This unknown God, Paul explained, gives life to everything on earth. This God is 'not far from each of us' within our very being—we are his children.

Richard Dawkins, who calls himself a deeply religious nonbeliever, writes, 'An atheist in the sense of philosophical naturalist is somebody who believes there is nothing beyond the natural, physical world, no supernatural creative intelligence lurking behind the observable universe, no soul that outlasts the body and no miracles—except in the sense of natural phenomena that we don't yet understand. If there is something that appears to lie beyond the natural world as it is now imperfectly understood, we hope eventually to understand it and embrace it within the natural. As ever when we unweave a rainbow, it will not become less wonderful.'[31]

Q. This rather beautiful and profound statement from an obviously very spiritual man can help paint an unusual picture of our Creator. For an interesting analysis, re-write the paragraph in your journal, taking out each negative and replacing it, or leaving it in the positive. Replace 'atheist' with 'theist' as someone who believes in God.

'God is somebody who believes there is something . . .' and finish your paragraph. Change or omit a word where necessary to make sense of your writing. What does this picture look like? Compare your versions with each other.

Acts 17: 29-33

Being then the offspring of God, we ought not to think that the Divine Nature is like gold, or silver, or stone, engraved by art and design of man. The times of ignorance therefore God overlooked. But now he commands that all people everywhere should repent, because he has appointed a day in which he will judge the world in righteousness by the man whom he has

---

31   Richard Dawkins "The God Delusion" Published by Bantam Press. Page14.

ordained; of which he has given assurance to all men, in that he has raised him from the dead.'

Now when they heard of the resurrection of the dead, some mocked; but others said, 'We want to hear you again concerning this.'

Thus Paul went out from among them. But certain men joined with him, and believed, among them were Dionysius the Areopagite, and a woman named Damaris, and others with them.

Later writings tell us that Dionysius converted to Christianity and became the Bishop of Athens. Damaris may have been an intellectual God-fearing woman who had listened to Paul before.

Paul continued to tell them that this God is made of stern stuff. He will not judge those who have never heard about him but will judge those who will not listen. The time of ignorance is over; the Day of Judgment will come. To prove his point God allowed Jesus to appear in some form to his friends after death. Paul's story of the resurrection of Jesus sparked the inquiring minds of the non-scoffing scholars—some were eager to know more.

Q. Put your journalist's hat on again, and in about one hundred words, report the resurrection of Jesus for your local newspaper, as if it had happened in your area this week.

Summary of Chapter 17

Paul and his companions travel on down the Egnatian Way to Thessalonica where they stay for only three weeks. Paul manages to establish a church in that time, which was to bring him great comfort for its faithfulness later on. However, the Jews feel threatened again and trouble brews, so off to Berea this time, fifty miles away. The fanatical Jews follow them from Thessalonica to Berea and hound them out of there, too, so Paul and his party continue on to Athens, where he is brought before the Court of Areopagus to explain the life and resurrection of Jesus. Some of them listened and believed, while others sneered, but more Christian seeds had been sown.

CHAPTER 18

Third Missionary Journey—
Paul Shaves His Head

Acts 18: 1-4

After these things Paul departed from Athens, and came to Corinth. He found a certain Jew named Aquila, a man of Pontus by race, who had recently come from Italy, with his wife Priscilla, because Claudius had commanded all the Jews to depart from Rome. He came to them, and because he practiced the same trade, he lived with them and worked, for by trade they were tent makers. He reasoned in the synagogue every Sabbath, and persuaded Jews and Greeks.

Corinth was a new city with a great commercial harbor. Paul knew how important it was to establish a church there. Corinth was destroyed by the Roman army under General Mummius in 146 BC, and it remained in ruins for a hundred years until Julius Caesar rebuilt it as a Roman colony in 46 BC. Corinth. Like Thessalonica, it had a reputation of loose living, which was to cause the new church much trouble.

Aquila and Priscilla, who were probably Christians before this time, proved to be such a help to Paul. He stayed with them in Corinth for eighteen months, earned his keep working by making tents, while he preached in the synagogue every Sabbath. Nothing was left to chance as Paul met the right people at the right time to help him.

If there is a predestined plan for our liveswhich we follow, I believe God will present the tools and opportunities to achieve the goal. If we deny our part, our piece of the plan may never be filled.

Q. What is the dream you have for your life? Have you done it, are about to do it, or are still waiting to find out what it is? Share your dreams.

Acts 18: 5-6

But when Silas and Timothy came down from Macedonia, Paul was compelled by the Spirit, testifying to the Jews that Jesus was the Christ. When they opposed him and blasphemed, he shook out his clothing and said to them, 'Your blood be on your own heads! I am clean. From now on, I will go to the Gentiles!'

Silas and Timothy caught up with Paul in Corinth. They brought financial gifts from the new churches. This enabled Paul to do less tent making and more preaching. It is thought that after a while, Silas was sent back to support the church in Philippi, and Timothy went back to Thessalonica.

Paul had been quite successful in the synagogue in Corinth for a while, but frustrated by the Jews' constant abuse, he turned away to the gentiles. This was no chance incident. The great spread of Christianity to the gentiles may never have happened if the Jews had not repeatedly pushed Paul away.

Acts 18: 7-11

He departed there, and went into the house of a certain man named Justus, one who worshiped God, whose house was next door to the synagogue. Crispus, the ruler of the synagogue, believed in the Lord with all his house. Many of the Corinthians, when they heard, believed and were baptized. The Lord said to Paul in the night by a vision, 'Don't be afraid, but speak and don't be silent; for I am with you, and no one will attack you to harm you, for I have many people in this city.'

He lived there a year and six months, teaching the word of God among them.

Crispus, the Jewish synagogue administrator, was a useful ally to Paul through this difficult and seemingly unproductive time.

Paul was going through a low ebb—he seemed to be making no headway with the people in the synagogue. At the moment he needed a boost—he saw Jesus again in a vision, giving him the reassurance and confirmation he needed that he was to stay in Corinth, with the added bonus of living next door to the synagogue with friends around him.

Q. Take a quiet few moments to think if there is anyone you know who may be feeling a bit low today and needs a boost. Share it if it feels comfortable.

Acts 18: 12-16

But when Gallio was proconsul of Achaia, the Jews with one accord rose up against Paul and brought him before the judgment seat, saying, 'This man persuades men to worship God contrary to the law.'

But when Paul was about to open his mouth, Gallio said to the Jews, 'If indeed it were a matter of wrong or of wicked crime, you Jews, it would be reasonable that I should bear with you; but if they are questions about words and names and your own law, look to it yourselves. For I don't want to be a judge of these matters.' He drove them from the judgment seat.

Junius Gallio was the provincial governor; he had a reputation for fairness. From an inscription to him found in Delphi, it is known that he was proconsul of Achaia (the area of Greece south of Macedonia) from AD 51-52 allowing the date of Paul's visit to be identified accurately.

The suspicious Jews were on the attack again and tried to influence the Roman court by pointing out that Christianity was not the same religion as Judaism. As mentioned previously, the Jewish religion had special protection by Roman law, but as yet, there was no such protection for the Christian religion. Therefore governor Gallio was not prepared to delve into religious differences.

His decision was very important, setting a precedent for future governors dealing with Christian issues, enabling them as well to reject dealing with Christian matters under Roman law. This protected Christianity from Roman intervention for the next ten vital years. Another piece in the perfect jigsaw puzzle drops into place.

In Paul's eyes, Gallio's statement was a sign of Roman protection for Christian preachers and gave Paul the confidence to appeal to Caesar later on when he was in strife again.

Acts 18: 17

Then all the Greeks laid hold on Sosthenes, the ruler of the synagogue, and beat him before the judgment seat. Gallio didn't care about any of these things.

It is believed that Sosthenes later became a Christian even after that beating, poor chap. The fact that the Greeks dared to beat the Jewish ruler of the synagogue outside the courthouse shows the strong anti-Jewish feeling of the Greeks and the level of tension that lay just below the surface in Corinth.

Q. Living with tension can be detrimental to health and happiness. Is there a tension in your life that needs attention? Is this a good moment to talk about it? Make a list of up to five strategies for coping with tension, beginning with "take a deep breath . . . ."

Acts 18: 18-22

Paul, having stayed after this many more days, took his leave of the brothers, and sailed from there for Syria, together with Priscilla and Aquila. He shaved his head in Cenchreae, for he had a vow. He came to Ephesus, and he left them there; but he himself entered into the synagogue, and reasoned with the Jews.

When they asked him to stay with them a longer time, he declined; but taking his leave of them, and saying, 'I must by all means keep this coming feast in Jerusalem, but I will return again to you if God wills,' he set sail from Ephesus.

When he had landed at Caesarea, he went up and greeted the assembly, and went down to Antioch.

Paul's time in Corinth was over. In his vision, Jesus had vowed to look after Paul—to keep him from harm. Shaving the head was a Nazirite custom of thanksgiving, marking the end of a certain period of danger. It required a visit to the temple in Jerusalem to complete the commitment of gratitude.

Cenchreae was the eastern port in Corinth. The three friends, Priscilla, Aquila, and their shaven-headed friend Paul, set off by boat to Ephesus. Priscilla and Aquila stayed on in Ephesus, while Paul promised to come back, which he did, a few months later.

Paul was in a hurry to get to Jerusalem, not only to complete his vow but also to be there for the Passover, which was early in April that year. The sea was closed for navigation until 10 March, due to the weather, so that left only three to four weeks to reach Jerusalem. It involved two sea trips, one from Corinth across to Ephesus and a second to Caesarea, and finally a walk down to Jerusalem.

Q. Apart from wedding vows, the custom of vows is rather out of fashion nowadays. We make, break, and keep promises, which is not quite the same thing. List six vows or principles that you hold dear—ones you will try to adhere to all your life. Sharing them could be rewarding.

Acts 18: 23-26

Having spent some time there, he departed, and went through the region of Galatia, and Phrygia, in order, establishing all the disciples. Now a certain Jew named Apollos, an Alexandrian by race, an eloquent man, came to Ephesus. He was mighty in the Scriptures. This man had been instructed in the way of the Lord; and being fervent in spirit, he spoke and taught accurately the things concerning Jesus, although he knew only the baptism of John. He began to speak boldly in the synagogue. But when Priscilla and Aquila heard him, they took him aside, and explained to him the way of God more accurately.

After a time in Antioch, Paul set off to revisit the churches he had initiated on his first missionary journey. While he was away, Priscilla and Aquila met Apollos, the Jewish preacher from Egypt. Apollos came from Alexandra, which had a large Jewish population. Apollos may have known one of John the Baptist's followers from Galilee and therefore had heard about the promise of the coming Messiah.

Imagine Priscilla and Aquila's surprise as they listened to this excellent speaker in the synagogue, feeling a thrill as they realized Apollos was talking about Jesus.

Afterwards Priscilla and Aquila approached Apollos with glowing excited faces. They invited him home, bursting to tell him the rest of the story of the crucified and resurrected Christ.

Q. What a buzz. Like Paul, Priscilla and Aquila, is there a similar story of an unexpected amazing coincidence you would like to record and share?

Acts 18: 27-28

When he [Apollo] had determined to pass over into Achaia, the brothers encouraged him, and wrote to the disciples to receive him. When he had come, he greatly helped those who had believed through grace; for he powerfully refuted the Jews, publicly showing by the Scriptures that Jesus was the Christ.

How rewarding for Priscilla and Aquila to be able to give Apollos good contacts in the Corinth Church, where this excellent preacher would be a great strength and help to the new Christians.

We are beginning to see the fruits of Paul's earlier struggle to establish Christianity in the Middle East. It was a superhuman task in the first place, tackled with courage and faithfulness.

What a joy Apollos' story must have been to Paul as he heard about the Christians in Ephesus, encouraging and helping to strengthen the church there.

Summary of Chapter 18

Paul leaves Athens and has a wonderful trouble-free eighteen months in Corinth where he meets and stays with the tent maker Aquila and his wife Priscilla. The Jews stir up trouble again and bring Paul before the Roman court to try to stop him preaching, but the Roman Governor Gallio snubs the Jews and ejects them from the court.

Before leaving, Paul shaves his head as a sign of thanksgiving for his trouble-free time in Corinth. He sails away to Ephesus with Priscilla and

Aquila before going on to Jerusalem. Priscilla and Aquila stay behind in Ephesus and meet Apollos, an excellent preacher and follower of John the Baptist. Excitedly, they tell him the rest of the gospel story of the risen Christ. Apollos goes off and helps the new church in Corinth.

Map of Paul's Third Missionary Journey

CHAPTER 19

Paul Upsets the Silversmiths' Union

Acts 19: 1-7

It happened that, while Apollos was at Corinth, Paul, having passed through the upper country, came to Ephesus, and found certain disciples. He said to them, 'Did you receive the Holy Spirit when you believed?'

They said to him, 'No, we haven't even heard that there is a Holy Spirit.'

He said, 'Into what then were you baptized?'

They said, 'Into John's baptism.'

Paul said, 'John indeed baptized with the baptism of repentance, saying to the people that they should believe in the one who would come after him, that is, in Jesus.'

When they heard this, they were baptized in the name of the Lord Jesus. When Paul had laid his hands on them, the Holy Spirit came on them, and they spoke with other languages and prophesied. They were about twelve men in all.

Paul made his way back overland to Ephesus in the autumn of AD 52. He stayed there for two and a half years until the spring of AD 55. He arrived after Apollos had left for Corinth but met some other followers of John the Baptist, who probably had heard about Jesus too but were still waiting for the promised Messiah. They knew nothing of the coming of the Holy Spirit at Pentecost. This is the only time that we hear of anyone being baptized twice, first with John the Baptist and secondly in the name of Jesus.

Q. These ceremonies, such as baptism are important milestones in our journey. You probably don't remember your baptism, but if you were confirmed in the church, how important was this moment to you?

Those who were not confirmed, is there any important ceremony (perhaps excluding weddings) which made a significant impression on you? Please tell the group about it.

Acts 19: 8-10

He entered into the synagogue, and spoke boldly for a period of three months, reasoning and persuading about the things concerning the Kingdom of God.

But when some were hardened and disobedient, speaking evil of the Way before the multitude, he departed from them, and separated the disciples, reasoning daily in the school of Tyrannus. This continued for two years, so that all those who lived in Asia heard the word of the Lord Jesus, both Jews and Greeks.

Paul was very faithful to his synagogue. It must have hurt him dreadfully every time he failed to make headway with the Jews and was driven off again to preach to the gentiles.

Tyrannus, a philosopher, probably had his own school or lecture hall.[32] One Greek manuscript tells us Paul taught from eleven o'clock in the morning to four o'clock in the afternoon every day. This would have been during the heat of the day, a time nobody else wanted the hall. Despite this obstacle, people were not put off, and the message spread far and wide.

Paul's task was so huge, and after all, he only had one short precious lifetime to spread a new philosophy throughout a vast region with no media back up. He had so many close shaves in his life he often didn't even know if there would be a tomorrow for him.

Q. If you realized there may be no tomorrow, would it make a difference to the way you lived today? For fun, try jotting down a schedule for your last day. What important jobs would you do? Who would you contact to tell them something really important? You have twelve short hours to fill.

---

[32] The lecture hall of Tyrannus, probably a school used regularly by Tyrannus, a philosopher and rhetorician. The actual location of the hall in Ephesus is unknown. NIV Study Bible page 1683 and 1789. Published by Zondervan Bible Publishers 1985.

Acts 19: 11-16

God worked special miracles by the hands of Paul, so that even handkerchiefs or aprons were carried away from his body to the sick, and the evil spirits went out. But some of the itinerant Jews, exorcists, took on themselves to invoke over those who had the evil spirits the name of the Lord Jesus, saying, 'We adjure you by Jesus whom Paul preaches.' There were seven sons of one Sceva, a Jewish chief priest, who did this.

The evil spirit answered, 'Jesus I know, and Paul I know, but who are you?' 'Then the man with the evil spirit leaped on them and gave them such a beating,' that they fled out of that house naked and wounded.'[33]

It seems that seven naughty sons of the Jewish chief priest were trying to imitate Paul, by trying to cash in on miraculous works, with very interesting results. Luke's humor comes through in this amusing account of the punishment they received. Seven streakers!

Q. There is no doubt that the word 'holiday' derives from the words 'Holy Day'—a day which is inexplicably related to having spiritual fun. Sees, when was the last time you laughed in church on a holi-day?

Acts 19: 17-20

This [the exorcist's story] became known to all, both Jews and Greeks, who lived at Ephesus. Fear fell on them all, and the name of the Lord Jesus was magnified. Many also of those who had believed came, confessing, and declaring their deeds. Many of those who practiced magical arts brought their books together and burned them in the sight of all. They counted their price, and found it to be fifty thousand pieces of silver. So the word of the Lord was growing and becoming mighty.

How strange to value the books that they were just about to burn. However, the NIV Study Bible says, 'The high price was not due to the quality of the books but to the supposed power gained by their secret

---

33   Quote from the NIV Study Bible page 1684 study notes 19:19.

rigmarole of words and names.'[34] Ephesus was well-known for its trade in sorcery. The scrolls were the textbooks for magic.

This fear that repeatedly seized the people seem to be the recognition that God is serious about how we live our lives, and we need to be mindful of the consequences of it.

Q. Wincs and Sees, how serious are you about witchcraft? Do the *Harry Potter* books offend? I wonder what God thinks about them.

They may not have been such a success if 'someone up there' disapproved. The books have brought so much joy, and encouraged vast numbers of children to read prolifically. In this modern scientific age, can we handle a bit of magic for children? Does it do any harm?

From Ria: Could not the same question be leveled at the Da Vinci Code for adults? Q. Any answers?

Acts 19: 21-22

Now after these things had ended, Paul determined in the spirit, when he had passed through Macedonia and Achaia, to go to Jerusalem, saying, 'After I have been there, I must also see Rome.'

Having sent into Macedonia two of those who served him, Timothy and Erastus, he himself stayed in Asia for a while.

The Christian Gentiles in Ephesus had collected funds (1 Cor. 16: 1-4) to send to the mother church in Jerusalem. Some of the members were going to deliver it soon. Apparently this was a good opportunity for Paul to go with them, so he waited. This stay marked the end of Paul's Aegean and third missionary journey. Paul's ultimate goal in life was to reach Rome to evangelize at the center of the Roman Empire, but little did he know the circumstances in which he was to achieve his goal.

---

[34] Quote from the NIV Study Bible page 1684 study notes 19:24.

Acts 19: 23-27

About that time there arose no small stir concerning the Way. For a certain man named Demetrius, a silversmith, who made silver shrines of Artemis, brought no little business to the craftsmen, whom he gathered together, with the workmen of like occupation, and said, 'Sirs, you know that by this business we have our wealth. You see and hear that not at Ephesus alone, but almost throughout all Asia; this Paul has persuaded and turned away many people, saying that they are no gods that are made with hands. Not only is there danger that this trade come into disrepute, but also that the temple of the great goddess Artemis will be counted as nothing, and her majesty destroyed, whom all Asia and the world worships.'

Demetrius was probably the leader of the silversmiths' guild. The Artemis Temple was one of the wonders of the ancient world and the biggest source of trade. Their beloved goddess Artemis, the Greek name for Diana, was the great mother goddess of the Ephesians.

The idol is thought to have been an interestingly shaped meteorite resembling a 'many breasted image' dropped from heaven[35] with objects like ostrich eggs. The silver trinket trade of this fascinating image was big business, and any discredit to their story would have far-reaching commercial implications. At the trade union meeting, Demetrius sanctimoniously suggested Paul was denigrating their goddess.

This meant trouble was looming for the followers of the Way again; however, there was no way Paul could explain the gospel of only one God without criticizing the citizen's beloved and lucrative idol, Artemis.

Acts 19: 28-31

When they heard this [the temple of the goddess Artemis will be counted as nothing] they were filled with anger, and cried out, saying, 'Great is Artemis of the Ephesians!' The whole city was filled with confusion, and they rushed with one accord into the theatre, having seized Gaius and Aristarchus, men of Macedonia, Paul's companions in travel. When Paul wanted to enter in to the people, the disciples didn't allow him. Certain

---

[35] Quote from the NIV Study Bible page 1684 study notes 19:27

also of the Asiarchs, being his friends, sent to him and begged him not to venture into the theatre.

Another ugly crowd scene. This time Paul's companions were in the firing line and were dragged into the open-air amphitheater, where the council was having its meeting. The theater could hold about twenty-five thousand people, so there was plenty of room for a rampaging crowd. It is interesting that the disciples were mentally strong enough to stop Paul from rushing in. The officials of the province, who warned Paul to stay out of it, were Greek men of wealth and influence. Paul, it seems, had friends in high places.

Acts 19: 32-34

Some therefore cried one thing, and some another, for the assembly was in confusion. Most of them didn't know why they had come together. They brought Alexander out of the multitude, the Jews putting him forward. Alexander beckoned with his hand, and would have made a defence to the people. But when they perceived that he was a Jew, all with one voice for a time of about two hours cried out, 'Great is Artemis of the Ephesians!'

They must have been hoarse after all that shouting. Again we see the ethnic tension between the Gentiles and the Jews. Alexander was a Jew, but not one of the Christians. He was probably pushed forward to tell the crowd that the Jews wanted to divorce themselves from any association with the Christians, but actually the crowd wasn't fussed by such refinements. A Jew was a Jew, fair game to be bellowed at, no matter what their internal religious differences may be. Most of the shouting people didn't know why they were there anyway. A nice touch of Luke's gentle humor again.

Q. Humor plays such a vital role in our lives. With it, we grow and feel mentally stimulated; without it, we shrink.

A recent newspaper article told of a girl who was expelled from her church school because she put minnows in the holy water. Surely God smiled. I hope her parents were able to laugh after a while. Do you have a good, clean joke to bring to the group?

Acts 19: 35-41

When the town clerk had quieted the multitude, he said, 'You men of Ephesus, what man is there who doesn't know that the city of the Ephesians is temple keeper of the great goddess Artemis, and of the image which fell down from Zeus? Seeing then that these things can't be denied, you ought to be quiet, and to do nothing rash. For you have brought these men here, who are neither robbers of temples nor blasphemers of your goddess. If therefore Demetrius and the craftsmen who are with him have a matter against anyone, the courts are open, and there are proconsuls. Let them press charges against one another. But if you seek anything about other matters, it will be settled in the regular assembly. For indeed we are in danger of being accused concerning this day's riot, there being no cause. Concerning it, we wouldn't be able to give an account of this commotion.' When he had thus spoken, he dismissed the assembly.

What a sensible man. The city clerk was an important person; he was the chief executive officer of the free municipal assembly or council that met three times a month. The clerk was also the go-between for the Greek community and the occupying Roman provincial government. The Romans would not tolerate violent and riotous behavior. Gentiles, Jews, and Christians alike would have been accused and in big trouble if the Roman officials arrived on the scene.

Actually there was no one to take the Assizes at that moment, which was another lucky break for Paul and his companions. The last Roman proconsul, Junius Silanus, had recently been assassinated late in AD 54, and the new one had not yet arrived. Thankfully, the city clerk had no option by to dismiss them. Another small piece of the perfect jigsaw puzzle has just dropped into place.

Summary of Chapter 19

In Ephesus, Paul comes across some people who had been baptized by John the Baptist; they were waiting for the Messiah. Paul is able to tell them the Messiah had already come. He baptizes them for the second time.

Paul is soon in trouble with the Silversmiths' Trade Union by suggesting they should not worship idols. Riots erupt, but Paul is protected by his friends, Gaius and Aristarchus. Paul's travelling companions are rescued from aggressive crowds by the sensible town clerk. Paul pines to go to Rome.

CHAPTER 20

Sad Farewells

Acts 20: 1-3

After the uproar had ceased, Paul sent for the disciples, took leave of them, and departed to go into Macedonia. When he had gone through those parts, and had encouraged them with many words, he came into Greece. When he had spent three months there, and a plot was made against him by Jews as he was about to set sail for Syria, he determined to return through Macedonia.

Paul wanted to see Titus in Troas and collect the donations from the new churches to take back to Jerusalem for the Christians in Judea. Paul went across to Corinth and probably had to stay there for the three winter months because no boats would have sailed until the weather improved. It is thought that Paul wrote his letter to the Romans in early AD 57 while he was waiting to sail in the spring. He slipped across from the port of Cenchrea and went back, mainly by land, to visit his old friends in the new churches before hopping across the sea to Troas.

Q. It must have been depressing for Paul to be rejected again and again. Have you ever been in a similar situation of having to battle a rebuff repeatedly? What, or who was it, that kept you going?

From Ria: Try being a part of the women's movement for forty years!

Acts 20: 4-6

These accompanied him as far as Asia: Sopater of Beroea; Aristarchus and Secundus of the Thessalonians; Gaius of Derbe; Timothy; and Tychicus and Trophimus of Asia. But these had gone ahead, and were waiting for us at Troas. We sailed away from Philippi after the days of Unleavened Bread, and came to them at Troas in five days, where we stayed seven days.

These men seem to have been appointed by the new churches to accompany Paul and to carry the donated money back to Jerusalem. Although Paul was in a hurry to get to Jerusalem for Pentecost, he stayed in Troas for seven days. This may be to wait for the next ship or to wait for the next Sabbath service, to break bread with the local Christians on the first day of the week before he left.

The winds must have been very gentle, as it took them five days this time to sail from Philippi to Troas, and they only took two days coming across the other way (Acts 16: 11).

The Feast of Unleavened Bread began with the Passover and lasted a week. So they sailed away at Easter time in the spring of AD 57 with good friends to accompany them.

Acts 20: 7-12

On the first day of the week, when the disciples were gathered together to break bread, Paul talked with them, intending to depart on the next day, and continued his speech until midnight. There were many lights in the upper room where we were gathered together. A certain young man named Eutychus sat in the window, weighed down with deep sleep. As Paul spoke still longer, being weighed down by his sleep, he fell down from the third story, and was taken up dead. Paul went down, and fell upon him, and embracing him said, 'Don't be troubled, for his life is in him.'

When he had gone up, and had broken bread, and eaten, and had talked with them a long while, even until break of day, he departed. They brought the boy in alive, and were greatly comforted.

Paul, the dynamic speaker, had so much to say that poor Eutychus just couldn't keep awake. Another version of the Bible records the little detail of smoky, warm oily lamps causing a stuffy atmosphere that increased the drowsiness of the young man. Maybe he was leaning against an unfastened window and tumbled out. This was no ordinary Sunday service.

Luckily, there was a doctor in the house. Luke, the physician, would have been the first on the pavement scene to examine Eutychus. Paul's confidence in his ability to bring him back to life is amazing. Although Paul used his God-given healing power to help others, he interestingly never used it on his own disease.

Paul had never resuscitated anyone before, and just as Peter revived Tabitha in Acts 9: 40, Paul revives Eutychus. You'd think a few bones may have been broken from a fall from a three-storey building. Luke probably sat with the lad to keep an eye on him, while Paul talked on into the early hours of Monday morning.

Eutychus was a common name among the freedmen, persons released from slavery. Maybe he needed a life-changing experience for some reason. He certainly got it.

Sankara Saranam says, 'Not only are miracles used in dubious ways to increase one's sense of security . . . but they cast a dangerously misleading model of the universe—one that spiritual investigators would question.'[36] Miracles can be a stumbling block to would-be believers, although the two thousand-year-old survival of the Bible is a great miracle in itself.

We know the Gospel writers had a huge task to try to persuade the Jews that Jesus was the Messiah, but the story of Paul reviving of this dead boy who received no broken bones after a fall from a three-storey building is a bit difficult to swallow today but maybe that is what was needed at the time.

Q. These miracles are being a bit of a worry. Should we look for the meaning within the miracles, rather than lingering on the stark facts?

What do you all think about the miracles?

Acts 20: 13-16

But we who went ahead to the ship set sail for Assos, intending to take Paul aboard there, for he had so arranged, intending himself to go by land. When he met us at Assos, we took him aboard, and came to Mitylene.

---

[36] Sankara Saranam, 'God without Religion: Questioning Centuries of Accepted Truths,' published by Simon & Schuster, pp 32-33.

Sailing from there, we came the following day opposite Chios. The next day we touched at Samos and stayed at Trogyllium, and the day after we came to Miletus. For Paul had determined to sail past Ephesus, that he might not have to spend time in Asia; for he was hastening, if it were possible for him, to be in Jerusalem on the day of Pentecost.

Luke and the money-carrying companions started hopping from port to port down the coast. Paul decided to walk the twenty miles to Assos from Troas, half the distance of the sea journey. The walk would not take much longer.

Back on board, they sailed straight across the Ephesian Gulf for two reasons. One, although Paul had many friends in Ephesus, after the riots he had caused the previous year, he would be exposed to serious danger again if he was seen (1 Cor. 15: 30; 2 Cor. 1: 8-10). Two, he decided to avoid any possible delay in getting to Jerusalem in time for Pentecost.

Q. Can you relate to that feeling of being late, with the possibility of missing the train, plane, doctor's appointment, or even just getting the meal on the table to put the children to bed in time? We live in such a busy world; is there a resolution you would like to make to help slow down the pace of your life? Will you share it, so that you have witnesses?

Acts 20: 17-21

From Miletus he sent to Ephesus, and called to himself the elders of the assembly. When they had come to him, he said to them, 'You yourselves know, from the first day that I set foot in Asia, how I was with you all the time, serving the Lord with all humility, with many tears, and with trials which happened to me by the plots of the Jews; how I didn't shrink from declaring to you anything that was profitable, teaching you publicly and from house to house, testifying both to Jews and to Greeks repentance toward God, and faith toward our Lord Jesus.'

Is Paul trying to justify himself here? He sounds nervous. '*I didn't shrink from* . . .' Perhaps he was still unhappy with himself for persecuting the early Christians and was talking himself through it.

Paul had missed visiting the elders in Ephesus, so he asked them to meet him further down the coast in Miletus instead. It sounds as though

Paul was trying to get something important off his chest. Elders had been appointed in the newly established churches, and it was important to keep in touch with them whenever possible.

Paul wanted to leave them with two basic teachings of the Christian life. Keep your debit account short with God and adhere to the teaching of Jesus by trusting him with the luxury of a clear conscience.

Acts 20: 22-25

Now, behold, I go bound by the Spirit to Jerusalem, not knowing what will happen to me there; except that the Holy Spirit testifies in every city, saying that bonds and afflictions wait for me. But these things don't count; nor do I hold my life dear to myself, so that I may finish my race with joy, and the ministry which I received from the Lord Jesus, to fully testify to the Good News of the grace of God.

'Now, behold, I know that you all, among whom I went about preaching the Kingdom of God, will see my face no more.'

Paul was walking into danger by going to Jerusalem, not against his will, but with complete confidence in the Holy Spirit. He was fully aware of the dangers that lay ahead, for the Jews in Jerusalem were out to kill him. (Acts 9: 23) Although he realized the risks, he knew that if he were going to fulfill his dream to get to Rome and Spain, he had to go to Jerusalem first.

There is a glimpse of his apprehension and deep sadness as he prepares to leave.

Q. Paul had a burning ambition to get to Rome. What is or are your burning ambitions?

Acts 20: 26-27

Therefore I testify to you this day that I am clean from the blood of all men for I didn't shrink from declaring to you the whole counsel of God.

Here is the 'something' he wanted to get off his chest. Paul recognized that God had forgiven him for his persecution of the Christians, but he had sincerely repented—to God, to Peter and the apostles, and, I'm sure, if he met them, he'd repented to any of those whom he persecuted. He'd had a complete change of heart.

However, he was saying here that having said sorry to as many people as possible, he was now free from guilt. If some of those people wouldn't or couldn't accept his apology, so sad, too bad, but it was no longer his problem. 'I am clean from the blood of all men.'

Q. In a few quiet moments reflect if there is someone to whom you could say sorry. No need to share.

Acts 20: 28

Take heed, therefore, to yourselves, and to all the flock, in which the Holy Spirit has made you overseers, to shepherd the assembly of the Lord and God which he purchased with his own blood.

Now that Paul had made his peace with himself, he gives them a message. Having resolved any outstanding issues, they needed to put them behind and get on with looking after their flock and their church family.

We each belong to a flock—it may be a little circle or a large group of people for whom it is our privilege to care.

Christianity gives us the tools to live a life of even moderate—on the Richter scale—harmony, and to enjoy the richness of close relationships.

Q. With Paul, let us struggle with a bit of problem solving. Could you research the tools—a few simple rules the professionals use to help resolve conflict and guilt. The best five could be laminated for the fridge door with the other. This could be a life changing exercise.

Acts 20: 29-31

For I know that after my departure, vicious wolves will enter in among you, not sparing the flock. Men will arise from among your own selves, speaking perverse things, to draw away the disciples after them. Therefore watch, remembering that for a period of three years I didn't cease to admonish everyone night and day with tears.

Paul reminded his flock that his latest missionary journey had taken nearly three years. He had met plenty of vicious wolves who had even tried to kill him along the way, but he wasn't thinking of himself; he was trying to warn his listeners of 'vicious wolves' who would come to ravage them, false prophets who would try to destroy their faith.

Even among our own family and friends, there can be vicious wolves—people who love to snipe, criticize, to destroy the harmony, or gossip and ready to pass on an unsavory story, whether it be true or false. And if we are honest, the savage wolf in most of us sometimes delights in a bit of juicy gossip, almost without realizing it.

Q. Can you identify any vicious wolves in your circle of acquaintance? Avoid them.

Acts 20: 32-36

Now, brothers, I entrust you to God, and to the word of his grace, which is able to build up, and to give you the inheritance among all those who are sanctified. I coveted no one's silver, or gold, or clothing. You yourselves know that these hands served my necessities, and those who were with me. In all things I gave you an example, that so laboring you ought to help the weak, and to remember the words of the Lord Jesus, that he himself said, 'it is more blessed to give than to receive.'

When he had spoken these things, he knelt down and prayed with them all.

These words from Jesus, *'It is more blessed to give than to receive,'* are only quoted in Luke's writing.

Paul was justifying himself here for some reason, by saying, 'I did not sponge on you when I stayed with you. I earned my keep.' Perhaps he was still carrying a little of that guilty feeling. It is so hard to forgive oneself.

Luke expressed again the deep sadness of their final goodbyes. We all know the feeling.

Q. Has any particular issues jumped out for you in this chapter that has not surfaced for discusssion?

Summary of Chapter 20

The chapter begins in uproar in Ephesus. Paul leaves for Macedonia to get away from the troublesome Jews again. Paul, on his way back to Jerusalem for Pentecost, says his farewells along the way. He fully realizes the danger he faces in Jerusalem. After many tearful farewells, he sails off across the Mediterranean with his companions, heading for Jerusalem, to try and arrive there before the feast of Pentecost.

CHAPTER 21

Storms Brewing in Jerusalem

Acts 21: 1-6

When it happened that we had parted from them and had set sail, we came with a straight course to Cos, and the next day to Rhodes, and from there to Patara. Having found a ship crossing over to Phoenicia, we went aboard, and set sail. When we had come in sight of Cyprus, leaving it on the left hand, we sailed to Syria, and landed at Tyre, for there the ship was to unload her cargo.

Having found disciples, we stayed there seven days. These said to Paul through the Spirit, that he should not go up to Jerusalem. When it happened that we had accomplished the days, we departed and went on our journey. They all, with wives and children, brought us on our way until we were out of the city. Kneeling down on the beach, we prayed. After saying goodbye to each other, we went on board the ship, and they returned home again.

The ship sailed away, after another heart-rending farewell, leaving families standing on the shore, feeling empty. Anxious for Paul's safety, they resolved with renewed vigor to carry on his work. Paul had become an important leader to the new Christian churches, with many friends. The thought of losing him filled them with fear.

This level of concern highlights the strong bonds that had developed between the early Church congregations, like a strong fortress to sustain them against the trouble that was to buffet Christians for centuries to come.

Q. Are there other organizations which provide nurturing in quite the same way as a good church family? What a privilege it is, if you have a mixed group, to ponder on this caring nature which must be one of the greatest strengths of religions.

Wincs, your input is particularly important here.

Acts 21: 7-9

When we had finished the voyage from Tyre, we arrived at Ptolemais. We greeted the brothers, and stayed with them one day. On the next day, we, who were Paul's companions, departed, and came to Caesarea. We entered into the house of Philip the evangelist, who was one of the seven, and stayed with him. Now this man had four virgin daughters who prophesied.

Paul comes across as a tough man's man. He certainly didn't hang around Philip's four unmarried daughters for long. Having four unmarried daughters would have been fairly unusual, they were possibly dedicated in some way to God's service.

Philip was last mentioned in chapter 8 after he met the Ethiopian reading Isaiah in the chariot. Philip stayed on and preached there for twenty-five years. Philip, along with Stephen, was one of the seven chosen to be the first deacons of the church, distributing funds and food to the widows and poorer members of the church.

What a lot had happened since then. Philip had an easier road than Paul but had established a strong church in Caesarea.

Q. Do you think Paul was ever tempted to settle down and get married? Can you find anyone in today's world who remotely resembles Paul—his lifestyle and dedication to his task? Please share your heroes.

Acts 21: 10-16

As we stayed there some days, a certain prophet named Agabus came down from Judea. Coming to us, and taking Paul's belt, he bound his own feet and hands, and said, 'Thus says the Holy Spirit: "So will the Jews at Jerusalem bind the man who owns this belt, and will deliver him into the hands of the Gentiles".'

When we heard these things, both we and they of that place begged him not to go up to Jerusalem. Then Paul answered, 'What are you doing, weeping and breaking my heart? For I am ready not only to be bound, but also to die at Jerusalem for the name of the Lord Jesus.'

When he would not be persuaded, we ceased, saying, 'The Lord's will be done.'

After these days we took up our baggage and went up to Jerusalem. Some of the disciples from Caesarea also went with us, bringing one Mnason of Cyprus, an early disciple, with whom we would stay.

Agapus would have been an elder or vestryman in the church in Judea with the gift of prophecy. Earlier in Acts, he prophesied the coming famine, fifteen years before it happened (chapter 11). This acting out, or charade-like prophecy, was common practice in the Old Testament.

Picture the scene as Agapus takes Paul's belt off to begin to prophesy. When he bound Paul with a belt, they knew that chains and jail would be waiting for him in Jerusalem. The people, including Luke this time, tried again to persuade him not to go on, until they realize that it was the Holy Spirit's plan; Paul must go.

There is a series of incidents in Paul's journey to Jerusalem that shadow the events Jesus experienced on his final journey before his crucifixion. The words 'The Lord's will be done' are the words used by Jesus in the Garden of Gethsemane. (Luke 22: 42) The Jewish authorities were waiting to pounce on both occasions, and like Paul's friends, Jesus's disciples were fearful for his safety. Look what happened to Jesus in Jerusalem. No wonder they were all afraid for Paul. Was it God's will?

Q. After the tsunami on Boxing Day 2004, when more than three hundred thousand people died, somebody said to a friend of mine, 'It is all in God's plan.' My friend made a very uncharacteristic strong response to that statement, 'Well, what a bastard your God must be.' When good things happen, Christians are very happy to say, 'it is God's will', but then, what is the response when bad things happen? Is there a lesson here? What is it? Please help us Wincs.

Acts 21: 17-21

When we had come to Jerusalem, the brothers received us gladly. The day following, Paul went in with us to James; and all the elders were present. When he had greeted them, he reported one by one the things which God had worked among the Gentiles through his ministry. They, when they heard it, glorified God. They said to him, 'You see, brother, how many thousands there are among the Jews of those who have believed, and they are all zealous for the law. They have been informed about you, that you teach all the Jews who are among the Gentiles to forsake Moses, telling them not to circumcise their children neither to walk after the customs.'

Paul had made the journey to Jerusalem in time for Pentecost. The travellers were greeted warmly, not only for themselves but also for the gifts of money they had brought to Jerusalem from the new churches. The travellers went to see the boss, James, the brother of Jesus. Apparently, none of the original twelve disciples were living in Jerusalem. Paul reported the progress made since his last visit. The elders told him of the rumor that Paul was encouraging the Jewish Christians not to circumcise their children.

Circumcision was a very hot issue for the Jews. It was one of the root causes of all the antagonism Paul had experienced from the Jews on the way around the Middle East. The rumor was not factual. Paul had never encouraged the Jews to turn away from their tradition, and Paul himself hadn't turned away either. Malicious gossip.

Allegations, or even subtle suggestive remarks, can be so damaging. One of the speakers at the 2009 Parliament of World Religions (notes were taken hurriedly, so forgive me, but I cannot remember the name of the speaker) suggested this recipe:

* Face up to the allegation and confirm the details by finding out the facts.
* Pray for the person that no harm comes to them.
* Write the incident down, then burn it, and forget it.
* And/or talk with the accusing person gently, trying to make your words non-personal. For example, try not to say, 'Why did *you* do/say . . . whatever?' Rather, say, 'when you did/said . . . whatever, it was not helpful. You may not have meant it, but those words/that action *(not you)* . . . hurt me. If there is something I have done to hurt you, I am so sorry.'

Q. Do you agree or can you improve on these four points?

Acts 21: 22-25

What then? The assembly must certainly meet, for they will hear that you have come. Therefore do what we tell you. We have four men who have taken a vow. Take them, and purify yourself with them, and pay their expenses for them, that they may shave their heads. Then all will know that there is no truth in the things that they have been informed about you, but that you yourself also walk keeping the law. But concerning the Gentiles who believe, we have written our decision that they should observe no such thing, except that they should keep themselves from food offered to idols, from blood, from strangled things, and from sexual immorality.

James and the elders—all zealous for the law—asked Paul at this meeting to try to dispel the rumor that he had discouraged Jews from being circumcised, but he had certainly told the gentile Christians that it was not necessary.

The Jews were still very sensitive about the circumcision issue. Innocent Paul, to defuse the rumors, was asked to pay the expenses for the four men, who had taken a vow of penance. (We are not told what their crime had been.)

This would somehow prove to the Jews that Paul was innocent of their accusations. The elders acknowledged they had already passed a motion allowing non-Jewish new Christians exemption from being circumcised, but this did not apply to Jews.

Acts 21: 26

Then Paul took the men, and the next day, purified himself and went with them into the temple, declaring the fulfilment of the days of purification, until the offering was offered for every one of them.

Paul was risking recognition by going to the temple for seven consecutive days, but he had to go with the faulty four to complete his vow, and to demonstrate that he was not trying to persuade them or anyone else to turn against the Jewish law, but was encouraging them to keep it.

Paul chose to maintain the Jewish tradition all his life. 'To the Jews I became a Jew, in order to win Jews,' he says in 1 Corinthians 9: 20. The Jewish authorities wanted to get rid of Paul by any means. The elders had hoped to dilute this hate and fear by going through this strange, and untruthful scheme. No such luck.

Q. Once a lie is uttered, however beneficial or 'white', it usually needs another to help out. The situation is apt to grow like a cancer. Can you think of an example? Did the lie achieve anything? What happened?

Acts 21: 27-29

When the seven days were almost completed, the Jews from Asia, when they saw him in the temple, stirred up all the multitude and laid hands on him, crying out, 'Men of Israel, help! This is the man who teaches all men everywhere against the people, and the law, and this place. Moreover, he also brought Greeks into the temple, and has defiled this holy place!' For they had seen Trophimus, the Ephesian, with him in the city, and they supposed that Paul had brought him into the temple.

Paul and the Christian elders may have held their breath as each of the seven days went by. They were nearly there when disaster struck. The scheme may have worked, if only those nasty Jews from Asia hadn't turned up.

Gentiles were forbidden to go into the temple. There are engraved stones to this day announcing the fact.

There is no recorded evidence that Paul had taken Trophimus into the temple. Anyone was allowed into the outer court, but to go any further was to risk being set upon and killed, like an intruder into a nest of bees.

The persistent, troublesome Jews from Asia had hounded Paul wherever he went, trying to get rid of him. Trophimus, not Paul, should have been the target of the allegation had it been true. The Jews were prepared to go down any devious path to stamp out Christianity, if only they could find a way.

Q. 'If only the Jews from Asia hadn't turned up . . .' would you share an 'if only . . .'event in your life?

Acts 21: 30-32

All the city was moved, and the people ran together. They seized Paul and dragged him out of the temple. Immediately the doors were shut. As they were trying to kill him, news came up to the commanding officer of the regiment that all Jerusalem was in an uproar. Immediately he took soldiers and centurions, and ran down to them. They, when they saw the chief captain and the soldiers, stopped beating Paul.

The Roman barracks were attached to the northern end of the temple, up two flights of steps, so the crowd would have immediately seen the soldiers coming out.

Claudius Lysias was the centurion at the time. The centurions were in charge of a hundred soldiers, who came stomping down the two flights of steps into the temple's crowded outer court to rescue Paul. No wonder the Jews stopped in their tracks. They were already in trouble for being involved in a riot, whoever the perpetrator was.

Poor Paul, although protected by the Romans, he had a rough time. It was a good thing for Christianity that Israel and the whole of the Middle East were occupied by Rome at this time. Christianity may never have got as far as the walls of Jerusalem if the Jews could have prevented it.

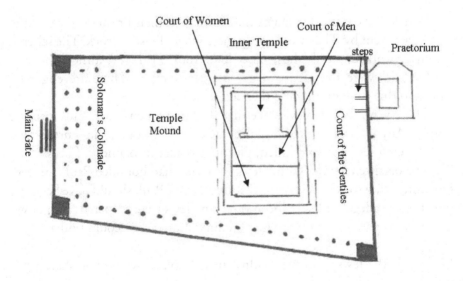

Diagram of the Temple in Jerusalem

Hand drawn but copied from map in
the NIV study Bible.

Plan of the Temple

Acts 21: 33-36

Then the commanding officer came near, arrested him, commanded him to be bound with two chains, and inquired who he was and what he had done. Some shouted one thing, and some another, among the crowd. When he couldn't find out the truth because of the noise, he commanded him to be brought into the barracks.

When he came to the stairs, it happened that he was carried by the soldiers because of the violence of the crowd; for the multitude of the people followed after, crying out, 'Away with him!'

Here is another shadow of the Jesus story here, as Luke describes the frightening scene of the seething mob. Paul, chained by each hand to a soldier on either side, had to be carted off before the crowd beat him to death. 'Who is he, and what has he done?' Claudius asks the screaming mob, in the same way that Pilate asked the crowds on that last precious day as they screamed for Jesus to be crucified.

How the creator must shake his/her head in despair at the awful things we do to each other.

Summary of Chapter 21

There are many sad farewells in this chapter as Paul continues to make his way through familiar towns in Asia Minor before he sets sail again for Caesarea and then walks down to Jerusalem with some of his friends from Caesarea. Controversy arises again over the circumcision issue, but eventually everything settles down, and Paul completes his vow and pays the expenses for four others who had made vows. The troublemakers from Asia catch up with Paul again, more rioting, so the Roman commanding officer arrests him to save his life from those with evil intent.

CHAPTER 22

Roman Citizenship Saves the Day

Acts 21: 37-22: 2a

As Paul was about to be brought into the barracks, he asked the commanding officer, 'May I speak to you?'

He said, 'Do you know Greek? Aren't you then the Egyptian, who before these days stirred up to sedition and led out into the wilderness the four thousand men of the Assassins?'

But Paul said, 'I am a Jew, from Tarsus in Cilicia, a citizen of no insignificant city. I beg you; allow me to speak to the people.'

When he had given him permission, Paul, standing on the stairs, beckoned with his hand to the people. When there was a great silence, he spoke to them in the Hebrew language, saying,

'Brothers and fathers, listen to the defence which I now make to you.' When they heard that he spoke to them in the Hebrew language, they were even more quiet.

Paul was a charismatic speaker, calm and confident enough to be able to quieten this mob. Claudius thought Paul was an Egyptian agitator who had recently been in the area professing to be a second Moses. The Egyptian had escaped the fury of the Jews and abandoned his followers, only to be cut to pieces by a murdering group of 'dagger men'.

Claudius was surprised when Paul referred to his citizenship of Tarsus. Paul had impeccable credentials; yet again he did not mention that he was a Roman citizen. Even so, Claudius realized he had to be careful. He was impressed by Paul, who was able to speak fluently in either Greek or the native tongue of the Jews—Hebrew.

Well-educated Paul had many privileges, and he used them skilfully to help the cause for his saviour, Jesus Christ.

Q. It can truly be said that Paul usually achieved whatever task he tackled. He may not have worn a pristine ironed shirt, he may even have looked pretty scruffy with the sort of life he led, but he was hugely successful. Only yesterday, someone said she had been thinking about people who were successful in life and recognised that most of them seem to have a faith. Can you think of a few and respond to that statement?

Can you write a definition of a successful life? All your answers will be interesting.

Acts 22: 2a-5

Then Paul said, 'I am indeed a Jew, born in Tarsus of Cilicia, but brought up in this city at the feet of Gamaliel, instructed according to the strict tradition of the law of our fathers, being zealous for God, even as you all are this day. I persecuted this Way to the death, binding and delivering into prisons both men and women. As also the high priest and all the council of the elders testify, from whom also I received letters to the brothers, and travelled to Damascus to bring them also who were there to Jerusalem in bonds to be punished.

Paul knew the story of his early Jewish upbringing would appeal to the Jewish crowd. They would also enjoy hearing that he had persecuted the Christians, the 'followers of the Way'with the high priest's blessing.

At the time Paul was hounding the Christians, the high priest had been Caiaphas, the man who condemned Jesus to death. Caiaphas had died, but the current high priest was able to testify to Paul's story.

Acts 22: 6-9

It happened that, as I made my journey, and came close to Damascus, about noon, suddenly there shone from the sky a great light around me. I fell to the ground, and heard a voice saying to me, 'Saul, Saul, why are you persecuting me?' I answered, 'Who are you, Lord?' He said to me, 'I am Jesus of Nazareth, whom you persecute.'

'Those who were with me indeed saw the light and were afraid, but they didn't understand the voice of him who spoke to me.'

Multilingual Paul continued to tell the story of his encounter with Jesus. Luke does not tell us which language Jesus used to speak to him on the road to Damascus; he only wrote that the soldiers heard the sound but did not understand the words.

Paul's short encounter with Jesus was probably not more than a minute or two, but it led him down paths he could not have imagined in his wildest dreams—to preach a gospel that, sadly, would alienate him from his people forever.

Q. Do you have a similar story—a time when your life was changed and a relationship was broken forever by your conviction? If this is too painful, just pass.

Acts 22: 10-13

I said, 'What shall I do, Lord?' The Lord said to me, 'Arise, and go into Damascus. There you will be told about all things which are appointed for you to do.'

Paul dropped in every detail that would help soften his message to get the crowd on his side. The description of the highly respected and law-abiding Ananias would be important to the Jews and give credibility to his story. Paul, standing between his Roman soldier guards, high on the steps of the barracks, had managed to quieten the crowd to the relief of the Romans—so far, so good . . .

Q. When you have an issue to solve, to whom do you turn to ask, 'What shall I do?' Do they know how important they are to you?

Acts 22: 14-16

He [Jesus] said, 'The God of our fathers has appointed you to know his will, and to see the Righteous One, and to hear a voice from his mouth. For you will be a witness for him to all men of what you have seen and heard.

Now why do you wait? Arise, be baptized, and wash away your sins, calling on the name of the Lord.'

What a no-nonsense God we have. 'Now get up and get on with it,' Jesus had said to him. Paul had the advantage of hearing Jesus audibly, an encounter most of us do not have the privilege to enjoy. However, we have the New Testament to tell us how to live. God is still saying, 'Now get on with it,' which is hopefully what you and I are doing at this minute.

Q. After a quiet moment of contemplation, ask that deep inner voice if it is trying to tell you to get on with something. Maybe now is the time.

Acts 22: 17-21

'It happened that, when I had returned to Jerusalem, and while I prayed in the temple, I fell into a trance and saw him saying to me, "Hurry and get out of Jerusalem quickly, because they will not receive testimony concerning me from you." I said, "Lord, they themselves know that I imprisoned and beat in every synagogue those who believed in you. When the blood of Stephen, your witness, was shed, I also was standing by, and consenting to his death, and guarding the cloaks of those who killed him".'

'He said to me, "Depart, for I will send you out far from here to the Gentiles".'

Three years after Paul's conversion, it would be interesting to know how he felt about telling the story of his previous violent behaviour. But knowing full well that he was forgiven, there was no need to feel guilty, God just said to him again, 'Now get on with the job I've given you to do!'

Q. Sees and Wincs, has your conscience, ever had to repeat this statement to you, too—*get on with it?* Can you share your story?

Acts 22: 22-24

They listened to him until he said that; I will send you out far from here to the Gentiles then they lifted up their voice, and said, 'Rid the earth of this fellow, for he isn't fit to live!'

As they cried out, and threw off their cloaks, and threw dust into the air, the commanding officer commanded him to be brought into the barracks, ordering him to be examined by scourging, that he might know for what crime they shouted against him like that.

However much Paul tried to get the crowd on his side; he knew the testing time would come at the mention of the word *Gentiles*. He was right—all hell was let loose again. It was blatantly obvious that Paul was only too willing to talk about Jesus at every possible occasion to anyone who would listen to him, so it seemed a bit harsh to have him beaten to find out what the crowd was so angry about.

The Romans used a lethal whip, which was not allowed to be used on a Roman citizen, but could legally be used on a wretched slave or foreigner. The pain of it often killed the victim.

Rejected by his people and beaten unbearably, one wonders how much more Paul could bear. Jesus must surely have felt this same emotional pain, on top of the physical pain of torture.

Q. Do you know a modern story where physical and emotional pain has been almost unbearably endured?

Acts 22: 25-26

When they had tied him up with thongs, Paul asked the centurion who stood by, 'Is it lawful for you to scourge a man who is a Roman, and not found guilty?'
When the centurion heard it, he went to the commanding officer and told him, 'Watch what you are about to do, for this man is a Roman!'

Up to this point, Paul had only mentioned that he was a citizen of Tarsus but not that he was a Roman citizen. As was mentioned before, under Roman law, a Roman citizen was privileged and not permitted to have any degrading punishment, such as being put in chains, beaten with rods, flogged, or crucified without trial.

If Jesus had been a Roman citizen the gospel story could not have materialized. But he wasn't, and Paul was. Paul needed that privilege to achieve the work he had been given.

How perfect are the pieces of God's planning, down to the smallest detail, which holds good for us too, I suppose. Charles Roderick in his little book of sermons, *Listen to the Wind*, says, 'Every one of us is in the Bible somewhere on one page or another, doing something or not doing something . . . '[37]

Q. Who are you? A Martha, Mary, Ruth, or Priscilla? A Peter, Luke, Job, or Moses? Or another? Having identified your 'twin' from the Bible, record why you relate yourself to this figure.

Acts 22: 27-29

The commanding officer came and asked him, 'Tell me, are you a Roman?'

He said, 'Yes.'

The commanding officer answered, 'I bought my citizenship for a great price.'

Paul said, 'But I was born a Roman.'

Immediately those who were about to examine him departed from him, and the commanding officer also was afraid when he realized he was a Roman, because he had bound him.

'You must be joking. How could someone like you afford citizenship?' was Commander Claudius Lysias's cutting, sarcastic remark. Claudius was the commander's first name, which indicates that he had bought his citizenship during the reign of the Emperor Claudius.

There were three ways of obtaining Roman citizenship:

1) A reward for outstanding service to the Romans.
2) Buying it for a high price.
3) Inheriting citizenship from father to son, like Paul. How Paul's father or forebear received it is not known.

---

[37] The late Rev. Charles Roderick, formerly chaplain to the queen, 'Listen to the Wind,' p. 37, 1984.

Claudius Lysias realised he was guilty of ordering an illegal flogging and putting a Roman citizen in chains.

Those around Paul melted away, fearful of being involved in the crime. It is interesting how quickly people disappear from a scene if they feel they may become involved in some unpleasant dispute. Moral fibre can disintegrate very quickly.

Q. Do you have such a tale to tell?

Acts 22: 30

But on the next day, desiring to know the truth about why he was accused by the Jews, he freed him from the bonds, and commanded the chief priests and all the council to come together, and brought Paul down and set him before them.

Paul had suddenly become an embarrassment, and if Claudius was to get away without serious consequence for his blunder, he'd have to get rid of him as soon as possible.

As we saw earlier, the Roman authority respected the Jewish religious law and allowed the Jews to judge their own religious issues. Therefore, punishment couldn't be administered by the Romans without Jewish approval, so Paul was sent straight to the Jewish Sanhedrin court for their approval.

Summary of Chapter 22

Paul, while still in trouble in Jerusalem, tries to explain the Ggospel message to the Jews causing more uproar. The commander tries, and fails, to find the reason for the disturbance. Paul is about to be flogged illegally when he mentions that he is a Roman citizen. This leads him to the Sanhedrin to settle the Jewish religious issue.

CHAPTER 23

Clever Paul

Acts 23: 1-3

Paul, looking steadfastly at the council, said, 'Brothers, I have lived before God in all good conscience until this day.'

The high priest, Ananias, commanded those who stood by him to strike him on the mouth.

Then Paul said to him, 'God will strike you, you whitewashed wall! Do you sit to judge me according to the law, and command me to be struck contrary to the law?'

Paul stood up proudly, faced the Sanhedrin fearlessly, and professed, as he often did, that he had done a good job. Paul exuded self-confidence. He got slapped in the face for it and retaliated strongly by using that great expression, '*you whitewashed wall!*' implying that you look okay on the outside, but inside, your mind is pretty filthy. The members of the Sanhedrin may have gasped at Paul's impertinence.

How humiliating for the high priest, how satisfying for Paul, but what a disgraceful display of arrogance from the high priest! This incident highlights the patriarchal, hierarchal attitude that has haunted the religious world forever and continues in dark spots today.

Chris Mulherin made a point when he wrote in a newspaper article called 'Thank God for the Rise of Atheism conference,' reporting the Melbourne, 2010 World Atheists Conference, 'I wondered how much anger at the convention was rooted in pain for crimes and misdemeanors committed by the church, and I remembered that Jesus rejected no one *except those who thought themselves righteous.*'[38]

The late Bishop John Wilson wrote in his book *Christianity alongside Islam*, ' . . . devout Muslims are a rebuke to the casual, often self-centered and self-satisfied attitude which many Christians adopt.'[39]

Q. In the above bible verses, it was the Jews who were demonstrating a self-righteous attitude. What crimes and self-righteous attitudes have been evident in the Western church in the last half century? What affect has it had overall?

Acts 23: 4-6

Those who stood by said, 'Do you malign God's high priest?'

Paul said, 'I didn't know, brothers, that he was high priest. For it is written, "You shall not speak evil of a ruler of your people".' But when Paul perceived that the one part were Sadducees and the other Pharisees, he cried out in the council, 'Men and brothers, I am a Pharisee, a son of Pharisees. Concerning the hope and resurrection of the dead I am being judged!'

There are several reasons why Paul may not have recognized the high priest. One suggestion is that he had poor eyesight, (Gal. 4: 15; 6: 11) or he may not have recognized this new man as high priest. Or perhaps he was being sarcastic, implying that no decent high priest would have ordered someone to have their face slapped. Whichever it was, Paul quoted from Exodus 22: 28 and apologized to the office, as opposed to the person, of the high priest. Then he appeals to the Pharisees.

The Pharisees were the administrators and keepers of the temple. They believed in a life after death. They were able to become Christians and still

---

[38]   The Rev. Chris Mulherin, an Anglican minister writing a doctorate on science and theology. In his article 'Thank God for the Rise of Atheism conference,' he commented on his appreciation for the voice of atheists to make the Christian church reflect on its own frailties against humanity. The Rise of Atheism convention was held in Melbourne, Australia, in March 2010.

[39]   Bishop John Wilson, 'Christianity alongside Islam,' p. 338.

remain Pharisees. The Sadducees were the high priestly party and ruling class of the Jews who did not believe in the resurrection and so were unable to convert to Christianity and remain Sadducees. Paul was able to put the proverbial 'cat amongst the pigeons' deliberately creating division to avoid disaster.

Q. Can you recall a situation when you had to seriously defend yourself against an unjust accusation? Or, alternatively, have you ever misjudged a situation and accused someone unfairly—even a child maybe? How was it resolved?

Acts 23:7-8

When he had said this [concerning the hope and resurrection of the dead], an argument arose between the Pharisees and Sadducees, and the assembly was divided. For the Sadducees say that there is no resurrection, nor angel, nor spirit; but the Pharisees confess all of these.

Recounting the story of the resurrection of Jesus was the very central point of Paul's life's work. He knew, of course, that his comments on the resurrection would divide the Sanhedrin because the Pharisees and Sadducees could not agree, so the court would be unable to condemn Paul. It looks as though clever Paul was about to escape through the slippery net again.

Acts 23: 9-11

A great clamour arose, and some of the scribes of the Pharisees part stood up, and contended, saying, 'We find no evil in this man. But if a spirit or angel has spoken to him, let's not fight against God!'

When a great argument arose, the commanding officer, fearing that Paul would be torn in pieces by them, commanded the soldiers to go down and take him by force from among them, and bring him into the barracks.

The following night, the Lord stood by him, and said, 'Cheer up, Paul, for as you have testified about me at Jerusalem, so you must testify also at Rome.'

The Roman commander Claudius Lysias, watching quietly in the wings, had enough trouble on his plate without a murdered Roman citizen to add to it. He ordered Paul to be rescued again and brought back to the barracks. Paul felt depressed and alone, hated by his own people, passionate about his cause, yet feeling he wasn't making headway—but there was Jesus again and this time, he was toldl his dream to go to Rome would come true. How exciting—Paul had waited for this moment for so long.

It often seems amazing how a mood can swing in a moment by some remark, good news, unexpected visit, phone call, or, in this case, a visit from Jesus; but no wonder Paul's state of mind changed in a flash.

Q. Can you recall such a moment of a sudden mood swing from feeling a bit low and depressed to instantly being wonderfully happy?

Acts 23: 12-15

When it was day, some of the Jews banded together, and bound themselves under a curse, saying that they would neither eat nor drink until they had killed Paul. There were more than forty people who had made this conspiracy. They came to the chief priests and the elders, and said, 'We have bound ourselves under a great curse, to taste nothing until we have killed Paul. Now therefore, you with the council inform the commanding officer that he should bring him down to you tomorrow, as though you were going to judge his case more exactly. We are ready to kill him before he comes near.'

A hunger strike was pretty drastic. It indicates how fearful the Jews felt about the introduction of Christianity. We're not told how many of them died of starvation, but I doubt there were many.

If someone like Paul decided to preach unconventional spirituality today, would we hate him passionately, even if we did not agree? In Paul's case, he wasn't even trying to hurt or threaten anyone; he was just preaching about the love of God through the teaching of compassionate Jesus

Q. Is there an injustice you feel passionately about? Will you all share your tales?

Acts 23: 16-19

But Paul's sister's son heard of their lying in wait, and he came and entered into the barracks and told Paul. Paul summoned one of the centurions, and said, 'Bring this young man to the commanding officer, for he has something to tell him.'

So he took him, and brought him to the commanding officer, and said, 'Paul, the prisoner, summoned me and asked me to bring this young man to you, who has something to tell you.'

The commanding officer took him by the hand, and going aside, asked him privately, 'What is it that you have to tell me?'

Paul's nephew sounded a good lad, bravely willing to help his uncle at considerable risk to himself. I wonder if he began to regret his action when he was carted off to Commander Claudius Lysias. Was this a good idea after all? Or was he heading into trouble? Claudius sounds like an understanding and gentle man, who took the probably nervous nephew by the hand to a quiet corner where he wouldn't feel overheard.

Acts 23: 20-22

He [Claudius] said, 'The Jews have agreed to ask you to bring Paul down to the council tomorrow, as though intending to inquire somewhat more accurately concerning him. Therefore don't yield to them, for more than forty men lie in wait for him, who have bound themselves under a curse neither to eat nor to drink until they have killed him. Now they are ready, looking for the promise from you.'

So the commanding officer let the young man go, charging him, 'Tell no one that you have revealed these things to me.'

Good and faithful nephew, well done. He took action and stood up for what he believed in a dangerous situation. Claudius's dilemma continued. He realized the danger the boy was in and cautioned him. Now what to do with Paul? This was not an easy case. The deviousness of the Jewish authorities was frustrating. He'd have to think of another plan, other than allowing the Sanhedrin to decide Paul's fate. To send him off to a higher authority may be the answer. This case was getting beyond him.

Acts 23: 23-30

He called to himself two of the centurions, and said, 'Prepare two hundred soldiers to go as far as Caesarea, with seventy horsemen, and two hundred men armed with spears, at the third hour of the night.' He asked them to provide animals, that they might set Paul on one, and bring him safely to Felix the governor. He wrote a letter like this:

'Claudius Lysias to the most excellent governor Felix: Greetings. "This man was seized by the Jews, and was about to be killed by them, when I came with the soldiers and rescued him, having learned that he was a Roman. Desiring to know the cause why they accused him, I brought him down to their council. I found him to be accused about questions of their law, but not to be charged with anything worthy of death or of imprisonment. When I was told that the Jews lay in wait for the man, I sent him to you immediately, charging his accusers also to bring their accusations against him before you. Farewell".'

Claudius took no chances here. To give Paul such an enormous escort seems to be taking a hammer to crack a walnut, but Claudius obviously recognized the seriousness of the situation. It could have easily have got out of hand and reflected back on him. He wrote a concise report, but didn't confess to his 'faux pas' of almost chaining and nearly flogging a Roman citizen.

Claudius sent the accusers along to Felix too, and must have been glad to be shot of the lot, or so he thought.

Acts 23: 31-35

So the soldiers, carrying out their orders, took Paul and brought him by night to Antipatris. But on the next day they left the horsemen to go with him, and returned to the barrack. When they came to Caesarea and delivered the letter to the governor, they also presented Paul to him. When the governor had read it, he asked what province he was from. When he understood that he was from Cilicia, he said, 'I will hear you fully when your accusers also arrive.' He commanded that he be kept in Herod's palace.

The fact Paul came from Cilicia was another extraordinary coincidence in the Great Arranger's jigsaw puzzle, adding yet another twist in the story to protect Paul, as we shall see.

Governor Antonius Felix and his brother Pallas had been slaves, then freed men, and finally risen to become government officials. Felix was in a good position to obtain the ear of the emperor, because his brother was one of Claudius's favorite ministers. It is an impressive rags-to-riches story—from slave to governor in one lifespan. Perhaps both brothers were stunningly handsome young men. But the fairytale like story does not stop there.

Felix married three queens, his present wife, Druscilla, daughter of King Herod Agrippa, came from Cilicia. If Antonius Felix did not pay attention to a citizen from his wife's birthplace, he may find himself in trouble with her. Antonius Felix could have passed Paul's case on to a lesser court but chose to hear the case himself. He wanted neither a riot nor the death of his prisoner on his hands, so to cover himself both ways, he kept Paul under house arrest in Herod's palace for the time being.

Herod the Great (the villain who tried to murder Jesus as a baby) had built a palace for himself. It had subsequently become the Roman praetorian, the place where the official business of the emperor was carried out.

Having come from a near flogging and jail in Jerusalem, Paul was now comfortably settled in Herod's palace.

Q. When you are in a 'pickle' like Felix, how true is the saying 'It is not what you know but who you know.' Any examples?

Summary of Chapter 23

Chaos reigns in court among the Sanhedrin in the temple. Paul cleverly divides the court as he talks about the resurrection—the Pharisees believed in a resurrection, and the Sadducees did not—so they were unable to agree on a verdict. The crowd riots, so the Roman commander rescues Paul. The Jews plot to kill him. Paul's nephew hears about it and goes to tell his uncle and the Roman commander Claudius Lysias. The whole case is getting too much for Claudius to deal with, so he sends Paul off to the higher court of Governor Felix. Felix proceeds with caution and waits for Paul's accusers to arrive. Paul has a welcome rest in Herod's palace. God works in mysterious ways to bring comfort to those who are about his business.

CHAPTER 24

To Prison Again in Caesarea

Acts 24: 1-4

After five days, the high priest, Ananias, came down with certain elders and an orator, one Tertullus. They informed the governor against Paul. When he (Paul) was called, Tertullus began by saying, 'Seeing that by you we enjoy much peace, and that excellent measures are coming to this nation, we accept it in all ways and in all places, most excellent Felix, with all thankfulness. But, that I don't delay you, I entreat you to bear with us and hear a few words.'

Paul would have five days of blissful relaxation, while a messenger rode sixty miles to Jerusalem to deliver his message—the Sanhedrin had to choose their delegates and then ride back to Antipatris. Ananias the high priest, renowned for his cruelty and violence, came back to Antipatris himself.

The 'second-rate orator'[40], Tertullus, started the proceedings by trying to butter up Felix. Governor Felix, the ex-slave, was having a wonderful time. He no longer needed to be beaten into submission; he had the power to do the beating these days but maybe not for much longer.

So here we have Paul, the Jew, being tried in court again by a Roman governor, who was lawfully not allowed to interfere in Jewish religious matters. This whole conundrum was heading for the 'too difficult box', or

---

[40]   The New Commentary of the Bible Revised, published by Inter-Varsity Press, chapter 24:1-27, p. 1004.

maybe the Great Arranger was organizing something very clever again for Paul.

Q. In your opinion should governments take a more active part when considering new, often dangerous and fanatical, sects we have in our communities? Should the state look into the ethics of new religions before giving them a license to carry on? Or is this infringing on democratic rights? What do you all think?

Ria's comment: I hope you have a long enough session planned—you could do a whole course on this issue.

Acts 24: 5-9

The orator Tertullus continues:

For we have found this man to be a plague, an instigator of insurrections among all the Jews throughout the world, and a ringleader of the sect of the Nazarenes. He even tried to profane the temple, and we arrested him. By examining him yourself you may ascertain all these things of which we accuse him.

The Jews also joined in the attack, affirming that these things were so.

Felix, whose administration as governor was not considered effective, had been peppered with troublesome groups of bandits.

The Roman captain, standing at the top of the steps overlooking the courtyard, imagined Paul was the escaped Egyptian leader who had caused so much trouble previously. (Acts 21: 38)

To be a leader of any sect was a treasonable offence against Caesar. Any group formed without Roman approval was liable for heavy penalties.

Q. What were the three false charges brought against Paul? How similar were they to the charges that were brought against Jesus at his trial before Pilate?

Acts 24: 10-12

When the governor had beckoned to him to speak, Paul answered, 'Because I know that you have been a judge of this nation for many years, I cheerfully make my defence, seeing that you can recognize that it is not more than twelve days since I went up to worship at Jerusalem. In the temple they didn't find me disputing with anyone or stirring up a crowd, either in the synagogues, or in the city.'

Felix silenced the accusing Jews and nodded to Paul to speak. Paul acknowledged that he was confident of a fairer hearing from Felix than in the Sanhedrin court, went straight to the allegations:

Firstly, if Paul had been in Jerusalem only seven days this was hardly enough time to have caused riots throughout the world v.5.

The second charge—causing a disturbance in the temple was untrue; the disturbance had been caused by the Jews who attacked Paul, and had to be rescued from them by the Roman soldiers.

The third allegation that he had tried to desecrate the temple was obviously absurd.

People look so stupid and dishonored when they are caught lying that it seems strange to subject oneself to such discomfort.

Acts 24: 13-16

Nor can they prove to you the things of which they now accuse me. But this I confess to you, that after the Way, which they call a sect, so I serve the God of our fathers, believing all things which are according to the law, and which are written in the prophets; having hope toward God, which these also themselves look for, that there will be a resurrection of the dead, both of the just and unjust. Herein I also practice always having a conscience void of offence toward God and men.

Although the Old Testament has plenty of promises of fire and brimstone for the evildoers, the New Testament brings a different message—one of love, not vindictiveness, and it brings the revelation of hope that there truly is life after death. This relaxed way of thinking way of thinking caused the Jews concern. Were they right?

Q. Has the Christian faith become too relaxed and undisciplined? The spoiled undisciplined child is not a happy one. This may be a painful thought for the Sees, but perhaps it needs addressing in the church. The Jews and Muslims maintain a firmer self-discipline.

Sees, and friends do you have any comments, thoughts or suggestions here?

Acts 24: 17-21

Now after some years, I came to bring gifts for the needy to my nation, and offerings; amid which certain Jews from Asia found me purified in the temple, not with a mob, nor with turmoil. They ought to have been here before you, and to make accusation, if they had anything against me. Or else let these men themselves say what injustice they found in me when I stood before the council, unless it is for this one thing that I cried standing among them, 'Concerning the resurrection of the dead I am being judged before you today!'

Paul referred to the Jews from Asia who recognized him in the temple in Jerusalem and who started the riots against him. The fact that they were not there in court in Antipatris may indicate that the high priest, who had come to bear witness against Paul, couldn't see any substance in the Asians' accusations and therefore thought it was better to leave them behind.

Paul said the only cause for dispute was a theological difference, which should be of no interest to the Romans.

The idea of the resurrection was undeniably a hugely difficult issue to put across convincingly. Many of us have been brought up with the idea, but Paul had to convince many people who had never even considered a life after the grave. The joyful news of the resurrection is interestingly, often a stumbling block to prospective Christians.

Acts 24: 22-23

But Felix, having more exact knowledge concerning the Way, deferred them, saying, 'When Lysias, the commanding officer, comes down; I will decide your case.' He ordered the centurion that Paul should be kept in custody, and should have some privileges, and not to forbid any of his friends to serve him or to visit him.

While he was governor of Judea and Samaria for six years, Felix would certainly have heard about Christianity. Paul, his prisoner, was a Roman citizen. The charges seemed purely academic and religious. However, if he let Paul go altogether, there would undoubtedly be another riot, and the Jews would kill him. Felix stalled for time and called for Lysias, the Roman commander in Jerusalem, the person who sent Paul to him in the first place.

Lysias would not be in a hurry to come, hoping he had seen the end of Paul. It seems nobody wanted to attend to this case. In the meantime, Paul had a very pleasant time in the palace with his friends, writing letters, with few restrictions on him.

Q. Are you conscious that we are sometimes given unexpected treats, or call it lucky breaks? Have we talked at all about guardian angels? Do you feel we have a mother, father, or beloved friend keeping an eye out for you? Who is yours?

Acts 24: 24-25

But after some days, Felix came with Drusilla, his wife, who was a Jewess, and sent for Paul, and heard him concerning the faith in Christ Jesus. As he reasoned about righteousness, self-control, and the judgment to come, Felix was terrified, and answered, 'Go your way for this time, and when it is convenient for me, I will summon you.'

Felix, as we know was an ex-slave, having married three princesses. His current wife, Drusilla was a Jew and may well have influenced Felix's opinions. Drusilla had been married off to the King of Euresa at the age of fifteen, but a year later, she had bravely, and maybe foolishly, deserted him for Felix. Drusilla and Felix had a son who was killed in the eruption of Vesuvius in AD 79. Poor things. She was no mouse of a woman.

Felix listened to Paul talk about his faith and God's judgment to come. Reflecting on his own life of greed and selfish ambition, he was terrified; feeling he was not facing a very rosy future according to Paul's theory—go away, Paul!

We are not told what happened when the Roman commander Claudius Lysias arrived with his story or what happened to the high priest and his cronies. Supposedly, they all decided there wasn't enough substantial evidence to pin on Paul. However, Felix evidently was not game to let him go, so the Paul issue became a stalemate.

Q. Sometimes it is easier to ignore or deny an issue rather than face up to it. Jesus never procrastinated. Is there something you feel you ought to do but, have put it away for another day, like Felix? ☺ Remember the pass option.

Acts 24: 26-27

Meanwhile, he also hoped that money would be given to him by Paul, that he might release him. Therefore also he sent for him more often, and talked with him. But when two years were fulfilled, Felix was succeeded by Porcius Festus, and desiring to gain favour with the Jews. Felix left Paul in bonds.

Because Paul had told Felix he was a Roman citizen, Felix thought Paul may have been wealthy enough to have paid for his citizenship, and also, having brought gifts of money for the poor in Jerusalem he apparently was not short of a bob. (Acts 24: 17) Perhaps Felix may be in luck and offered a hefty bribe to release Paul?

Felix really does appear to be a bit hopeless—laws about bribery were more often broken than kept by Roman administrators at the time. He was recalled to Rome two years later.

Felix suspected the Jews' report to Rome on Paul's case would not contain very complimentary remarks about him. Therefore, to please the Jews by leaving Paul in custody, he hoped to soften their comments in their report.

Anyway Paul was out of the way for now—unable to continue his troublesome preaching. Little did Felix know that during those two years, Paul was busy writing letters to the new churches that would go down in history influencing millions of people for the next two thousand years and beyond. These letters were miraculously kept safe to eventually leave their legacy in the Bible. The Great Arranger was still busily at work.

Q. However small, what legacy will you leave for the future? Forget humility to record and share your thoughts.

Summary of Chapter 24

Paul's accusers are called to Caesarea for the trial under Felix, the governor. They have an indecisive court hearing, and with little evidence and no witnesses, the court adjourns. As no decision is made about his future, Paul remains comfortably in Herod's palace for two years with his friends. Felix is sent back to Rome at the end of his term.

CHAPTER 25

The Court Case Continues before Festus and Agrippa

Acts 25: 1-5

Festus therefore, having come into the province, after three days went up to Jerusalem from Caesarea. Then the high priest and the principal men of the Jews informed him against Paul, and they begged him, asking a favor against him, that he would summon him to Jerusalem; plotting to kill him on the way. However Festus answered that Paul should be kept in custody at Caesarea, and that he himself was about to depart shortly. 'Let them therefore,' said he, 'that are in power among you go down with me, and if there is anything wrong in the man, let them accuse him.'

There is little written about the next governor, Festus, He arrived in Caesarea sometime in AD 59 and died in AD 62, so it was to be a short term of office. He was a nobler man than Felix and wasted no time in trying to establish a rapport with the Jewish authorities in Jerusalem. The Jews urgently brought up the case of Paul, hoping to get further with Festus than Felix.

The men who, two years ago, promised not to eat or drink until they'd killed Paul (Acts 23: 12-15) must have been pretty hungry by now. They were still out to kill him. Festus may have seen through their religious bigotry. He refused their request to bring Paul back to Jerusalem and shrewdly invited them to Caesarea to present their case against Paul.

The Jewish accusers hated Paul with enough fury to kill him. Professor William Loader referring to Jesus talking about the commandment *Thou shalt not murder* says Jesus shifts the focus from murder to anger which expresses itself in hate. The issue (or the danger) is not the *feeling* of anger but what we do with it."[41]

Q. How do you cope with anger? If you start with, 'Take a deep breath (again☺) . . .' please finish the sentence, and share your thoughts. It could be another of those laminated words of wisdom for the crowded fridge door.

Acts 25: 6-8

When he had stayed among them more than ten days, he [Festus] went down to Caesarea, and on the next day he sat on the judgment seat, and commanded Paul to be brought. When he had come, the Jews who had come down from Jerusalem stood around him, bringing against him many and grievous charges which they could not prove, while he said in his defence, 'Neither against the law of the Jews, nor against the temple, nor against Caesar, have I sinned at all.'

Fair-minded Festus got on with the job without wasting a minute. For two days Festus and his troop rode the sixty miles back from Jerusalem to Caesarea to reconvene the court the next day. Now that Festus was thereHe stood before the court and listened to the false charges he had heard before. Their evidence was thin. The Jews had no witnesses. Paul answered the old allegations again. He'd done no wrong in the temple or against Jewish law. This time he added his respect for Caesar, as Jesus had done at his trial. Paul may have felt that something good was going to happen at last.

John Donohue tells of an incident when the preacher at a Gospel Mass in New Orleans invited each person to turn to their neighbor and say, '*Something good is going to happen to you.*' The author says, 'It made me realize that there are such encouraging bouquets of words that we never offer each other . . . his words . . . blessed me for days.'[42]

---

[41]   Professor William Loader, 'The New Testament with Imagination,' published by Ridley Hall Books, p. 19.

[42]   John O'Donohue, 'Eternal Echoes: Exploring Our Hunger to Belong,' published by Bantam Books, P. 151.

Q. Are you game enough to say those words to someone today? 'Something good is going to happen to you today.' Is it a risky thing to say?

Acts 25: 9-12

But Festus, desiring to gain favor with the Jews, answered Paul and said, 'Are you willing to go up to Jerusalem and be judged by me there concerning these things?'

But Paul said, 'I am standing before Caesar's judgment seat, where I ought to be tried. I have done no wrong to the Jews, as you also know very well. For if I have done wrong and have committed anything worthy of death, I don't refuse to die, but if none of those things is true that they accuse me of, no one can give me up to them. I appeal to Caesar!'

Then Festus, when he had conferred with the council, answered, 'You have appealed to Caesar. To Caesar you shall go.'

Festus was Caesar's regional representative. He treated Paul respectfully by asking him if he would go back to Jerusalem. Paul knew there was little point in going over the same ground again by returning to Jerusalem and exposing himself to his bitterest enemies. He wouldn't get any fairer trial than he had last time, although Festus would conduct the trial himself. As a Roman citizen, Paul had the right to appeal to Caesar. He'd wanted to go to Rome for years; Jesus had promised him in his vision that he would go. (Acts 23: 9-11) Now was his chance.

By appealing to Caesar, he should get a fair hearing in the supreme court of the empire. Festus gladly accepted the opportunity to send Paul to Rome. However, he had a dilemma—what charges would he make against Paul which were sufficiently serious to warrant his being sent to the Supreme Court?

Q. What do you feel about the justice system in your country? Does it give you confidence? It is an interesting exercise to go and sit at the back of a court one day and listen to proceedings in a trial.

Ria: By the by, you will have difficulty getting into a family court and you need to be sure a trial is going to take place; otherwise you will waste a lot of time.

Acts 25: 13-22

Now when some days had passed, King Agrippa and Bernice arrived at Caesarea, and greeted Festus. As he stayed there many days, Festus laid Paul's case before the king, saying, 'There is a certain man left a prisoner by Felix; about whom, when I was at Jerusalem, the chief priests and the elders of the Jews informed me, asking for a sentence against him. To whom I answered that it is not the custom of the Romans to give up any man to destruction, before the accused has met the accusers face to face, and has had opportunity to make his defence concerning the matter laid against him.

When therefore they had come together here, I didn't delay, but on the next day sat on the judgment seat, and commanded the man to be brought. Concerning whom, when the accusers stood up, they brought no charge of such things as I supposed; but had certain questions against him about their own religion, and about one Jesus, who was dead, whom Paul affirmed to be alive.

Being perplexed how to inquire concerning these things, I asked whether he was willing to go to Jerusalem and there be judged concerning these matters. But when Paul had appealed to be kept for the decision of the emperor, I commanded him to be kept until I could send him to Caesar.'

Agrippa said to Festus, 'I also would like to hear the man myself.'

'Tomorrow,' he said, 'you shall hear him.'

Festus really did not understand why Paul should be sent to the Supreme Court in Rome, nor did he understand the charges that had been brought against Paul, or even why such a commotion should be caused by Paul's assertion that a man named Jesus who was dead, had been seen again. Maybe King Agrippa could fill in the facts and help him.

It may be helpful to go over the background of Agrippa and Bernice to put them into context to better understand Festus's dilemma.

It was customary for the local king, such as Agrippa, to pay his respects to a new procurator by visiting him soon after his appointment. King Herod Agrippa II was only seventeen years old when his father died in AD 44. So a Roman procurator had been appointed to guide the lad and administer the region until he was old enough to take over. This meant Agrippa had worked a great deal with the Romans. They ruled the area around the Sea of Galilee together and some territories beyond. During the Great Revolt of the Jews against the Romans in AD 66-70, Herod Agrippa was on the side of the Romans.

Herod Agrippa died in AD 100 at the ripe old age of seventy-three. He was known to be an expert on the theologically sensitive differences between the Pharisees and the Sadducees. He also had the authority of appointing (or disposing of) the high priest and was sometimes called the secular head of the Jewish church.

Festus thought Agrippa was just the man he needed to solve his problem.

Bernice was Agrippa's younger sister. When only thirteen years old, she was married off to their uncle Herod of Chalcis and had two sons. When her husband died, she lived with her brother Herod Agrippa. To silence rumors of incest, she married Poleman, the king of Cilicia, but she didn't like Poleman. After a year, she left him to become the mistress of the emperor's son Titus. With such close connections to the emperor, Agrippa needed to be sure of having a good case to send Paul to Rome.

Agrippa was interested in the story of Jesus. For some time, Agrippa had heard about Paul, too, and had been keen to meet them both.

Herod Agrippa was well portrayed in Andrew Lloyd Webber's musical *Jesus Christ Superstar* when he sang the verse 'And will you walk across my swimming pool, Jesus King of the Jews?' So here was Agrippa's chance. He hadn't got very far with Jesus, so perhaps Paul would perform for him.

Q. Who is the most exciting person you have met lately, excluding your partner? What were the qualities in that person that excite you? Will you share your experience?

Acts 25: 23-27

So on the next day, when Agrippa and Bernice had come with great pomp, and they had entered into the place of hearing with the commanding officers and principal men of the city, at the command of Festus, Paul was brought in. Festus said, 'King Agrippa, and all men who are here present with us, you see this man, about whom all the multitude of the Jews petitioned me, both at Jerusalem and here, crying that he ought not to live any longer. But when I found that he had committed nothing worthy of death, and as he himself appealed to the emperor I determined to send him. Of whom I have no certain thing to write to my lord. Therefore I have brought him forth before you, and especially before you, King Agrippa, that, after examination, I may have something to write. For it seems to me unreasonable, in sending a prisoner, not to also specify the charges against him.'

Festus rose to the occasion and held the interview—not in the courtroom, for this was not a trial, but in the auditorium, which was appropriate for the pomp of receiving the king and other high-ranking Jews and Romans.

There were five garrisons of Roman soldiers stationed in Caesarea, so their commanders would have automatically been included on the guest list. Festus appealed to Agrippa, hoping to get some help for his report to Rome. This was yet another given opportunity for Paul to spread his message in high places.

Summary of Chapter 25

Festus, the new governor, arrives in Caesarea where Paul is being held in semi-confinement. Festus goes to Jerusalem to meet the Jewish leaders, who ask him to send Paul back to Jerusalem to try him there under Festus's jurisdiction. Festus says, 'No, you come to Caesarea.' Festus talks to Paul and asks him if he'd go back to Jerusalem for another trial. Paul refuses, and Festus is at a loss as to what to do with him, just as Governors Felix and Claudius had been before him.

If Festus set Paul free, as he could see no crime in him, the Jews would undoubtedly murder Paul, but he could not leave him in prison without a conviction. Paul appeals to Caesar. Festus agrees but has difficulty writing the charge against Paul, because he cannot grasp the essence of the Sanhedrin's accusations. Herod Agrippa is an expert on Jewish religious matters, so Festus asks him for advice.

CHAPTER 26

Off to Rome at Last

Acts 26: 1-8

Agrippa said to Paul, 'You may speak for yourself.'

Then Paul stretched out his hand, and made his defence. 'I think myself happy, King Agrippa, that I am to make my defence before you this day concerning all the things that I am accused by the Jews, especially because you are expert in all customs and questions which are among the Jews. Therefore I beg you to hear me patiently.

'Indeed, all the Jews know my way of life from my youth up, which was from the beginning among my own nation and at Jerusalem; having known me from the first, if they are willing to testify, that after the strictest sect of our religion I lived a Pharisee. Now I stand here to be judged for the hope of the promise made by God to our fathers, which our twelve tribes, earnestly serving night and day, hope to attain. Concerning this hope I am accused by the Jews, King Agrippa! Why is it judged incredible with you, if God does raise the dead?'

With his hand, Paul motioned a greeting of respect to his distinguished audience, emphasizing how glad he was to stand before the well-informed King Herod Agrippa. Agrippa was allied to the Sadducees. Paul stressed the fact that he was brought up a strict Pharisee who believed in the resurrection.

Paul was excited to have the opportunity to witness his faith to this important audience and expressed his passionate belief that Jesus was the long-awaited Messiah. He explained that there is life after death. 'Why should anyone think this is incredible?' Paul asked.

Paul's enormous faith kept him buoyant through thick and thin. He'd been in custody for two years, having committed no crime, simply longing to go to Rome.

Q. How patient are you while waiting for a possible dream to come true? Waiting for a son/daughter, husband, or friend to come home from an overseas conflict comes to mind. Do you need someone to help keep your spirits up somehow? Who is it that helps you and how do they do it?

Acts 26: 9-11

'I myself most certainly thought that I ought to do many things contrary to the name of Jesus of Nazareth. This I also did in Jerusalem. I both shut up many of the saints in prisons, having received authority from the chief priests, and when they were put to death I gave my vote against them. Punishing them often in all the synagogues, I tried to make them blaspheme. Being exceedingly enraged against them, I persecuted them even to foreign cities.

Paul was honest enough to confess his earlier antagonism to the Christians. The reference 'I gave my vote against them [the Christians]' may indicate there was some system that entailed casting votes to pass the death penalty.

To blaspheme was an offence punishable by death.

Ria comments: Blasphemy is still punishable by death in some communities—think of the radical Islamists.

Q. How times have changed. We hear so many blasphemous swear words today. Can you think of the reason? Is it a sign something new is happening?

Acts 26: 12-18

'Whereupon as I travelled to Damascus with the authority and commission from the chief priests, at noon, O king, I saw on the way a light from the sky, brighter than the sun, shining around me and those who travelled with me. When we had all fallen to the earth, I heard a voice saying to me in the Hebrew language, "Saul, Saul, why are you persecuting me? It is hard for you to kick against the goads."

'I said, "Who are you, Lord?"

'He said, "I am Jesus, whom you are persecuting. But arise, and stand on your feet, for I have appeared to you for this purpose: to appoint you a servant and a witness both of the things which you have seen, and of the things which I will reveal to you; delivering you from the people, and from the Gentiles, to whom I send you, to open their eyes, that they may turn from darkness to light and from the power of Satan to God, that they may receive remission of sins and an inheritance among those who are sanctified by faith in me".'

The expression 'to kick against the goads' means resistance is useless. If an ox kicked against the goads, or his harness, he would be in bigger trouble than before.

Paul told his tale a third time. Each time it was slightly altered to accommodate his different audiences, but the pattern was the same. 'I am a Pharisee. Therefore, I believe in the resurrection. I persecuted the Christians. I had a vision of Jesus. This vision changed my life, my thinking, my speaking, and everything I do. I have done nothing wrong according to the Jewish law. Jesus told me Jew and Gentile alike are to be forgiven, loved, and cherished. Jesus commissioned me to spread this good news to the Gentiles.'

The Jews, loath to share their God with the Gentiles, would willingly kill anyone who threatened their exclusive status. They had readily killed Jesus, and others, and were ready and waiting to do the same to Paul by whatever means possible—foul or fair.

Q. Have you had the need to forgive someone unconditionally? Has it completely gone? The forgiving could be easier than the forgetting. Well done if it is really finished. It is such a hard thing to do. Pass if this one has been discussed before.

Acts 26: 19-24

Paul goes on to finish his story. 'Therefore, King Agrippa, I was not disobedient to the heavenly vision, but declared first to them of Damascus, at Jerusalem, and throughout all the country of Judea, and also to the Gentiles, that they should repent and turn to God, doing works worthy of repentance. For this reason the Jews seized me in the temple, and tried to kill me. Having therefore obtained the help that is from God, I stand to this day testifying both to small and great, saying nothing but what the prophets and Moses said would happen, how the Christ must suffer, and how, by the resurrection of the dead, he would be first to proclaim light both to these people and to the Gentiles.' As he thus made his defense, Festus said with a loud voice, 'Paul, you are crazy! Your great learning is driving you insane!'

Festus was completely out of his depth. Although Paul was probably a genius, Festus questioned his sanity. It is understandable for people to stumble over the resurrection, which cannot be proven. Jesus proved it to his friends, but that was a long time ago. Festus thought Paul was obsessive, and by anyone's reckoning, he probably was.

Like proponents of every new philosophy, Paul had to go to extremes to get his message across. We thought the Greenies were obsessive forty years ago. They had to go to extremes to make us realise that we humans are poisoning the world to extinction. Now we are generally all Greenies at heart.

Paul was saying everyone should be told that forgiveness is waiting for them, and there is a life after death as well. This news needed to be spread far and wide and still needs to be today.

Q. Do some or any of the group believe there is a life to come after death? If so, how are you able to spread the good news about it?

Acts 26: 25-32

But he said, 'I am not crazy, most excellent Festus, but boldly declare words of truth and reasonableness. For the king knows of these things, to whom also I speak freely. For I am persuaded that none of these things is hidden from him, for this has not been done in a corner. King Agrippa, do you believe the prophets? I know that you believe.'

Agrippa said to Paul, 'With a little persuasion are you trying to make me a Christian?'

Paul said, 'I pray to God, that whether with little or with much, not only you, but also all that hear me this day, might become such as I am, except for these bonds.'

The king rose up with the governor, and Bernice, and those who sat with them. When they had withdrawn, they spoke one to another, saying, 'This man does nothing worthy of death or of bonds.' Agrippa said to Festus, 'This man might have been set free if he had not appealed to Caesar.'

As Agrippa was an expert on religious matters, Paul acknowledged that Agrippa would understand what he was talking about. However, Agrippa was in a pickle. If he said 'yes', he believed that Moses prophesied Christ's resurrection; Paul would push him further to acknowledge that Jesus's resurrection was that fulfilment—then Festus will think Agrippa was insane too. But if he said 'no', he didn't believe in Moses prophesy he was in trouble with the Jewish Pharisees, whose teaching of the prophets was the very foundation of their faith.

Agrippa hedged the question by answering with another question, 'Does Paul really think he, Agrippa, can be persuaded to be a Christian on such a brief encounter?' Then he left promptly. This discussion had become too difficult.

Festus and Agrippa both realised that Paul had committed no crime worthy of death; however, he was still in danger from the Jews.

Paul solved everyone's dilemma by appealing to Caesar and remaining under Roman protection. If he had been released, he would certainly never arrive in Rome alive.

Summary of Chapter 26

Governor Festus invites King Agrippa and the district dignitaries to listen to Paul's case to help him work out the complex accusations brought against Paul. Paul tells the story of his conversion for the third time, pointing out that Jesus was the Messiah who was promised long ago by the prophets. King Agrippa is not sure how to handle the situation. He has been no help to Festus in finding a solution in writing a report to the emperor. Festus cannot set Paul free because he appealed to Caesar, the right of every Roman citizen. So to Rome he must go.

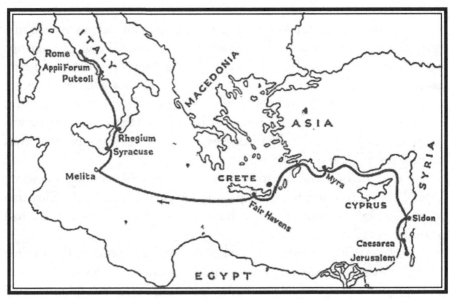

Map of Paul's Sea Voyage to Rome

CHAPTER 27

Storms at Sea

Acts 27: 1-2

When it was determined that we should sail for Italy, they delivered Paul and certain other prisoners to a centurion named Julius, of the Augustan band. Embarking in a ship of Adramyttium, which was about to sail to places on the coast of Asia, we put to sea; Aristarchus, a Macedonian of Thessalonica, being with us.

At last, after a two-year wait, Paul, Luke, and Aristarchus set sail. There was a long journey ahead, and it was already autumn. Julius needed to get a move on. They had to go north to Myra to find another ship for Rome. It was fortunate that faithful Luke was still with Paul. His accurate and descriptive writing, combined with his knowledge of seamanship, makes this a famous and exciting chapter in Acts, heralded as 'one of the most instructive documents for the knowledge of ancient seamanship.'[43]

Luke was not only a great colleague, author, and first-hand observer of Paul's life, but he was also the doctor that Paul needed. Paul records in 2 Corinthians 12: 7 that he had a severe medical problem. We're not told what it was. The perfect planner attended to every detail. Off they set for the adventure of their lives.

---

[43]   James Smith, 'The Voyage and Shipwreck of St. Paul, James Smith 'The Voyage and Shipwreck of St Paul, 4th edition. 1880. Information from F. F. Bruce, DD, formerly Rylands Professor of Biblical Criticism and Exegesis, University of Manchester. Contributor to the Acts of the Apostles, The New Commentary of the Bible Revised, published by Inter-Varsity Press, p. 1008.

Q. Have you had an overseas trip and felt a guardian of some description was keeping a careful eye on you? Were there any specific incidents to share?

Acts 27: 3

Thee next day, we touched at Sidon. Julius treated Paul kindly, and gave him permission to go to his friends and refresh himself.

Paul, this God-chosen Jewish Roman citizen was not only a fine speaker, a brilliant scholar, a fearless advocate, and a dynamite evangelist, but he also had excellent social skills. These were the gifts he needed to accomplish the enormous work he had been given to do.

Q. List the talents you have used this week, or if it is more comfortable pair up and list each other's talents.

Acts 27: 4-8

Putting to sea from there, we sailed under the lee of Cyprus, because the winds were contrary. When we had sailed slowly many days, and had come with difficulty opposite Cnidus, the wind not allowing us further, we sailed under the lee of Crete, opposite Salmone. With difficulty sailing along it we came to a certain place called Fair Havens, near the city of Lasea.

To avoid the winter storms, the centurion had to get his prisoner across the Mediterranean to Italy as soon as possible. It would have taken longer to go by land to Myra, so they sailed from Alexandria in a coaster carrying grain to Rome from Egypt, the great granary for the empire.

The strong westerly winds hampered their progress through the islands off Cnidus. They were beating into the wind, which is a very uncomfortable, slow course to sail. When they headed southward to Crete, the wind was on the beam (at right angles to the sails, which makes for a faster and more comfortable course). The pilot of the coaster probably wanted to get more sea room, away from the crowded islands, to take advantage of the shelter offered by mainland Crete. The trip to Fair Havens would take them about ten to fifteen days.

Q. Can you speculate how Paul and Luke may have been feeling on their first day at sea? Try giving as many reasons and examples of feelings as you can.

Acts 27: 9-12

When much time had passed and the voyage was now dangerous, because the Fast had now already gone by, Paul admonished them, and said to them, 'Sirs, I perceive that the voyage will be with injury and much loss, not only of the cargo and the ship, but also of our lives.' But the centurion gave more heed to the master and to the owner of the ship than to those things which were spoken by Paul. Because the haven was not suitable to winter in, the majority advised going to sea from there, if by any means they could reach Phoenix, and winter there, which is a port of Crete, looking northeast and southeast.

The Fast is the Jewish Day of Atonement fell on 5th October in AD 59. The sailing season lasted from Pentecost in May to the Feast of Tabernacles in October. To sail after mid-September was considered risky, and to sail after the 11th November was considered suicidal.

Fair Havens was the name for the modern city of Kalolimonias, whose coastal position was not protected from the winter's cold northwest winds. Apparently, Paul, the experienced traveller, was included in deciding the next move. But his warning fell on deaf ears, and the centurion, the senior officer on board, made the final decision. Understandably, Julius took the advice of the ship's captain to take the risk and dash across to Phoenix in order to find a more comfortable anchorage for the winter.

Q. Life would be very dull if we never took a risk or two (even writing a book is a risk). Do you have a story to tell about a risk that paid off, or did not pay off, that was significant in your life? I hope you have a laugh over some of these stories. Maybe it will be how you found your partner.

Acts 27: 13-17

When the south wind blew softly, supposing that they had obtained their purpose, they weighed anchor and sailed along Crete, close to shore. But before long, a stormy wind beat down from shore, which is called Euroclydon. When the ship was caught, and couldn't face the wind, we gave way to it, and were driven along. Running under the lee of a small island called Clauda, we were able, with difficulty, to secure the boat. After they had hoisted it up, they used cables to help reinforce the ship. Fearing that they would run aground on the Syrtis sand bars, they lowered the sea anchor, and so were driven along.

Oh, dear! They set sail, lured by the gentle wind. For historians and readers particularly from the armed forces, the small island of Clauda is the modern island of Gozo, off Malta. It is in the same area in which the Battle of Matapan was fought on 28th March 1941, during World War II.

The northeaster, mentioned in some translations, is a typhoon-like gale—the Euroclydon, which blew them off course, away from Phoenix. The lifeboat was towed along behind the coaster and was therefore in danger of being smashed against the ship in the storm. In the shelter they found behind the island of Clauda, they pulled the lifeboat aboard, in the driving wind and rain, to secure it safely.

If it was feared that a wooden ship might break up in a gale, '*They used cables to help reinforce the ship.*' Two men went up to the bow to pass a cable, or rope, under the ship, each holding one end. They flung the centre of the cable over the bow, allowing the ship to sail over it. Both men walked back, pulled the cable, and fastened it at the appropriate place—quite a job in the middle of a storm. Running aground on the sandbar of Syrtis would not be much fun for it is full of quicksands.

Q. Have you ever been in a storm at sea with a tale to tell?

Acts 27: 18-20

As we labored exceedingly with the storm, the next day they began to throw things overboard. On the third day, they threw out the ship's tackle with their own hands. When neither sun nor stars shone on us for many days, and no small storm pressed on us, all hope that we would be saved was now taken away.

Desperate measures were needed. Battered by the storm, shivering in the driving rain, they somehow coped with the violent movement of the ship, as the sailors tipped some of the precious wheat, and anything else they could lay their hands on, into the sea.

Relentlessly the storm raged on. Navigating with no moon or star to guide them, they had no idea where they were going or which way they should turn, all they knew was facing death by drowning was a real possibility.

Q. Have you faced death? When? What were your thoughts?

Acts 27: 21-26

When they had been long without food, Paul stood up in the middle of them, and said, 'Sirs, you should have listened to me, and not have set sail from Crete, and have gotten this injury and loss. Now I exhort you to cheer up, for there will be no loss of life among you, but only of the ship. For there stood by me this night an angel, belonging to the God whose I am and whom I serve, saying, "Don't be afraid, Paul. You must stand before Caesar. Behold, God has granted you all those who sail with you." Therefore, sirs, cheer up! For I believe God, that it will be just as it has been spoken to me. But we must run aground on a certain island.'

There may be several reasons why the men had gone without food. The difficulty of cooking in the galley in these conditions wouldn't have helped; seasickness and salt water in the stores may also have contributed to the lack of meals. Morale was low. Where were the centurion, the owner, and the helmsman? It seems that in the moment of crisis, Paul was the only one to take control.

Although no one had listened to Paul's warning at Fair Havens, he was human enough to say, 'I told you so!' But he also had good news for them all. Inspired by his vision, he told them to have courage, fear not, trust God, and trust me; we must run aground, but every one of you will be saved.

What a relief to have a strong leader in times of disaster, a tower of strength like Paul whose calm authority relieved the inevitable feeling of panic.

Q. Have you been in a situation of near panic, like Paul? Did you, or someone else, have to take control?

Acts 27: 27-29

But when the fourteenth night had come, as we were driven back and forth in the Adriatic Sea, about midnight the sailors surmised that they were drawing near to some land. They took soundings, and found twenty fathoms. After a little while, they took soundings again, and found fifteen fathoms. Fearing that we would run aground on rocky ground, they let go four anchors from the stern, and wished for daylight.

The Adrian Sea, not to be confused with the Adriatic Sea, is charted well south of Italy on the maps of the time. After fourteen hideous days of storm, they may have felt and heard a different tempo in the waves and surf, which made them sense that land was near. They anxiously took soundings to avoid the ship from breaking up on rocks.

Four anchors were dropped over the stern to allow the ship to point toward land as the tide came in. Should the anchor drag, the ship would at least be heading in the right direction.

We are not told who prayed, but regardless of religion, people seem to pray to something, someone, anyone when in grave danger.

Q. No one quite knows who God is, but the mystery of a spirit friend has been the center of attention of religion for billions of people for thousands of years.

It is a big request, but write a sentence or two to describe your God to the Wincs. Who or what are God, the Son, and the Holy Spirit?

A and A's, did you have a faith at one time? Can you share how you lost it? Other faiths, can you describe the one you worship?

Acts 27: 30-32

As the sailors were trying to flee out of the ship, and had lowered the boat into the sea, pretending that they would lay out anchors from the bow, Paul said to the centurion and to the soldiers, 'Unless these stay in the ship, you can't be saved.' Then the soldiers cut away the ropes of the boat, and let it fall off.

Letting the lifeboat float away would certainly stop the sailors from escaping, but it meant nobody else could use it either. Maybe they were all in such a state of jitters that some idiot cut the ropes in panic, as some of the sailors tried to save their own skin by sneaking off in the only lifeboat—leaving the rest to sink or swim.

Maybe Judas felt like the frightened sailors when he betrayed Jesus to the authorities. He may have thought at least by looking like a goodie goodie he would escape the brewing trouble. These sailors were luckier. They did not pay such a high price as Judas for their cowardice.

Acts 27: 33-35

While the day was coming on, Paul begged them all to take some food, saying, 'This day is the fourteenth day that you wait and continue fasting, having taken nothing. Therefore I beg you to take some food, for this is for your safety; for not a hair will perish from any of your heads.' When he had said this, and had taken bread, he gave thanks to God in the presence of all, and he broke it, and began to eat.

Paul saw to the crew's physical needs, aware they had had no regular meals for two weeks. He encouraged them not only to eat before the ordeal ahead, for heaven only knew when they would get their next meal, but also reassured them again that they would all be saved. It was a huge undertaking to confidently assure two hundred and seventy-six men, some of who could probably not swim, that no one would drown in those frightful conditions.

Paul had not a clue what God had in mind, without even a lifeboat to help them get ashore. He demonstrated his great faith as he publicly gave thanks to God, in whom he had complete trust.

Q. Proverbs 29: 25: 'Fear of man will prove to be a snare, but whoever trusts in the Lord is kept safe.' Can you find, and share, an example in your own life when you, or someone you know, was very afraid but trusted their safety entirely to a Greater Being?

Acts 27: 36-38

Then they all cheered up, and they also took food. In all, we were two hundred seventy-six souls on the ship. When they had eaten enough, they lightened the ship, throwing out the wheat into the sea.

Nothing like a bit of food inside to make everyone feel better. You can feel the different atmosphere on board, as everyone tucks into food and busily prepares for a landing. The poor ship owner is about to lose his coaster with the rest of his cargo of wheat as well. It is interesting that in moments of great danger or threatened health, our priorities change dramatically and things like money and possessions cease to be important.

Survival, health, and people are really the only things that matter. Why does it take such dramatic events to bring us to our senses?

Q. It always seems miraculous the way grizzling, hungry children perk up the instant they are given some food. Is there a parallel here with people who have experienced the food from an awesome spiritual experience? Can you think of an example?

Acts 27: 39-41

When it was day, they didn't recognize the land, but they noticed a certain bay with a beach, and they decided to try to drive the ship onto it. Casting off the anchors, they left them in the sea, at the same time untying the rudder ropes. Hoisting up the foresail to the wind, they made for the beach. But coming to a place where two seas met, they ran the vessel aground. The bow struck and remained immovable, but the stern began to break up by the violence of the waves.

The number of people on board indicates that Paul's ship must have been pretty big.

They prepared to beach. The ancient ships had a steering paddle at either side of the rudder, which had been roped to the stern. So with four anchors dragging behind and the foresail billowing, they headed straight for the sandy beach. Feelings must have been very tense on board. I wonder where that centurion, Julius, was all this time. He's very quiet.

To Paul's great credit it sounds as though there was no panic. Trusting their leader, Paul, whose faith was rooted in the promise Jesus gave to him in his vision, the ship ploughed ahead through the surging sea, for better or worse. Well, it was a bit worse than better because they hit a sand bar, and the stern broke up, but they were now within swimming and floating distance to the shore; the incoming tide helped sweep them along.

Acts 27: 42-44

The soldiers' counsel was to kill the prisoners, so that none of them would swim out and escape. But the centurion, desiring to save Paul, stopped them from their purpose, and commanded that those who could swim should throw themselves overboard first to go toward the land; and the rest should follow, some on planks, and some on other things from the ship. So it happened that they all escaped safely to the land.

Aha, the centurion has come out of hiding at last. No wonder he didn't want anything to happen to Paul, for that would leave him in charge of this lot alone at this unbelievably dangerous moment. There seemed to be some remarkably impractical soldiers on board. First, they cut the lifeboat adrift (it would have been very handy at this moment), and then they tried to kill the only person on board who is doing anything to save them.

At least the centurion seemed to have come to his senses at last. With the ship in pieces, they swam, floated, and clung to flotsam and jetsam to land safely on the beach.

Summary of Chapter 27

This amazing chapter gives a graphic picture of Paul's journey by ship from Caesarea in Israel, up the coast to Turkey, down and across to Crete. After a tumultuous storm, spending weeks at sea, and against enormous odds, including a shipwreck, Paul, trusting faithfully in God, manages to land nearly three hundred people safely ashore, on a beach in Malta, known at the time as Melita by the Greeks and Romans, appropriately named by a Phoenician word meaning 'refuge'.

CHAPTER 28

The End of a Journey?

Acts 28: 1-4

When we had escaped, then they learned that the island was called Malta. [From the NIV Bible: 'Once safely on shore, we found out that the Island was called Malta.'] The natives showed us uncommon kindness; for they kindled a fire, and received us all, because of the present rain, and because of the cold. But when Paul had gathered a bundle of sticks and laid them on the fire, a viper came out because of the heat, and fastened on his hand. When the natives saw the creature hanging from his hand, they said one to another, 'No doubt this man is a murderer, whom, though he has escaped from the sea, yet Justice has not allowed to live.'

The thoughtful islanders quickly built a large fire for the nearly three hundred people, as they squelched around in sopping clothes, cold in the October or November rain and wind. Moving about to gather wood would warm them up a bit. Mercifully, there were no children, women, or elderly people among them. Poor Paul, how much more can he take? How terrifying for him to see a snake suddenly sink its fangs into his hand.

Q. Unless you have already done it, what is the most frightening experience you have had in your life? Will you write and share it?

Acts 28: 5, 6

However he shook off the creature into the fire, and wasn't harmed. But they expected that he would have swollen or fallen down dead suddenly, but when they watched for a long time and saw nothing bad happened to him, they changed their minds, and said that he was a god.

Luke, the doctor, is the only New Testament writer to talk about swelling after the snakebite. It is thought that the snake was a *Coronella leopardinus*, which can be found in Malta. There are no poisonous snakes on the island today,[44] but there may have been at that time. Paul nonchalantly shakes the snake into the fire, poor thing. Then, horror of horrors, from the ridiculous to the sublime, the islanders change from thinking Paul must be a murderer to thinking he must be one of the gods.

This is the second time it has happened, to Paul's great discomfort. The Lystrans thought Paul and Barnabas were gods in

Acts 14: 11-13.

Q. What was the end of your frightening story? Have you shared it?
Did anyone 'hero worship' you?

Acts 28: 7-10

Now in the neighborhood of that place were lands belonging to the chief man of the island, named Publius, who received us, and courteously entertained us for three days. It happened that the father of Publius lay sick of fever and dysentery. Paul entered in to him, prayed, and laying his hands on him, healed him. Then when this was done, the rest also who had diseases in the island came, and were cured. They also honored us with many honors, and when we sailed, they put on board the things that we needed.

---

44   Snakes on the island of Malta. Information from F. F. Bruce, DD, formerly Rylands Professor of Biblical Criticism and Exegesis, University of Manchester. Contributor to the Acts of the Apostles, The New Commentary of the Bible Revised, published by Inter--Varsity Press, p. 1010.

liii Quoted from the Wikipedia Internet web site The Sonnini Manuscript.

Can you imagine this kind man, Publius, entertaining and probably feeding, nearly three hundred shipwrecked people for three days? Maybe being the chief man (with such an appropriate-sounding name), he was able to use the resources of the island.

One wonders what they did for clothes. It would be unlikely they had the right currency to buy more. Maybe the local residents sorted out their 'to give to the Op-Shop' clothes. Paul and Luke proved useful, running a medical clinic for the sick.

Q. What a joy to have Publius nearby. Was this another miracle/coincidence? Have you had any such miracle/coincidence recently?

Acts 28: 11-14

After three months, we set sail in a ship of Alexandria which had wintered in the island, whose sign was 'The Twin Brothers.' Touching at Syracuse, we stayed there three days. From there we circled around and arrived at Rhegium. After one day, a south wind sprang up, and on the second day we came to Puteoli, where we found brothers, and were entreated to stay with them for seven days. So we came to Rome.

It was February AD 60 by now. Spring was in the Mediterranean air as they sailed away from Malta. Luke's observant eye gives us a picture of the ship's figurehead of the heavenly twin gods Castor and Pollux, sons of the god Zeus, the guardian patrons of sailors.

From Malta, they probably sailed in another grain ship, to Syracuse/ Sicily, on to Rhegium on the toe of Italy, and finally up to Puteoli, called Pozzuoli today, in the Bay of Naples, the chief port for Rome. There were both Jews and Christians living there. We can only guess that these Christians were a result of the great explosion of Christianity at Pentecost some twenty-five years earlier.

Q. Can you think of five things that, in the past twenty-five years, have changed the way we live in the world?

Acts 28: 15-16

From there the brothers, when they heard of us, came to meet us as far as The Market of Appius and The Three Taverns. When Paul saw them, he thanked God, and took courage. When we entered into Rome, the centurion delivered the prisoners to the captain of the guard, but Paul was allowed to stay by himself with the soldier who guarded him.

How exciting for the Christians in Rome to hear that the great leader Paul was almost there. He'd written to them some three years earlier to say he wanted to come one day, not knowing how he'd get there or in what circumstances. The Roman Christians had to travel more than thirty miles to greet him.

No wonder Paul was encouraged and grateful that he'd made it at last. It would have been a thrill to spend time and worship with them, even if he was in chains and trotting around lightly handcuffed to his guard. Perhaps the guards had become Christians by this time, for they had spent months in Paul's company, and he never missed an opportunity to convert people to his passion for Christianity—even the shallow-spirited centurion Julius may have succumbed.

Having said a sad farewell to all the crew who had survived this frightening journey with him, Paul was probably exhausted after the ordeals of the past months. However, he was in Rome!!!! He enthusiastically welcomed 'the brothers.'

Q. How long does Luke tell us that Paul's journey had taken since leaving Jerusalem?

Acts 28: 17-20

It happened that after three days Paul called together those who were the leaders of the Jews. When they had come together, he said to them, 'I, brothers, though I had done nothing against the people, or the customs of our fathers, still was delivered prisoner from Jerusalem into the hands of the Romans, who, when they had examined me, desired to set me free, because there was no cause of death in me. But when the Jews spoke against it, I was constrained to appeal to Caesar, not that I had anything about which to accuse my nation. For this cause therefore I asked to see you and to speak with you. For because of the hope of Israel I am bound with this chain.'

Luke switches here from the lovely warm welcome of the Christians to the ordeal of explaining his situation to the leaders of the Jewish temple. Paul calls them together before the pack of lies from the scheming accusers in Jerusalem reached them.

Diplomatically, Paul called the Jewish leaders 'brothers,' emphasizing his strong connection with them as fellow Jews, as he tells them his story.

Paul respected the Jewish tradition all his life. He never intended to change religions; he only wanted the Jews to acknowledge that Jesus Christ was the Messiah, the one for whom they had been waiting for so long.

Thought: This man's life work changed the history of the world. Let's not underestimate the power of one. Do you have a story about the power of one?

Q. Have you ever thought about the people whose lives you have influenced or changed? Forget humility; who are they?

Acts 28: 21-22

They said to him, 'We neither received letters from Judea concerning you, nor did any of the brothers come here and report or speak any evil of you. But we desire to hear from you what you think. For, as concerning this sect, it is known to us that everywhere it is spoken against.'

Many Christians in Rome who would have heard about the great Paul and been excited to see him. Now was their chance. However as they had not heard about Paul's troubles with the Jewish authorities in Jerusalem, they were very surprised to see him in chains.

Q. Do you have an exciting story to tell about longing to meet a famous or great mentor—and then been given the chance? Have a good time sharing your stories.

Acts 28: 23-27

When they had appointed him a day, many people came to him at his lodging. He explained to them, testifying about the Kingdom of God, and persuading them concerning Jesus, both from the Law of Moses and from the prophets, from morning until evening. Some believed the things which were spoken and some disbelieved. When they didn't agree among themselves, they departed after Paul had spoken one word, 'The Holy Spirit spoke rightly through Isaiah, the prophet, to our fathers, saying,

"Go to this people, and say, in hearing, you will hear, but will in no way understand.

In seeing, you will see, but will in no way perceive.

For this people's heart has grown callous.

Their ears are dull of hearing.

Their eyes they have closed.

Lest they should see with their eyes, hear with their ears, understand with their heart, and would turn again, and I would heal them".'

Paul was proving to be a big draw card. Imagine a similar case today—a leader of a new religious, in chains, comes to explain his doctrine to the church. Very strange.

Maybe the nearest to this situation is the preaching and writing of Bishop Spong, the retired Episcopalian bishop. Not that he is in chains, but he has very confronting Christian views. When he visits anywhere, like Paul, mobs of people flock to hear him. And in the same way plenty of people believe and agree with him, and a few don't.

How often do we hear, but choose not to understand when it comes to change? How much easier it seems to be to say, 'No, it won't work.' I once suggested a BBQ for our local elderly residents, and was told, 'No because they tried it twelve years ago, and it rained.'

Q. Have people's 'hearts grown callous. Their ears dull/eyes closed'? Or are we all just waiting for a change? But it won't change unless we change it. Have you seen any encouraging signs, locally or globally, that this is happening?

Acts 28: 30-31

Paul stayed two whole years in his own rented house, and received all who were coming to him, preaching the Kingdom of God, and teaching the things concerning the Lord Jesus Christ with all boldness, without hindrance.

This feels like the unfinished symphony. We can only speculate about the reason Luke stopped writing the story so suddenly. Perhaps he died while they waited two years in semi-confinement for Paul's accusers to arrive from Jerusalem for the court hearing.

It's strange that if something had happened to Luke, Paul did not record it in one of his letters.

Paul was busy writing to the earlier established churches—to the Colossians, Corinthians, and his friends Timothy and Philemon. Luke, too, may have been writing his Book of Acts just now.

The accusers eventually arrived. Apparently, they were not in a hurry and weren't any more successful in their effort to destroy Paul than they had been with Governors Felix, Festus, or Claudius beforehand.

It was Clement of Rome (listed as the second or third bishop of Rome after St. Peter) who suggested in early literature that Paul was released after two years and went on to Spain. Apparently, Paul went back to Asia to revisit his earlier established churches at some stage.

The lost chapter of the Acts of the Apostles, also known as the Sonnini Manuscript,[45] is a short text which claims to be the translation of a manuscript containing the twenty-ninth chapter of the Acts of the Apostles. This chapter is said to detail St. Paul's journey to Britain, where he preached to a tribe of Israelites on Ludgate Hill, the site of St. Paul's Cathedral. However, there is little conclusive evidence to substantiate the claim.[2]

Whatever the reason for Luke's abrupt ending, the Peter and Paul story finishes with the statement that God's salvation is for every single person on earth who wants it.

Paul had preached the Gospel story in Jerusalem, across the Middle East, penetrating Europe, certainly as far as Rome, and maybe farther. Peter remained preaching to the Jews until he and Paul were crucified in

---

[45]   Quoted from the Wikipedia Internet web site The Sonnini Manuscript.

Rome between AD 67 and AD 68, during the reign of the cruel Roman Emperor Nero.

In apparent harmony, these saints proclaimed the promised Messiah—a new Kingdom of God on earth—laying the foundation stones for the Christian faith, at enormous personal sacrifice. It is a legacy, and a miracle, that Luke's writing has been preserved for two thousand years.

All there is to say, to finish this chapter, is a heartfelt

thank God for these brave men and the message they delivered.

Summary of Chapter 28

Having arrived safely at Malta, wet and soggy from their shipwreck adventure, a snake leaps from the fire to attach itself to Paul. The chief of the island, appropriately called Publius, takes care of nearly three hundred survivors for three months. They all set off for Italy and arrive in Rome to the joyful welcome of the Jewish Christians. Paul explains why he is in chains, which does not deter him from preaching daily from his lodgings for two years. The story comes to an abrupt end, and there is only speculation as to what happened to him until his crucifixion with Peter during the reign of the cruel emperor Nero in AD 67/68.

events during the first century

Paul appeals to Caesar and is shipwrecked on the Way to Rome. Under house arrest for two years waiting for accusers to arrive from Jerusalem. Writes letters to Ephesians, Colossians, and Philippians. Luke abruptly finishes the Book of Acts – Perhaps he died, but maybe he did't!

Paul's unsubstantiated 4th missionary journey to Spain, travelled on to revisited the churches in Asia Minor, Crete and Greece. Returns to Rome, imprisoned. Writes letters to Colossians, Corinthians, and to his friends Timothy and Philemon. Paul and Peter were martyred in Rome. Ist is believed Paul was beheaded and Peter crucified during the reign of the cruel Emperor Nero in 67/68 AD

Paul's third missionary to Turkey and Greece with Timothy and Silas. Imprisoned in Jerusalem and sent on to Caesarea. He writes Corinthians I and II. and Romans.

Paul's second Missionary journey via Cyprus, to Turkey and Greece with Mark and Barnabas. Paul writes his letters to the Thessalonians and Galatians. Returns to Jerusalem, imprisoned and appears before the fair minded Roman pro-consul Gallio.

Herod Agrippa dies. Paul trips to and from Jerusalem. Paul begins his journey to Jerusalem his first missionary Mark and with Barnabas Asia Minor. Cyprus and Mark to first missionary journey He writes a letter to the Galatians. Jerusalem Council.

Early Persecutions. James martyred Peter in prison. Paul's conversion on the road to Damascus. Stephen stoned to death. Christians persecuted and scatter all over the Middle East.

Jesus Christ was crucified. John Baptist begins. Jesus ministry begins. a Jesus was probably born Saul was later than year Jesus. Christ was born.

"Good people rooted in the sun... you shine ...so finely encircled by the arms of God."
Hildegard of Bingham
12th century mystic

60 ad

59 ad

62-67ad 67-68 ad

53-57ad

52ad

51ad

46-50 ad

43-44ad

35 ad

27 ad

5bc

Diagram of important events during the first century AD.

SOME MAJOR EVENTS DURING THE LAST TWO MILLENNIUM

First Century. 5 BCE approx. Jesus Christ was born.

26 A.D Jesus baptised as his ministry begins.

28/29 A.D John the Baptist was beheaded.

26 A.D Jesus was crucified.

30 A.D Pentecost and conversion of St. Paul.

46-61 A.D Paul's Missionary journeys establishing churches in Turkey, Greece and Italy.

2nd to 3rd Centuries—Christians burned alive, and fed to the lions until the end of 3rd century.

Polycarp 69-155 A.D Bishop of Smyrna, understandably regarded as a saint, was persecuted for his great faith. He is said to have hidden in a farm house, where he had a vision of a pillow on fire. He turned and said, "It must needs that I shall be burned alive". He refused to try and escape. When his captures arrived he greeted them graciously, ordered food for them, before he was led away. He was bound to the stake and set alight, but when the fire appeared not to burn him, he was stabbed to death.

Augustine of Hippo 350-430 A.D, an influential philosopher, and the patron saint of brewers, printers, theologians, the alleviation of sore eyes, and many cities and diocese.

Quintus Tertullian, 160-220 A.D, a prolific author from Carthage in Africa, and often called "the father of Latin Christianity and founder of Western theology". Perhaps he is most famous for using the term 'Trinity', which at first was rejected as heresy. The Trinity was later accepted so he narrowly avoided martyrdom.

4th-6th Centuries – Christianity is accept—the long struggle for survival is over.

Emperor Constantine 272-337 A.D. was exposed to Christianity by his mother, Helena. He experienced a dramatic event in 312 at the Battle of Milvian Bridge. Reputedly, Constantine looked up and saw a cross of light above the sun, and with the words, "by this, win!" after which he commanded his troops to adorn their shields with a Christian symbol and thereafter they were victorious. In 313 A.D. Constantine announced religious freedom and tolerance, while returning all confiscated land and church possessions.

325 A.D Original of the Nicene Creed—was a statement of the Christian faith dedicated in Nicaea Italy. "I believe in . . ." with strong statements that its design will not be changed.

570 ad—632 ad Life of the Prophet Muhammad. Section two contains further details of the life of this prophet.

598 A.D St Augustine, a Benedictine monk was chosen by Pope Gregory the Great, to lead a mission to "Christianize" the English Kingdom of Kent under King Ethelbert from his Anglo-Saxon paganism. Augustine was to become the first 1st Archbishop of Canterbury in 598, and considered to be the founder of the Church in England.

7th to 9th Century—Christianity "comes of age" with the Roman Empire becoming the *Holy* Roman Empire and the writing of the Liturgy.

710 A.D Constantine was the last pope to visit to Constantinople's Orthodox Church until Pope Paul VI visited again in 1967. Constantine's primary motivation for the trip was to "forestall" a rift between Rome and Constantinople.

800 A.D Charlemagne was the first roman emperor to be crowned by the pope. But it is Otto I the Great, crowned in 962 who is considered to be the first *Holy* Roman Emperor. This title remained until the end of the Holy Roman Empire in 1806 during the Napoleonic Wars.

861 A.D Missionary expansion through the Middle East by St Cyril and Methodius, the two Byzantine Greek brothers born in Thessaloniki who worked as Christian missionaries across the Middle East, particularly among the Slavic people, for which they received the title *"Apostles to the Slavs"*.

10th-14th Centuries—an age of exploration & travel, and massive social changes through feudal system. Greed for power and wealth among church leaders, with grumblings & crumbling within the Church of Rome. 1054 ad **Great Schism**—East/ Orthodox church splits from the West/Roman Catholic church—one of the issues being whether to use leaven or unleavened bread in the Eucharist.

1066 Invasion of England organized by the Pope, led by Normandy Duke William carrying the crusade banner to protest against the erring English church.

1075 Dictatus papae—27 statements gave the Pope extreme powers.

1095-1272 The Crusades (from the Latin word for *cross*) were a series of wars between European Christians and Muslims fighting for the Holy Land (Palestine, especially the city of Jerusalem.) Regaining control over the Holy Land was not the only goal, Christians were concerned by the rapid Islamic expansion.

1170 Thomas Becket was murdered on the steps of Canterbury Cathedral in England for irritating the King Henry II. His story has been immortalized in the play by T.S.Elliot, *Murder in the Cathedral*.

1302 Papal bull Unam Sanctam declares submission to the Pope is necessary for salvation.

1379-1418 The Great Schism within the Roman Church. Three rival Popes were asked to resign in 1417, the matter was resolved with a re-election.

15th-16th centuries—Renaissance brings rapid change, spiritual renewal, new hope, but religious persecution continues.

1525 William Tyndale translates the New Testament into English—and was burned at the stake as a heretic for his trouble.

1530 & 1541 The Confession of Ausberg— a controversial and important statement of faith of the Lutheran Church caused the last conference between Roman Catholic & Protestant churches for four centuries.

1533 Henry VIII breaks with Rome—and heads the Church of England.

1536 Calvin and others introduce an austere religious philosophy.

1483-1546 Martin Luther, a German priest and professor of theology, whose life's work was translating the Bible into language the people could understand. Outraged, he wrote his famous *Ninety-Five Theses* in 1517 to expose the corruption and fraudulent financial practices in the church. Lutheran services became popular, replacing the Roman Catholic services, giving him the title of Father of the Protestant Church, but resulting in his being excommunication by the pope and condemned as an outlaw by the emperor.

1556 Archbishop Cramner translated the English book of Prayer before being burned at the stake for his work.

1555-1558 "Marian martyrs" were protestants, and if discovered and found guilty, were first excommunicated, then handed over for execution or burned. Scotland's Roman Catholic Queen earned the name of Bloody Mary.

17th-19th Centuries—political revolutions from 1789-1917. Many died for "liberty, equality and fraternity"

1611 King James version of the Bible's first print.

1703-91 The Wesley brothers wrote hymns.

1789 the French Revolution.

1830 John Newman's "high church" Oxford Movement tried to reverse the Church of England back to Rome.

1859 Charles Darwin's "Theory of the origin of species" rocked the religious world.

1863 Abraham Lincoln– the Emancipation Proclamation freed and prohibited slavery.

1867-69 The Papal state merged with the Kingdom of Italy and the Vatican Council endorsed papal infallibility.

20th-21st centuries

1964 Patriarch Athenagoras 1 of the Greek Orthodox Church and Pope Paul VI met in Jerusalem for the first official act of friendship by the two churches since the Schism in 1054.

1965 Pope John XXIII & Paul VI "opened the windows" to all Christians at the Vatican Council.

4th April 1968 Rev. Dr. Martin Luther King Jr. was assassinated. A Baptist minister who devoted his live to racial discrimination through nonviolent protests in the United States. His impromptu famous speech, "I dreamed a dream . . ." was deliver during a rally, when the gospel singer Mahalia Jackson shouted from the crowd, "tell them about the dream, Martin!" Dr. King stopped his speech and began to speak from his heart, punctuating his points with "I dreamed a dream . . ." He was assassinated by a prison escapee, James Earl Ray on April 4th, 1969. He is immortalized by an annual holiday near his birth date on the third Monday in January each year.

1948 the State of Israel is announced. After the horrors of World War II the United Nations sanctioned a British resolution to divide Palestine into two states, one Jewish and one Arab, to address their conflict. On 14th May 1948 the Jewish community in Palestine published a *Declaration of Independence* announcing the creation of the State of Israel, hoping to mark the end of the Arab-Israeli conflict.

1974 the Ordination of Women into the Anglican Church. The first woman was ordained in the Anglican Church in Hong Kong, then came Canada in 1975, USA and NZ in 1977, England in 1994—and then the flood gates opened—but what next? Women began to be ordained and consecrated Bishops in 1989 in Massachusetts USA.

1980 Pope John Paul II greeting to all Christians "in love and truth" on the 450th Anniversary of the slit of the Protestant and Roman Catholic Churches at the Confession of Ausberg in 1530.

1995 Pope John Paul II (1978-2005) issued the *Orientale Lumen,* encouraging reunion between East and West churches.

2001 September 11—a devilish event—so huge—it changed the world forever, and the search for a world in harmony continues.
When will we ever learn? When will we ever learn?

Information for these events is gratefully obtained from the amazing and generous Wikipedia Encyclopedia website.

Diagram of Significant Events during the Last Two Millennia

SECTION TWO

A Glimpse of Twelve Major Religions and Beliefs

The information for this section, unless stated, is obtained from the web sites of the various religions or from books identified in the bibliography.

The Abrahamic Faiths:
1. Judaism 2200 BCE
2. Christianity AD 40
3. Islam AD 600
4. Baha'i faith AD 1817

Vedic or Indian Faiths:
1. Hinduism 2500-1500 BCE
2. Jainism 600 BCE
3. Buddhism 500 BCE
4. Sikhs AD 1500

Chinese Traditions:
1. Confucian 550 BCE
2. Daoism, sometimes called Taoism 500 BCE

Japanese Traditions:
Shinto 712 BCE

Original traditions of Africa, Australia, and North America whose origins stretch too long ago to identify.

ABRAHAMIC RELIGIONS

1. Judaism 2200 BCE

If you and I were born in Israel, we may be Jews and believe in *Judaism*.

Founder: The Jews originated from nomadic groups about four thousand years ago. Abraham is said to be the father of the Jewish people. The tribes were not originally called Jews, but *bene* Abraham or Jacob or *bene* Israel—*bene* means 'descendants' or 'sons of' whoever. Jacob was sometimes called Israel, hence the name given to the Israelites. These groups settled on the east coast of the Mediterranean Sea, which was later called Judaea, from which the names Judaism and Jews derived.

The Holy Book of the Jews is called the Tanach or, more commonly, the Torah. The writing of the Old Testament in the Christian Bible and the Muslim Holy Book, the Koran, originated from the Torah. All record the stories of creation, the Exodus, and the early establishment of the Jews in Israel.

The Jews' great festival is the Feast of the Passover (the Christians' Easter occurs roughly at the same time).

The Jews believe that God will send his messenger to establish his perfect kingdom to rule and nothing can defeat the will and purpose of God. There is little mention of a life after death in the Jewish faith, simply that 'the souls of the faithful are in the hand of God, where shall no torment touch them'.

God's laws were given to the prophet Moses on Mt. Sinai on the Saudi Arabian peninsula, as the Jewish people were making their way out of slavery from Egypt. They travelled across the desert to the Promised Land, Israel, with the promise that their descendants would be God's chosen people and become a great nation.

The laws or commandments given to Moses state:

You shall have no other gods before me.

You shall not have idols but will show love to a thousand generations
of those who keep my commandments.

You shall not swear or blaspheme.

Keep holy the Sabbath Day, the last day of the week shall be a day of
rest.

Honor your father and mother.

You shall not murder, commit adultery, steal, or tell lies.

You shall not covet or be jealous of other people's possessions. (Ex. 20: 6)

2. Christianity 40 AD

If you and I were born in Europe, America, Australia, or many other
countries that were influenced by Christian missionaries, we may believe
in *Christianity.*

Founder: Jesus Christ, born in Bethlehem about two thousand years
ago. Jesus claimed to be the Christ, meaning messiah or savior, the
promised messenger from God, which was foretold by the prophets of the
Old Testament. He has the title of Jesus Christ, meaning Jesus the messiah
or savior.

Jesus, like Muhammad, who was born some six hundred years later,
was concerned at the hypocrisy of the religious leaders and the falling
away of the Jews from God's true message. Love, forgiveness, and the
resurrection of Jesus three days after his death, proving the ultimate
glorious message that there is life after death, are the center messages of
the Christian faith.

Jesus preached openly and critically about his concerns until the
situation with the Jewish authorities became so tense—they crucified
him.

The Bible is the Christians' holy book. Christians focus particularly
on the New Testament, which records the story of Jesus' life and includes
letters written by his followers to the new churches after his crucifixion.

During the fourth century, there was a major split in the Christian
camp over doctrine and the defining nature of Jesus. Was he divine, human
and divine, or simply human? And what was the nature of Mary, the

mother of Jesus? During this controversy, the Orthodox Church was born and moved its headquarters from Rome to Constantinople. The Orthodox Church spread east to many countries across northern Europe, as far north as Russia. Centuries later in AD 1054, the final separation of the Orthodox and Catholic churches, sometimes known as the Great East-West Schism, was formalized.

During the 16th century a further split occurred, the *Protest Reformation,* caused four more divisions, the Lutheran, Reform, Baptist and Anglican. From these roots, over thirty thousand denominations are recorded, reputedly making Christianity the largest religion, which includes the Roman Catholic and Orthodox churches, of two billion people worldwide.

Summary of Christianity in the words of Jesus: 'The first commandment is to love your God with all your heart and with all your soul, and with your entire mind. And the second is like it: Love your neighbor as yourself.'

3. Islam AD 600

If you and I were born in Iraq, Iran, Asian Malaya, Indonesia, or many Middle Eastern countries, we would likely be Muslim and believe in Islam, which is the second largest religion in the world with more than 1.25 billion followers worldwide. Islamic beliefs were grounded in Judaism and Christianity, that there is only one God—Allah. Moses and Jesus were God's messengers, but Muhammad was the last and most perfect messenger.

Ramadan, the Muslims' main annual event, is intended to teach patience, humility, and spirituality. It is held in the ninth month of the *Islamic calendar,* which lasts 29 to 30 days, during which time Muslims refrain from *eating* and *drinking* before sunset each day.

Founder: Muhammad was an Arab born in Mecca, Saudi Arabia, in AD 570 and died in AD 632. Muhammad was an orphan, reared by his uncle, and became a camel driver, trader, husband, and father. Muhammad was concerned by the lawlessness of his people and the fact that they worshiped many gods.

When Muhammad was about forty years old, he was praying in a cave near Mecca. He believed God spoke to him through an angel and asked him to be his prophet. Thereafter, he preached his central message that

'There is no other god but Allah—Muhammad is his messenger.' Whenever Muslims say Muhammad's name, they also say 'Peace be upon him'.

Islam is an Arabic word meaning 'to submit'. The Qur'an is the holy book of Islam, believed to be the words that Allah revealed to Muhammad, which makes Allah, not Muhammad, its author.

The five Pillars of Islam is the term used for the duties incumbent on every Muslim.

Salat: the name for the formal prayer, with set movements, to be conducted five times a day; praising Allah and asking for his guidance.

Zakah: is the name for an obligation to give a portion of one's wealth to the poor.

Hajj: is the commitment to journey to Mecca, a pilgrimage to be made at least once in a lifetime; it will include a visit to the Ka'bah, a small building believed to have been built by Abraham and one of his sons, Ishmael. Muhammad restored the building in his lifetime.

Sawm: means fasting from dawn to dusk during the month of Ramadan. This is a time to reflect on self-discipline and charity.

Jihad: or ijihad when translated means 'striving to serve God'. It demands the need for personal struggle to overcome temptation, to enable a human being to live a good life. For many Muslims, the Jihad also includes the holy duty to try to win others over to Islam by setting a good example in their lives. They believe, as Christians once believed, that the solution to world problems would be a worldwide state of their religion.

The six beliefs of Iman.

1. Belief that Allah is the one and only God
2. Belief that there are many angels, although we are often not aware of them.
3. Belief in the holy books, the Dawsud, Torah, Gospel and Qur'an.
4. Belief in the prophets. There have been over 124,000 messengers sent to mankind since the beginning of time.

5. Belief that we will be resurrected after we die and we shall be judged on the day of Oiyamah.
6. Belief that Allah has predestined all things. Even if you fail to see him, he sees you.

Various Traditions in Islam

There was much fighting between factions before and after Muhammad's death, when two main parties emerged—the Sunni and the Shia Islam or Shi'ites dynasties. A third and smaller group, the Sufis also emerged.

Sunni means 'the path shown by Muhammad'. This group represents about 90 per cent of the world's Muslims. The Sunnis believe the successor to Muhammad should come from the person best qualified to do the job.

The Shi'ites although the smaller group, are dominant in Iran and exist in southern Iraq, Lebanon, and Bahrain. The Shi'ites believe that the caliph or successor to Muhammad came from a direct descendant of 'the House of Muhammad' Ali, Muhammad's cousin and son-in-law.

The main difference between the two groups is their allegiance to their founders.

Sufism is characterized by brotherhoods that practice their own rituals. Sufis organize themselves into 'orders', or groups, called Tariqas.

Sufism seeks a closer personal relationship with God through special spiritual disciplines. Singing and dancing may be introduced, which lasts much longer than the usual daily prayer—often in a trance or ecstasy.

In Summary—from the Qur'an : 3: 104: 'Let there arise among you an ummah advocating all that is good, enjoining what is right and forbidding what is wrong. They are the ones to attain peace and prosperity.'

4. Bahá'í Faith AD 1817

Bahá'í, is a worldwide community of some five million people, represented in most of the nations in the world. If you or I were looking for an unaffiliated religion away from the mainstream faiths, we may choose the *Bahá'í Faith*.

It is the youngest of the world's Abrahamic-independent religions. Its founder, Bahá'u'lláh (1817-1892), is regarded by Baha'is as the most recent in the line of God's messengers that stretch back beyond recorded time, that include Abraham, Moses, Buddha, Krishna, Christ, and Muhammad.

The central theme of Baha'u'llah's message is that humanity is one single race and that the day has come for its unification in one global society. God, or Baha'u'llah, has set in motion historical forces that are breaking down traditional barriers of race, class, creed, and nation and that will, in time, give birth to a universal civilization. The principal challenge facing the peoples of the earth is to accept the fact of their oneness and to assist the process of unification.

The Baha'i Faith was founded in Persia, called Iran today, in the nineteenth century. Religious history is seen to have unfolded through a series of divine messengers, each of whom established a religion that was suited to the needs of the time and the capacity of the people. Baha'i believes each messenger taught the next. The role of humanity is need for the gradual establishment of peace, justice, and unity on a global scale.

VEDIC FAITHS

If you and I were born in India, we may belong to one of the oldest known religions in the world, the *Vedic faiths*, whose origins are believed to stem more than four thousand years ago. We may be a Hindu, Buddhist, Jain, or Sikh, among others.

The word *Veda* means 'sacred knowledge'. In the Vedas, Brahman is the name given to the source of all and is the power that brings the universe into being. Brahman is 'one without a second'—beyond anything that can be known and cannot be described. Brahman establishes a place beyond the world for the soul and equates with God, the creator.

The Vedas have timeless hymns and chants addressed to the gods or goddesses of all creation, those of the wind, sea, sun, fire, and more. The sacred cow sums up the generosity of nature.

The five gifts that are used in worship include milk, curds, ghee (fat), urine, and dung—the cow is a reminder that human life is dependent on the non-human.

The rules and sacrificial rituals of the Vedas, which are believed to have no human origin, have been passed down through the ages.

All three Vedic faiths view life as cyclical, being an endless cycle of birth, growth, decline, and death, leading back to the cycle of rebirth and reincarnation.

1. Hinduism 2500-1500 BCE

Hinduism is based on the Vedas. The term *Hindu* comes from 'Sindhu', the Greek word for *Indus*, which is the river in the northwest of India. The Muslims, after their conquest of northern India from the twelfth century on, called the non-Muslim people Hindus, a name adopted by the British in the nineteenth century. It is the dominant religion of India.

Hinduism is a diverse system of thought with beliefs involving devotion to a single god while accepting the existence of others. Most Hindus believe that the spirit or soul—the true '*self*' of every person—is eternal and is ultimately indistinct from the supreme Brahman spirit. Whoever becomes fully aware of the true self (*ātman*) as the innermost core of one's own self reaches total freedom.

For many Hindus, their most revered book is Bhagavad Gita, 'The Song of the Lord,' which contains lessons on how human lives should be conducted without thought for oneself through devotion to God in the form of Krishna.

In the Hindu tradition, there are four purusharthas, or aims that motivate people to find the way to a purposeful and fulfilling life—to be contributors to the good of society.

Dharma is the pursuit of righteousness and means to learn to uphold and to know how to behave in whatever circumstances.

Karma literally means "deed" or "act", which determines the destiny of a human according to his past actions, and binds the soul to this physical world and to the cycle of rebirth and reincarnation.

Artha is the accumulation of wealth to be able to support the family and give to charity.

Moksha means to 'release', or 'let go' to allow ones awareness to find a pathway to God.

The family is the foundation of Indian life, and although women had limited roles in public life, their influence in the home is paramount.

Animals, particularly cows, are protected, as they play such an important religious and economic role in traditional Hindu life.

2. Jainism 600 BC

If you and I were born in the south of India, we may belong to the Jainism religion, the second oldest known religion in the world.

The name Jain comes from Jina, which means 'victor', to overcome the passions of self-centeredness, promote positive thinking and believe humans are the 'architects' of their own lives.

Jains have mainly divided into two sections, which may be identified by their dress. Non-violence, reverence for all life, positive attitudes and tolerance are high priorities. Karma **"(defined as the inevitable**

consequence of one's actions)" in Jainism is very different from the Hindu philosophy.

The Jains have built beautiful temples all over India and observe many festivals.

3. Buddhism 500 BC

If you and I were born in almost any country in the world, we may be a Buddhist.

Founder: The name Buddha, which means 'awakened' or 'enlightened', is given through the story of a prince of the Shakya clan in India, called Siddhartha Gautama. The son of a king in Kapilavastu, he led a sheltered life in the palace. One day he was driven through a park and saw an old decrepit man; on the second day, he saw a diseased man; and on the third, he saw a dead man. On the fourth day, he saw a man who seemed to be completely at peace. Gautama decided to seek that kind of peace. He left his wife and son Rahula and went into the forest to learn from two spiritual teachers. He practiced extreme austerity, but this did not bring him peace.

He, therefore, decided to try a middle way between the pleasures of the palace and the silence of the forest. After some days of meditation, he found enlightenment—he had found his way to peace of mind.

From this experience, the enlightened one, or the Buddha, began his ministry of teaching. The heart and foundation of Buddhist belief is summarized in the Four Noble Truths and the Noble Eightfold Path.

The Four Noble Truths

First Truth: Dukkha means one accepts that suffering exists and is a part of living in the world.

Second Truth: Dukkha, the world's suffering, exists due to the thirst for endless youthfulness and the craving for material worldly possessions.

Third Truth: There is a way to end this thirst and craving.

Fourth Truth: The path to end suffering may be found by following the Eightfold Path, which, when practiced, achieves the path to peace of mind which is the philosophy of Buddha.

The Eightfold Path

1) Right understanding of the Four Noble Truths.
2) Right behavior by gentleness, courtesy, thoughtfulness, and avoiding the craving for material wealth.
3) Right speech—tell the truth and speak kindly with openness and honesty.
4) Right action—no stealing, lying, drug taking, drunkenness, or cheating.
5) Right living—earning a salary through work that does not hurt or harm anybody.
6) Right effort—positive thinking in all situations.
7) Right mindfulness—meditation with active thoughts, focusing on issues that affect our world now and in the future. This is in contrast to yoga in which the mind is stilled.
8) Right concentration—brings one to that place of peace or enlightenment, if the correct path is followed.

New Buddhists have spiritual leaders to instruct and guide them along the path.

Buddhism is found worldwide but mainly in India, Southeast Asia, Tibet, China, Korea, and Japan.

In summary of the Vedic faiths 'There are many paths in the Vedic faiths that lead to release or liberation from reincarnation . . . the final release can be described as union with God, . . . returning to the supreme peace or the quenching of all desires.'[46]

4. Sikh AD 1500

The Sikh faith began in the Punjab, northern India. The word means 'follower' or 'disciple' of the original guru, Guru Nanak, who was succeeded

---

[46]   Susan Meredith's 'The Usborne Book of World Religions,' p. 161.

by ten further teachers until the writings were instituted in 1708. A Sikh man may always be distinguished by his beard and the turban swathed around his head, which is a symbolic sign of the need to serve others, regardless of status. Devotees must meditate to progress toward enlightenment. Music and poetry play a major part in the worship of a Sikh service.

In many places, the Sikhs give food to hundreds of thousands of poor people from their free kitchens that are attached to the temple.

As with most religions, there have been times of tension and violence between the religions of Sikh and Hindu and Muslim.

CHINESE BELIEFS

If we were born in China, we may be a *Confucianist*, a *Daoist*, or a *Buddhist*.

There are many strands of religions in China, with no one single national creed. There are three major philosophies of Confucius, the Daoists, and Buddha. There is also a growing following of Christianity and Islam. The quest for immortality is central to Chinese belief.

1. Confucianism 550 BC

Confucius was a Chinese philosopher whose writings were intended to advise the rulers of China during his time, 551-479 BC.

His writings stress the following needs: to show dignity to all people, to behave appropriately, to work hard to achieve 'beautiful conduct', to respect your ancestors and be considerate to others, to aim for peace and harmony with the world, and to be in contact with the spiritual forces of the universe, including those of nature.

Confucius wrote: 'Heaven is the author of the virtue that is in me.' Although Confucianism is not classified as a religion for some reason, it appears to have all the essential hallmarks.

2. The Daoists 500 BC

Daoism began from the scripts of two writers, Laozi and Zhuangzi, of which very little is known. Daoism is a combination of religion and philosophy, following the contrasting energies of yin, and yang. Yin is the clam, representing the feminine gentle energy of water, clouds, and the moon; while yang represents the hard, aggressive masculine elements of sun, stone, and storms. These two elements, although seemingly opposite, are necessary for human existence and survival.

From the Dao De Jing:

> You look at it, but it is not to be seen:
> Its name is formless.
> You listen to it, but it is not to be heard: its name is soundless:
> You clutch it, but it is not to be held:
> These three escape analysis, and therefore they
> Merge and become one.
>
> The great Dao flows everywhere.
> It may go to the left or the right.
> The countless things that there are owe their existence to it,
> And it does not disown them.
> When its work is finished, it does not take possession,
> It clothes and feeds everything,
> But it does not take over as Master.
>
> Because it never makes any claim to greatness,
> Therefore it completely achieves greatness.

What a wonderfully original picture of God.

JAPANESE TRADITIONS

If you and I were born in Japan, we may believe in *Shinto* or *Buddhism* or a bit of both.

As with the Chinese, it is difficult to find a definite path for religions in Japan, with many original and different strands of spiritual beliefs.

After World War II many new religions were introduced in Japan, so it is difficult to identify one above another in today's world.

A clearer picture began to emerge in AD 574-622, as Buddhism was endorsed by the central government. The Japanese Prince Shotoku became known as the father of Buddhism; however, the local native religions remained important to Prince Shotoku.

Shinto 712 BC

The word *Shinto* meaning "Way of the Gods" is the oldest spirituality of the Japanese people. Shinto practices were first recorded in the 7th and 8th century. Shinto today is a term that applies to public shrines suited to various purposes such as war memorials, harvest festivals, romance, and historical monuments, as well as various sectarian organizations. The vast majority of Japanese people who take part in Shinto rituals also practice Buddhism.

Christianity was introduced to Japan in 1549 but was banned in 1612 and banned again in 1638 as Western influences were believed to be diluting the Japanese culture. Christians were persecuted and went underground.

When a Shinto warrior dies in battle, his soul always returns to Japan. This belief had a dramatic effect during World War II when the Kamikaze pilots wore white scarves—a white cloth worn by previous Japanese warriors. It was believed that only these special Shinto pilots' souls would return to the shrine in Tokyo.

This has caused considerable tension over the years between the Shinto and Buddhists during formal ceremonies around this shrine.

In summary: The Kami of the spiritual world guides and binds families together.

ORIGINAL TRADITIONS.

If we originally came from North America, we may belong to one of the five hundred tribes of *Native American*, who have many languages and religions.

Native American

Most of these religions believe in a spiritual world above our own, in which the Great Spirit and all spirits live. They believe that there is constant communication between the two worlds, and many tribes carve large sacred poles to connect them.

The medicine men play an important role in leading prayer and dance. They also carry the responsibility of being mediators and communicators between the physical and spiritual worlds. Many tribes believe that the souls of the dead go to the spiritual world, where there is no hunger, cruelty, or sadness.

Australian Koori or Aborigines

If you and I were an original Australian, belonging to one of the five hundred or so Koori tribes with some two hundred separate languages, we would probably 'worship the sanctity of the land and pray to the great spirits', who came into the world in the form of men and women and animals and birds.

The Aboriginals had no written language, so spirituality has been handed down for thousands of years by stories and songs. The great spirits gave the people the law, which tells them how to live, whom to marry, and what ceremonies are to be held in which places. These special places are their sacred sites, to be seriously protected and preserved. The land, or Mother Earth, is supremely important to them.

Summary: Their belief is centered on the spirits of creation, of which each person is a part of the whole.

CHALLENGES AHEAD

It has been an inspiration to reflect collectively on these different religions and to see quite clearly that our creator has sent many messengers with the same underlying message.

Many people find religion simply too hard, particularly when looked through negative historical lens—seeing religion as the perpetrator of war. However, to look at the twenty wars over the past two hundred years, it is clear to see that many wars have been motivated by greed, while religion may sometimes have been thrown in as an excuse.

For billions of people religion provides a way of life that brings comfort, hope, friendship, and support in the world today, and it will continue as long as man walks the earth, but there are challenges ahead before we can leave a safer world for the grandchildren, and it would be helpful if the 'Whoever is up there' would send another Peter, Paul, Myrtle, Wilfred, or Harry to help us cope with these hurdles.

First Challenge—Religious Intolerance

Like spoiled children, many people of faith continue to create tension by saying, 'But my God is *the best*, or my Jesus is the *only one*, or my prophet is *better* than your prophet'. Perhaps one of the most dangerous of all is the dream of claiming the holy city, Jerusalem, exclusively—fanning the flames of war.

Religious intolerance is not confined of course to any one religion. When a solution can be found to begin to dissolve inter-faith hatred and obsession the world will be a safer place. Madeleine Albright asks in her book *The Mighty and the Almighty* why fanatics are acting as 'vehicles for sticks of gelignite on their way to holy oblivion. [and] . . . believe destruction is their sacred duty and only path to glory.'[47] President Bill Clinton promotes a peaceful theme, 'The challenge for our leaders is to use *what we have in common* as a basis for defeating the most extreme elements and draining support for terror. Once people acknowledge their common humanity, it becomes more difficult for them to demonize and destroy each other. It is far easier to find principled compromise with one of "us" than with one of "them".'[48]

And finally to the atheists, who need to be respected as any other. Our new found friend, Ria has a similar outlook to the great actress Katherine Hepburn who said, 'I'm an atheist, and that's it. I believe there's nothing we can know except that we should be kind to each other and do what we can for others.'[49]

This surely sums up the philosophy not only of most atheists but of most religions as well.

Yann Martel highlights this point beautifully in the *Life of Pi* when, as a child, he discovered his favorite teacher was an atheist, 'It was my first clue that atheists are my brothers and sisters of a different faith, and every word they speak speaks of faith. Like me, they go as far as the legs of reason will carry them—and then they leap.'[50] And so say most of us.

---

[47] Madeleine Albright's 'The Mighty and the Almighty: Reflections on Power, God, and World Affairs,' p. 208.

[48] President Bill Clinton wrote the introduction to Madeleine Albright's 'The Mighty and the Almighty,' p. xiv.

[49] Katherine Hepburn's web site.

[50] Yann Martel's 'Life *of* Pi,' originally published in Canada by Alfred A. Knopf, a division of Random House of Canada. 'Life *of* Pi' was the winner of The Man Booker Prize 2002. Pi is speaking with affection about his favourite teacher, Mr. Satish Kumar, p. 28. Yann Martel's 'Life *of* Pi,' originally published in Canada by Alfred A. Knopf, a division of Random House of Canada. 'Life *of* Pi' was the winner of The Man Booker Prize 2002 speaking with affection about his favourite teacher, Mr. Satish Kumar, p. 28.s

Second Challenge—Climate Warming

We need to apologize to the polar bears drowning in warmer seas and to the shameful number of species becoming extinct or endangered due to our human greed and thoughtlessness. We can only try, individually and collectively, to undo the damage. Rachel Kohn, writing on the vulnerability of the natural world, the massive oil spills, nuclear reactor fallout, gas leaks, etc. assaulting the natural environment reinforces the view "that the human race has reneged on its responsibilities to the earth."[51]

However Al Gore quoted the scientists Stephen Pacala and Robert Socolow on his DVD *An Inconvenient Truth*, saying, 'Humanity already possesses the fundamental scientific, technical, and industrial knowledge to solve the carbon and climate problem.'[52] Hooray, let us hope humanity has found it in time.

So the challenge of global warming seems to be addressed if *everyone* along with governments, contribute and do our best—conscientiously.

One simple idea to reduce carbon emissions would be to call on our politicians to encourage parliaments to lawfully enforce turning off lights in all office blocks at night around the world to make an enormous contribution to the reduction of carbon emission.

'Politicians are a renewable resource! The solutions are in our hands,'[53] said Al Gore. So what are we waiting for?

Third Challenge—the Pandora's Box: Over population

This must be the most silent and dangerous hurdle to overcome. In 1950, there were two billion people on earth; by the turn of this century, there were more than seven billion—nearly trebling in half a century. Even if we managed to achieve a fairer distribution of food and water, is the world big enough to cope with such a rapidly growing population—who all need energy, water, and heat to live?

---

51 Dr Rachael Kohn's 'New Believers: Re-imaging God,' chapter headed 'Redeeming Religion from Itself,' p. 189.
52 Al Gore's DVD 'An Inconvenient Truth.'
53 Al Gore's DVD 'An Inconvenient Truth.'

A torrent of forty thousand babies and children die each *day*, while even greater numbers are born. Apart from the United Nations Population Fund, which encourages and assists family planning in many underprivileged countries, with only moderate gestures from far too few governments, it would seem the human race faces a disastrous future.

Some responsibility must rest on the shoulders of religious leaders who previously did not understand the damage they were doing when forbidding contraception and birth control to their flock. They were presumably unaware that they were dangerously contributing to the extinction of the human race—but they do know now.

Welfare benefits for a maximum of two children per family would certainly curtail enthusiasm for larger families in many areas—perhaps a further call to the politicians is needed here.

Only when we replace ourselves—full stop—and allow natural attrition to cope with the rest, will future generations have a chance. Throughout history, the pendulum swings in balance with the exception, unfortunately, of population growth. A glimmer of hope appeared in The *Melbourne Anglican* newspaper's article headed, 'Overpopulate and perish, says Anglican body', which reported on the 2010 General Synod. The Public Affairs Commission 'urged Christians to become acutely aware of the issues that surround population and to be prepared "to make personal and corporate sacrifices for the common good of all creation".'[54]

This third hurdle may prove to be the hardest one of all to overcome.

To conclude with wise words from great minds

Mahatma Gandhi, Nelson Mandela, Martin Luther King Jr., and many other saintly people have opened doors to welcome renewed religious thinking to help arrive at a place of peace.

The great Mahatma Gandhi said, 'All through history, the ways of truth and love have always won. There have been thugs and murderers, and for a time they may seem to flourish, but in the end they always fall—always.'

Mahatma Gandhi's grandson, Arun Gandhi continues along the same vein, 'The common thread running through the lives of God's many

---

[54] *The Melbourne Anglican* newspaper, June 2010, no 482 on the front page article headed 'Overpopulate and perish, says Anglican body.'

messengers is love, compassion, understanding, commitment, and respect for all living creatures. It might therefore be assumed that by exhibiting these qualities, they were demonstrating to the rest of humanity the way our Creator expects us to live . . . I am convinced that at the root of the spiritual problem we face today is the intense competitiveness we have injected into religion. Each of us believes our religion is the best . . .'[55]

David Tacey finds a word for the self-righteous, 'Religion is sometimes full of itself and this is what Paul Tillich, the influential theologian, referred to accurately as "the sin of religion".'[56]

So it would seem that whether our spiritual mentor is called Yahweh, Elohim, Allah, Krishna, Buddha, Jesus, Brahman, Kami, God, Om, Waheguru, Vishnu, physics, nature, creation, Mother Earth, *someone up there*, or simply, *something but it is too big to understand* (probably the most accurate description of all), it is essential for our children, families and friends' happiness that these names be embraced unconditionally in harmony, devoid of superior possessiveness, but in love.

And now to use an old Irish verse to say goodbye—with just a little license—may the road rise up to meet you, may the wind be always at your back, may the sun shine warm upon your face, and the rain fall softly upon your fields, and until we meet again, may 'whoever it is up there who is too big to understand' hold you in the palm of His hand.

ooOoo

---

[55] Arun Gandhi, fifth grandson of the legendary Mahatma Gandhi in a foreword to Sankara Saranam's book 'God with Religion: Questioning Centuries of Accepted Truths,' p. xx.

[56] Associate Professor David Tacey, Reader in Arts at La Trobe University, Victoria, Australia, 'The Spirituality Revolution: Emergence of Contemporary Spirituality,' published by HarperCollins Publishers, p. 21.

SECTION THREE

Two year discussion program
series one and series two
dreams 7-12.

Notes for group leaders are found at the end of this section.

FIRST YEAR—
SUMMARY OF SERIES ONE

The first series is taken mainly from the author's book, *O my God! Where are You?* with commentary, questions and discussion reflecting on the gospel of St Luke from beginning to end.

    a.   This book is available from *www.theworldinharmony.com*

No.7 the Advent dream of Joy from *O My God! Where are You?* x three weeks. Chapters 1-2.

Sample: Week 1 Ch. 1: v 46-56 "My soul praises the Lord . . ."

Take about ten minutes or so, and join Mary by writing a song of thankfulness. It need not rhyme or be 'clever'. Just write down whatever it is for which you feel grateful . . . .

No.8 the Lent dream of Hope from *O My God! Where are You?* x six weeks. Chapters 20-24.

Sample: Ch.: 24 v 30-32 and v 33-35 *"Were not our hearts burning within us while he talked with us . . ."* *"They got up and returned at once to Jerusalem . . . ."It is true! The Lord has risen . . . ."* The elated friends, bubbling with excitement, rush off to tell their friends. What has been one of your greatest moments . . . .

No.9 the Ordinary Sundays dream of Miracles from *O My God! Where are You?* x twenty eight weeksChapters 3-19.

Sample: Ch.: 8 v 4-8 *"He who has ears to hear, let him hear."* We have all fallen into different categories during our life. Our spiritual seed may have been 'eaten by birds', withered from lack of 'moisture' choked by 'thorns', or flourished on good ground to bear fruit. Which of these . . . .

ooOoo

Second Year— Series Two

Notes for group leaders are found at the end of this section.

No.10—the Advent dream of Santa's Christmas Party.

Sometimes it is rewarding to look at an event from a different angle. In his Gospel, Luke concentrates particularly on prayer, rejoicing in the teaching of Jesus, the role of women, concern for the poor, the presence of the Holy Spirit, the family circle, and establishing the importance of including all people into the family of God.

These points not only highlight the spirit of Christmas, but also encompass the qualities of St. Nicholas, sometimes, or nearly always called, 'Santa'. This dream is about educating the community about the relevance of St. Nicholas, and connecting him to the Christmas story.

Week One: Planning Session

The focus for this plan is to invite, and involve families who would normally never be in church—or even perhaps a Christian church—on Christmas Day.

If you are able to find a quiet moment, write in your journal the answers to the following three questions on whether you found this Advent activity helped:

a) calm your pre-Christmas rush?

b) made your pre-Christmas time more helpful and 'holy' for your family and friends?

c) embraced people who may be lonely, disillusioned by the church, hurting, or not interested in religion, to have a happy time and 'give God a go' this Christmas?

1. Begin by gathering a few stalwart faithfulls, who have imagination and enthusiasm, to a coffee morning to discuss a Christmas celebration with a bit of a difference.

Explain the plan is to hold a party in a barn, a stable, a home or shed—preferably not in a church or chapel, centered around a scene of the Nativity, to tell children and adults the story of St. Nicholas—Santa. Santa is all over the place at Christmas time, but does anyone know why? Has he anything, or everything, to do with the birth of Jesus? There is a story about St Nicholas which can be found by 'contact us' on *www. theworldinharmony.com*

At this meeting plan and choose:

1. A venue
2. Who to invite—as many as will fit into the venue, from as wide a choice of church and 'non church' families as possible. Decide how the invitations will be sent out, or will you go public? Special invitations could be sent to 'outside the church family' ones.
3. Who will play the piano, and choose the songs and carols (it would be wonderful if you could possibly try to forget Rudolph please—he doesn't quite fit the atmosphere here).
4. Could someone type up and run off an appropriate number of song sheets. Would the church help?
5. Which format to use: will the children be invited to dress up as angels or shepherds, or even make it fancy dress? A few angels scattered about always makes for fun and a good atmosphere, and nobody need feel left out. Perhaps someone in the church could offer to have a Sunday Angel Making session to include all the especially invited families
6. Would you have a 'Santa' to read the story, or have a "and guess whose come to see you now" at the end of the story?
7. Who will organize a decorated Christmas tree?
8. Who will organize the nativity scene
9. Who could find a sensible sized figure of Santa to put in or beside the nativity scene?
10. Who is or will be Santa?
11. Finally the Feast! On the invitations or posters everyone could be invited to bring a small plate for the Feast. It would be good if

someone could make a Christmas cake, but as there will be too much food anyway, it is not important.

12. If you need an activity while the Mum's are meeting, ask a 'crafty' person to help make crackers, or bonbons, or whatever you call them, with the children. Collect little Santas, and anything that goes with your theme—trinkets, rubbers, pencil sharpeners, beads, bracelets, whistlers etc. There are a host of websites to help give fun ideas

13. Or making a home-made nativity scene could be the activity getting the children to write their names on something. Again there are thousands of patterns and designs by googling 'make your own nativity scene'.

14. Remember to think of all the things I have forgotten. Happy planning.

Week Two—Visit the venue, who and what go where, etc. Where does the Feast take place? What will you drink?

Week Three—cooking, sewing, typing/copying, drinks, decorations and lights, chairs, song sheets.

Week Four—party time preparation in the morning.

Suggested format for 'The Celebration'.

1. Welcome.

2. Everyone sits on hay bales, on rugs on the floor, or on BYO chairs for a few carols.

3. Settle the children down quietly. The reader asks them a few questions about their Christmas, talks about Christmas and Jesus' birthday, and why Santa seems to appear only at Christmas time. What has he got to do with Jesus—who knows his *real* name, and why does he come around to celebrate Jesus' birthday every year + any other good topical questions you can think of to involve the children. Then they listen to the story of St. Nicholas around the nativity scene. It would be beautiful if Santa told his own story—the children will never forget it.

4. Now it is time for the children to move about. Encourage the children to sing 'Away in a Manger' on their own, and other songs they may know. If someone could make up the words and actions

to a carol tune about St. Nicholas and Jesus please let us know so we could start a 'Santa loves Jesus' song book, with full recognition to the authors. Then the children could begin to sing words out of their own '*Santa loves Jesus*' songbook.

5. Santa may like to make a big circle with the children to pull a cracker/bonbons with arms crossed, singing "Happy birthday to Jesus" with the second verse being, "Happy Christmas to you x 2 and happy Christmas St. Nicholas, ...".

7. Then, with paper hats on let the Feast begin—'Food, Glorious Food!'

A merry Christmas to you all.

ooOoo

Another way to celebrate a community Christmas for warmer climates in the fields.

It is usually warm at Christmas time in Australia, and for over twenty years our family had a celebration every Christmas Eve in the paddock in front of our home. Everyone brought their own picnic and something to drink, and sat on the grass, while the nativity story was acted out between carols and short readings. Mary and Joseph surprised everyone—Mary, riding a donkey led by Joseph, came from the corner of the paddock. Later the 'shepherds' attached to a few tame sheep or goats, appeared at the side, 'in their fields abiding'.

Mary and Joseph disappeared behind in a car trailer filled with a hay bale 'stable', and reappeared miraculously with a real baby Jesus—with angels and shepherds all around. Some of the children were fascinated and would try to pier under the trailer to see what was going on.

It was twilight at the stage when the three kings arrived; one of the kings rode a wonderful old grey stallion, which had competed in dressage events for many years. The Kings rode up to the manger—everyone was asked to be very still and quiet as this magnificent stallion bowed down on one knee in front of the baby Jesus—in a hushed and beautiful moment. He came for years until his old knees grew too stiff to bow down any more (I know the feeling).

After a few years, over twelve hundred people would arrive on Christmas Eve. People would often ask 'Why do you have to have it on Christmas Eve?' The answer was always the same, 'because it is Christmas Eve'.

Others took it over the Country Carols when we left the area and it still goes on some thirty years later . . .

ooOoo

January to Lent: Free time

No.11—the Lent dream of Knowledge—studies several religions for six weeks. Members of the group are asked to research the questions for the couple of allocated religions each week, and record their findings in their journal to share with the group. Either divide the *religions* up between different members of the group to answer one question per week, or take one question per week covering all the religions at a time so that each person studies one subject. It will depend on how many people are in the group, as to which way works best.

Weekly research questions.

1. What are the origins of this faith and who was their founder?
2. Whom do they worship?
3. What are their main festivals?
4. Conflicts: a) Has there been a history of conflict within the faith? b) Have there been any attacks from without the faith?
5. Write a short summary of their main features and beliefs.
6. Which part of the world do they live, and in what numbers of population?

Week 1. Judaism 2000 BC and Christianity AD 40
Week 2. Islam AD 600 and Baha'i faith AD 1817
Week 3. Hinduism 2500-1500 BC and Sikh fifteenth century AD
Week 4. Buddhism 500 BC and Jainism 600 BCE
Week 5. Confucius, Shinto 712 BC
Week 6. Indigenous traditions of Africa, Australia, and North America.

As this special Christian Easter time arrives, reflect on Holy Week by inviting any members of the group who are interested, to each take one day of Holy Week and bring the story of that day, in a paragraph or two, to read consecutively during the last session.

A beautiful way to end this series may be to have a Seder meal with an informal ecumenical service, provided that the Wincs and A and A's are involved and happy with the content of the celebration.

ooOoo

No.12 the Ordinary Sundays dream of the Saints focuses on the commitment and bravery of Peter, Paul and others during their adventures in the Book of Acts by reading *Dreams for a World in Harmony* from beginning to end. This study would be particularly interesting if members of different religions, no religion or lapsed religion were included in the group.

This series takes "one chapter per week" dividing the weeks wherever convenience for a break.

ooOoo

No. 13 Dreams of young families meeting together.

This informal, yet powerful, dream already happens in some churches—how wonderful if it will spread to include other denominations, faiths, and non-church-going families. The families are predominantly young, but of course there is no age barrier. They meet together at a convenient family time, such as 4-5pm on a Sunday afternoon, sitting in an informal circle in a carpeted room for the children to crawl or play about with minimum pitter-patter noise. One rostered Mum or Dad choose a theme for the day, with an activity, reflection, a song or two, prayer, and discussion. The children are invited to contribute in discussion and activities, with no (abnormal) restraint.

This is a lovely, thoughtful way to cross barriers, share ideas, and start the week.

ooOoo

No. 14 Dreams of a Pilgrimage.

The Pilgrimage could last for up to a week during a warm school holidays. A back up van or truck is needed to bring the sleeping bags and gear to the new venue each afternoon.

The initial organisation needs careful planning to find a wonderful long walk, and a hall, church or club house with enough floor space in which to sleep each night. Our pilgrimage was organised by two energetic, young at heart, wonderful people with a gift for focusing on themes that really matter, during a quiet time after the evening meal each evening. We often lit a candle for someone precious.

Again an invitation to other denominations, faiths and non-church going families enriches the experience. However it is so popular, be careful to keep the numbers to a manageable size—more than twelve young people is ambitious, which give a group of over twenty people. Each person under 18 must be accompanied by a parent or adult.

Catering is kept to the simplest form with "help yourself to breakfast, and make your sandwich for lunch" every morning, with a roster of people to clear up. A take-a-way something, BBQ or just for once, fish and chips for an easy evening meal. The days walk covers up to ten kilometres which gives young people plenty of exercise, with a spiritual memory they will never forget—the older ones may never forget it either.

ooOoo

NOTES TO GROUP LEADERS

Please acknowledge to every group that Wikipedia have generously given permission for the Book of Acts to be printed in full from their version of the Bible, the World English Bible.

The plan for no.4 Q&A panel dream is to encourage leaders in the Christian community to invite an eclectic panel of guests to a Q and A—Questions and Answers—for an hour or so once a month or week, or whenever suits the group.

The debate will have greater value if it includes as many atheists, agnostics, lapsed Christians and members of other faiths as possible. Having other versions of the Bible at hand, as well as the Holy Book of other faith members adds to the value of the discussion.

How the historical pendulum of time swings—as Christian gentiles today invite friends from the Jewish and Muslim communities to come in and listen, which reverses the biblical scene as Paul and the Jews began to invite the gentiles to come in and listen.

Probably about eight would be a good number—but whatever works for you will work.

The invited group, or panel, meet anywhere (except in church or chapel) to get to know each other and share the thoughts which surface through either *O my God! Where are You?* or *Dreams for a World in Harmony.* The commentary and questions in each chapter become a catalyst to feed the debate.

The group members will need a book, or journal, to record their thoughts at home and bring to the session each week. Please remind everyone that 'pass' is always an option for a sensitive or painful subject.

A celebration, containing contributions and comments from members in the group during that series, would be a beautiful way to complete the last session to any of the series. At the end of Lent series, one or two—a Seder meal—would be particularly appropriate.

The subjective opinions in this text belong entirely to the author. Being a long way from pretending to be an academic, but having been blessed with a reasonably creative imagination and a passion for peace in this wonderful world, the material may be used creatively, in whatever way the leader feels fit. The printed words are only a shadow of the potential treasure of hope, joy, and comfort waiting to be explored in Luke's writing.

ooOoo

BIBLIOGRAPHY

Aboriginal Arts Board of the Australia Council. *Victims or Victors.* The story of the Koori People of Victoria. Hyland House Publishing, 1985.

Amy-Jill Levine. *The Misunderstood Jew* shows how Christians often misunderstand Judaism. HarperOne, 2006.

Brian May, Patrick Moore, and Christ Lintott. *Bang! The Complete History of the Universe*: The story of the evolution of the earth. Carlton Books Limited, London, 2006.

Charles E.M. Roderick. *Listen to the Wind.* A collection of sermons.

Nicky Gumbel. *Questions of Life.* Offering an opportunity to explore the meaning of life. David C. Cook Publishing Company, 2002.

Charles Taylor. *A Secular Age.* Examining our society in a 'Post Christian' era. The Belknap Press of Harvard University Press, 2007.

Charles Taylor. *The Secular Age.* Taylor seeks to prove that God is still very much present in the world, if only we look at the right places. The Belknap Press of Harvard University, 2007.

David Pawson. *The Challenge of Islam to Christians.* A courageous wake up call to Christians. Hodder Christian Books.

David Tacey. *The Spirituality Revolution—The Emergence of Contemporary Spirituality* argues that the growing popularity of alternative spirituality is a sign of a new phase in the spiritual development of the Western world. HarperCollins, 2003.

Elizabeth Breuilly, Joanne O'Brien, and Martin Palmer. *An Illustrated Guide to Origins, Beliefs, Traditions and Festivals.* Checkmark Books, 2005.

John O'Donohue. *eternal echoes—exploring our hunger to belong.* Explores the most basic of human desires—the desire to belong. Bantam Press, Great Britain, 1998.

John W. Wilson. *Christianity Alongside Islam* informs the Western World about some of the pressing issues about Islam. Acorn Press, Brunswick East, 2010.

Madeleine Albright. *The Mighty and the Almighty.* Reflections on America, God, and World Affairs. HarperCollins, 2006.

Nick Wells. *World Religions—An Illustrated Guide.* The faiths are the oldest surviving human institutions in the world. To know more about them, we need to do more than stand outside. Time Books HarperCollins, 2004.

Rachael Kohn. The New Believers—Re-imaging God explores some of the key questions concerning religion and spirituality today. HarperCollins, 2003.

Richard Dawkins. *The God Delusion.* A hard-hitting, impassioned rebuttal of religion. Bantam Press, 2006.

Sakara Saranam. *God without religion* questioning centuries of accepted truths. Simon and Schuster, Australia, 2005.

St. Teresa of Avila. *The Interior Castle.* Edited by Halcyon Backhouse. Comparing the human soul to a castle of many mansions, shows the entrance key to be prayer. Hodder and Stoughton, 1988.

Susan Meredith. *The Usborne Book of World Religions* explores the history and major beliefs of the world's major religions. Usborne Publishing, 2005.

The New Bible Commentary Revised. Inter-Varsity Press.

The NIV Study Bible. Zondervan Bible Publishers.

William Loader. *The New Testament with Imagination* offers a fresh approach to reading the New Testament. Wm B. Eerdmans Publishing Co., 2007.

Maps are printed with permission from New Bible Commentary. Edited by Gordon J. Wenham, J. Alec Motyer, and others. Copyright 1970 Inter-Varsity Press, UK. Used by permission of Inter-Varsity Press, PO Box 1400, Downers Grove, IL, 60515, http://www.ivpress.com.

The Bible text has been taken from Wikipedia's version of the World English Bible with generous permission and without change, except to remove the number of each verse to comply with the publishers guidelines. This translation is in the public domain.

About the Author

Nancy Hawkins is a practicing Christian. She had a nursing/teaching career, was a clinical supervisor for the Monash University Nursing Faculty, and completed a four-year Education For Ministry course. She lives in Australia with her husband and family. Her first book *O My God! Where Are You?* was published in 2004.